BUSINESS
ORGANISATIONS AND ENVIRONMENTS
BOOK 1

NEW B/TEC SPECIFICATION

MATTHEW GLEW

MICHAEL WATTS

RONALD WELLS

Heinemann Educational Books

Uniform with this title

Business Organisations and Environments
Book 2
   by Matthew Glew, Michael Watts and
   Ronald Wells (forthcoming 1987)

Heinemann Educational Books Ltd
22 Bedford Square, London WC1B 3HH

LONDON   EDINBURGH   MELBOURNE   AUCKLAND
SINGAPORE   KUALA LUMPUR   NEW DELHI
IBADAN   NAIROBI   JOHANNESBURG
PORTSMOUTH (NH)   KINGSTON

First published 1986
Reprinted 1987

British Library Cataloguing in Publication Data

Glew, Matthew
   Business organisations and environments.
   Bk. 1
   1. Business enterprises
   I. Title   II. Watts, Michael, *1943–*
   III. Wells, Ronald, *1947–*
   338.7   HD2731

ISBN 0–435–45905–8

Printed in Great Britain by Thomson Litho Ltd,
East Kilbride, Scotland

Contents

Preface

This book includes the requirements of the re-specified Common Core Modules 3 and 4 entitled 'The Organisation in its Environment', which represent an integral part of the Business and Technician Education Council National Award in Business Studies.

In accordance with the revised specification the book moves progressively from a consideration of the position of the individual, to the organisation, and then through to the organisation within the wider business environment. The book fully reflects the emphasis that BTEC have placed in the re-specification on the areas of change, technology and management skills. The book seeks to guide students towards an understanding of their roles within the business environment. It therefore provides them with a basis for understanding and later analysing the economic, legal, social and political problems that affect the business world. The material has been presented in accordance with the underlying BTEC philosophy of an interdisciplinary approach to business studies courses. A balance has been maintained throughout the book between the disciplines of economics, law, government and sociology, thus providing a complete view of the operations of the business organisation.

The book will also prove valuable for students requiring an introduction or conversion course to the BTEC Higher National Award. In addition, students engaged upon professional and managerial courses will find that the wide perspective it provides on the business environment can successfully augment their studies.

To the tutor

To help you we have included several ideas for integrated assignments on pages 158–65. These are in line with the requirements of Business & Technician Education Council, *Business and Finance, Distribution Studies and Public Administration: Core Unit Specifications and Sample Learning Activities* (BTEC Publications, 1985).

Matthew Glew
Michael Watts
Ronald Wells
June 1986

Acknowledgements

The authors would like to thank Rosalyn Clothier for the help which she provided on the legal aspects of employment.

The authors and publishers would like to thank all those who gave permission to reproduce the following figures:

Barclays Bank: Fig. 5.3.
Department of National Savings: Fig. 5.5.
Economic Progress Report: Fig. 5.2.
The Sunday Times: Fig. 2.7.
The Times: Fig. 2.6

Thanks are also due to the following who gave permission to reproduce tables:

British Business: Table 6.3.
Times Books Ltd: Tables 1.1 and 1.2.

Crown copyright material, as indicated in the sources, is reproduced with permission of the Controller of Her Majesty's Stationery Office.

The publishers have made every effort to trace copyright holders, but if they have inadvertently overlooked any they will be pleased to make the necessary arrangements at the first opportunity.

1. The Organisation

Introducing organisations

The individual and the organisation

Every individual has certain basic needs that have to be satisfied. These arise out of the individual's dual role as both consumer and producer. As consumers, people have certain material and collective needs; and as producers they have economic, social and employment needs. These basic needs may be classified under three main headings:

Material needs

These refer to items of consumption necessary to sustain the expected and accepted standard of living of the individual within the community. These will vary according to a country's relative wealth and stage of development. In a developing country they may be as basic as the provision of shelter, warmth, food and clothing, whereas in a highly developed economy they are likely to include freezers, microwave ovens and fashionable clothing.

Collective needs

These concern the general collective wants of society, the economic and social needs of both the individual and community at large. They include law and order, defence, public and general health facilities, transport and communications, and educational and social services.

Employment needs

All individuals need to live in an economic and social environment that enables them to satisfy their material and collective needs. This means that opportunities must exist for individual members of the community to find employment so that they can produce sufficient (1) to meet their own needs

and (2) to support those who are dependent upon them, for instance their families, the elderly and the sick.

An individual working alone cannot satisfy all of these needs, because he/she lacks the basic skills, knowledge and physical strength and the range of required resources to do everything for him/herself. Therefore people have to rely on each other for help. Generally this comes in the form of help from groups of people formed into informal or formal organisations; they co-ordinate their efforts and activities to achieve some specific purpose or solve some particular problem.

For example, the individual relies upon people working in factories for the supply of a car, a television, a washing-machine and dishwasher; he/she relies upon members of the armed forces for defence; upon the police and judiciary for law and order; upon teachers in schools and colleges for education, and upon doctors, nurses and health workers for health care. The individual also depends upon factories, offices, shops and other places of work for employment opportunities, and hence for the means of satisfying his/her own material needs.

Organisations help to satisfy individuals' material and collective needs. At the same time they provide people with the means of paying towards the satisfaction of these, through money earned from employment. See Fig. 1.1 on page 2.

Reasons for forming organisations

Organisations help the individual satisfy his/her basic needs. This is something that he/she could not achieve alone. But in a more general sense, if society is to make the best use of any of the natural resources available to it, then this may be achieved only through the development of appropriate organisations.

For example, take the case of the extraction of North Sea oil; the exploration of the Forties oil-field has involved working over 2000 metres below the sea-bed. This is a highly complex operation. A single rig on a nine-day exploration of the North Sea requires around 3000 tonnes of equipment in order to operate. Supplies of casing, fuel, mud and cement, as well as the necessary spare parts, food and clothing, must all be transported from a base located often more than 100 miles away. This large-scale and difficult operation has been possible only through setting up appropriate organisations to make the optimum use of the available oil.

Such organisations need to be capable of co-ordinating the discovery, drilling, refining and distribution stages of the oil operation. They must also be able to employ a variety of specialists from all over the world, such as civil engineers, surveyors and geologists. They must delegate authority to the specialists so as to ensure that the task is carried out efficiently. This responsibility, in the case of North Sea oil, has been shouldered by a combination of state-controlled and multinational organisations.

We can see, then, that organisations are formed because they help society make the best use of resources. That is, because their creation provides for the **co-ordination** of an operation, the **employment of specialists** and the appropriate **delegation of authority** to achieve the overall objective.

The reasons put forward for the formation of an organisation explain its initial conception. However, the continued existence of organisations and their growth are generally due to market forces and economic and social pressures, which provide advantages for expansion.

Characteristics common to all forms of organisation

All organisations, whether large or small, whether operating in a business or an administrative environment, have certain common features. These are illustrated in Fig. 1.2.

1. *All organisations are governed by certain rules and regulations*, which are either written down, verbally passed on, or assumed to be known. These provide guidance for those who are charged with the responsibility of ensuring the organisation's future and adherence to certain required standards or procedures.

For example, in the case of a small retailer these may merely be a question of handing down through the family the attitudes towards the business and the approach towards the customers that have been found to be most successful. But for a large manufacturing company the rules and regulations may be more formally expressed in the form of the Memorandum and Articles of Association, the organisation's manuals, the annual reports, or the employee's rulebooks.

Fig. 1.1: The individual and the organisation

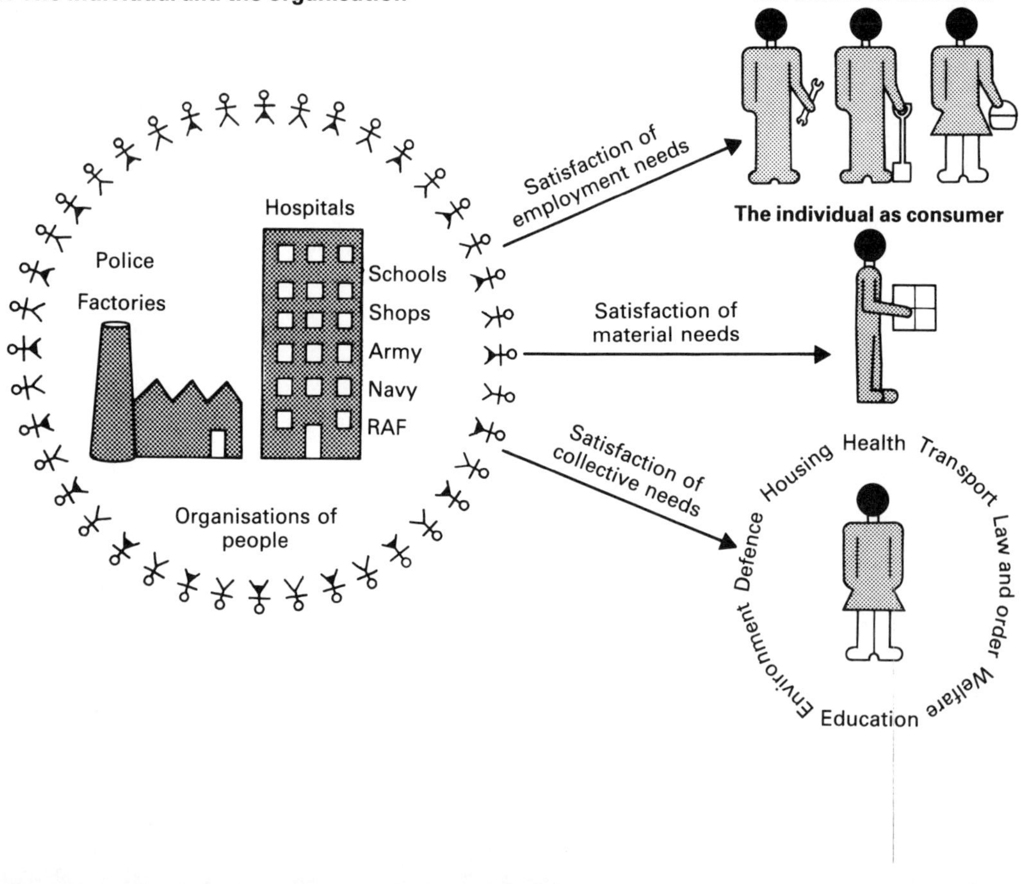

2. *All organisations share a system of positions, roles or jobs through which their work is carried out.* This means that everyone within an organisation has a role to perform. Large organisations require many specialist roles, whereas small organisations have individuals who are responsible for two or three functions.

For instance, in a large company there would probably be a marketing department in which one individual might have the responsibility for export sales; but in a smaller business one individual might have to combine the role of export manager with responsibility for advertising, market research, product planning and general domestic sales, under the umbrella title of marketing manager.

3. *All organisations require some sort of recognised chain of authority* regarding the carrying out of certain jobs or functions. There must be someone at the head of any organisation with ultimate responsibility for its relative success or failure. This person should then be able to delegate certain functions and tasks to other individuals beneath him/her, who in turn should be able to do the same.

The size of this structure will depend on the size of the organisation concerned.

For example, the sole trader running a shop may be ultimately responsible for his/her business and be able only to delegate some of the service in the shop to his/her spouse. But in a large company the managing director may take ultimate control, and he/she may then delegate to the directors such functions as marketing, finance, company secretary, production and personnel. They in turn will delegate to their subordinates, who in turn will delegate to the people beneath them, and so on.

4. *The power and authority within an organisation are vested in the hands of those who are capable of making decisions to ensure the achievement of the objectives of the organisation.* In the case of a nationalised industry such as the Coal Board, ultimate power is in the hands of Parliament, the Minister for Energy, the board and the chairman. All these people influence the policy of the industry in various ways to ensure that it meets its objectives.

'Authority' here means legalised authority, which generally comes from the owners of any

Fig. 1.2: Characteristics of organisations

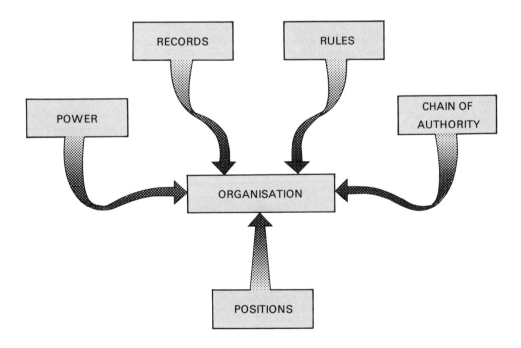

business, because they provide the resources to create the organisation. For example, legalised authority is vested in the shareholders of a company, who therefore earn a right to a say in how the company is run and its attempts to achieve its objectives.

5. *All organisations have some system of recording information relating to their activities, which provides guidance for future action.* In the case of organisations working in the North Sea oil-fields, regular records are required relating to such matters as geological structures, drilling operations, refining equipment, transport, personnel, costs and sales. This information is essential in order to develop production, purchasing, personnel, financial and marketing strategies based on past experience. It is also necessary for fulfilling legal requirements regarding taxation, employment records and so on.

Organisations in the UK economy

The type of environment in which the organisation operates in the UK is largely determined by its relationship with the government. This relationship involves a sharing of responsibility between the government and the business organisation in decisions involving the allocation of scarce resources, the methods by which those resources are turned into goods and services, and the way in which the rewards from production are distributed. Because in the UK responsibility for all these decisions rests jointly with both the government and business organisations, the UK system is said to be a mixed economy.

The mixed economy
A mixed economy is made up of aspects both of a free-enterprise capitalist system, and of a centrally controlled system. To understand how the mixed economy works, we must first consider the working of these two more extreme systems.

In a completely **free-enterprise capitalist system**, land and capital (two of the factors of production) are owned privately. These are used to earn profits for their owners (the entrepreneurs), who bear the risks associated with combining them with the other factor of production, labour, for the production of goods and services which are to be sold. Decisions about the allocation of resources are governed entirely by free market forces. Competitive pressures determine the methods of production employed by the business organisations. The distribution of rewards to the factors of production are decided entirely by their respective scarcity value. There is no country in the world which operates a pure capitalist system, although West Germany is probably the nearest to approaching it.

In a **centrally controlled system**, all decisions about the allocation of resources, methods of production and distribution of the rewards of production are taken by the central administration. This would result in a situation where the factors of production, including labour, would be directed by the state. The government would decide what should be produced, in what quantities and by which production outlet. The government's decisions on these matters would be based upon the planners' view as to what would be beneficial for the community and the state as a whole.

In this situation it would be easier for the government to achieve its objectives if it actually owned all the available resources. It is therefore usual under a controlled economy for there to be considerable, if not total, public ownership of wealth – and very few, if any, activities influenced by market forces. The nearest system to reflect this 'command economy' is that operating in the Soviet Union, although even this economy has traces of free choice and market forces in operation.

In a **mixed economy**, made up of elements of both free-enterprise capitalism and the centrally controlled system, the ownership of the means of production is shared between private individuals and the government. Decisions about the allocation of resources are made by a combination of market forces and government intervention and control. Decisions about methods of production are partly regulated by government controls and are made by a combination of government and private organisations. The distribution of the rewards of production is determined by several forces: (1) the personal accumulation and inheritance of wealth, (2) the share of rewards accruing to the different factors of production, (3) taxes and (4) social payments and services.

The mixed economy in the UK, we have said, combines elements from the two extreme systems. It therefore gives rise to a situation where there are two distinct sectors within the economy: namely the **public** and the **private**. The main types of organisations operating within each sector are shown in Fig. 1.3 and are described in detail in the second half of this chapter.

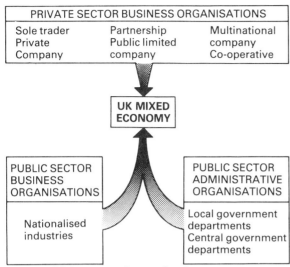

PRIVATE SECTOR BUSINESS ORGANISATIONS		
Sole trader	Partnership	Multinational
Private	Public limited	company
Company	company	Co-operative

UK MIXED ECONOMY

PUBLIC SECTOR BUSINESS ORGANISATIONS	PUBLIC SECTOR ADMINISTRATIVE ORGANISATIONS
Nationalised industries	Local government departments Central government departments

Fig. 1.3: Main types of organisation

The public sector

This is that part of the economic system controlled by the government. It is made up of both business and administrative organisations. The nationalised industries and mixed enterprises include those parts of the economy – such as energy, transport and communications – which have been taken under public control for economic, organisational, strategic or social reasons. Central and local government departments are responsible for running and administering government activities and services such as housing, health, education, defence and the environment. In general, organisations created in this sector are largely concerned with the maximisation of social welfare.

The private sector

This is that part of the economic system completely independent of government control. Business organisations in this sector operate as sole traders, partnerships, private companies, public limited companies, multinational companies and co-operatives. The specific objective leading to their creation tends to be the maximisation of profits. The actual type of organisation found is largely determined by the nature and size of the venture undertaken.

The objectives of organisations

Organisations are formed to accomplish some specific purpose or solve some particular problem. This means that the people involved in establishing an organisation are motivated by a wish to achieve certain goals, aims or objectives. In some cases they may be aiming to achieve a single objective such as making as much profit as possible. In other cases they may be attempting to achieve a number of different objectives, which could include establishing commercial security and power, bringing about technological advancement or enhancing the reputation, status and prestige of their organisation.

It is generally assumed that organisations in the private sector are created for the specific purpose of maximising profits, and those in the public sector for maximising social welfare. In reality, however, a range of objectives are open to organisations in both the private and public sectors.

Private sector objectives (Fig. 1.4)

1. *Maximisation of profits*

It is often assumed that within the market or private sector of a mixed economy, the sole pursuit of a firm is the maximisation of profits. This is an important assumption in that part of micro-economic analysis which seeks to demonstrate how a firm, under varying degrees of competition, will decide upon a level of output when this objective of maximum profits is secured. Such theory deals not only with the desire of the firm to achieve maximum profits but also with the aim of securing at least 'normal profits'.

A firm may be making profits after deducting the costs associated with production, but there is also a certain level of profit necessary in order to produce a return on capital that compensates the owners for the risks they have taken. The theory then suggests that this minimum return that owners are prepared to accept would be regarded as a 'normal' profit; if such a return is not forthcoming then capital will eventually be withdrawn from the enterprise and invested elsewhere.

What is regarded as a 'normal' profit will of course according to this definition differ between industries, because the degree of risk will depend upon the type of activity the enterprise is engaged in. If a firm is operating in a highly competitive and uncertain market, this normal profit will have to be far greater than the normal profit acceptable from a business venture in a more secure market. This normal profit is in fact likened to a cost, in that it must be covered. Any profits in excess of this level are regarded as 'pure' profit and are seen as an additional return to the owners of capital which more than compensates for the risk involved.

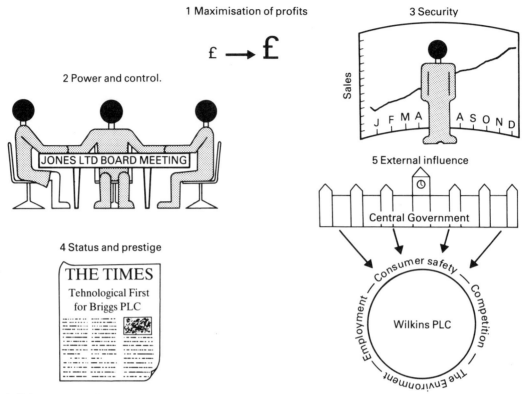

Fig. 1.4: Private sector business objectives

The level of profits achieved by an organisation also has another significance as an objective, in that it reflects the organisation's success or failure. This in turn will determine future prospects, because profits act as an important source of funds for investment purposes. Without new and improved techniques brought about through investment the competitive position of the organisation will deteriorate and result in a failure to achieve even normal profit.

2. *Power and control*
The owners of any business may enjoy the feeling of power associated with exercising direct control over a business venture. This could mean, in the case of a small family business, that their objective may be that of retaining this power rather than maximising profits. Under these circumstances, the family may recognise that in order to maximise profits they may need to expand and to seek additional funds; but they may not be prepared to do this because it could involve either forming a joint stock company or, for an existing joint stock

company, issuing more shares. In both cases such action could spread the ownership of the business and so reduce the family's power and control.

3. *Security*
Security may be another objective. The owners of any business organisation may be reluctant to strive for the maximisation of profits, because this may involve risks if it is associated with moving into new ventures that could prove unsuccessful. It might be considered more desirable to try to increase the volume of sales and thus achieve the objective of a more powerful and secure position in the market; this may be seen as a means of reducing the threat from both existing and potential competitors. This may result in the company expanding its volume of sales to a level that would not be justified if profit was the sole motive.

4. *Status and prestige*
This is an objective more likely to be pursued in a very large business organisation. In a public limited company, for example, there may be an apparent

divorce between the shareholders who own the business and the directors and managers who control it. Under these circumstances once a profit level has been reached that directors and managers believe will satisfy shareholders, chances arise to pursue other aims.

The board of directors may, for example, be dominated by personalities who seek to identify themselves with a very large company, and they may be interested in the company's growth – in terms of the volume of sales or turnover – for its own sake. This may help to secure greater prestige, but the result may not be a maximisation of profits. The extra units of output may add more to costs than to the firm's revenue; but as long as a 'normal' profit is produced the directors may be satisfying shareholders while still being able to satisfy their desire for status and prestige.

This non-monetary objective may also be furthered by emphasising the importance of product development and improved techniques. Although perhaps impressive from the purely technological point of view, such activity may not be directly geared to maximising profits. Research and development projects involve substantial sums of money and may be undertaken even though they yield a lower return than if the funds had been spent on less prestigious but more practical projects.

5. *External objectives and influences*
The objectives of the organisation may also be influenced by pressures from outside sources. In particular, pressure may come from governments seeking to achieve certain political, social and economic objectives through the activities of businesses. The environment within which the organisation operates will be partly a reflection of the current government's policies in these areas, and the organisation will have to take account of them in formulating its objectives. The pursuit of profit, power, security or prestige may have to be modified to take account of (a) its impact upon employment levels, either national or local, (b) the implications for industrial relations, (c) the effect upon the environment, (d) consumer safety and (e) the extent to which it complies with the government's interpretation of competition and monopoly. At the same time pressure may be exerted upon employers to consider the repercussions of their decisions upon the general economic climate and the course of economic events which such decisions may influence.

In the case of very large organisations, these pressures may work in the opposite direction. The organisation may be able to influence the overall political and economic environment in which it operates. It may seek to reduce the risks it sees arising out of an environment by exerting pressure upon governments to follow a policy in the company's own commercial interest.

This practice of 'political lobbying' is not restricted to the very large organisation; it can be pursued by smaller organisations that form their own trade and manufacturers' associations to communicate their opinions to the government. They will concern themselves with such issues as import duties, company taxation, prices and incomes policy, and industrial relations.

The extent to which a government is susceptible to such pressures depends upon both its integrity and the extent to which it can accommodate an organisation's or an industry's aims within the broader context of its economic, social and political programme. Increasingly, governments are obliged to make reference to the views of both organised labour and employers' associations in an effort to formulate their overall strategy. Nevertheless, this is a two-way process; governments will also seek to use organisations as a means of implementing their policies. Not only will a government adopt measures that influence the overall economic climate within which an organisation operates; it may also attempt to use organisations as a means of securing political, economic and social objectives in a more direct way. The objectives of the organisation and the means of achieving them may therefore be guided by the need to comply with the government's aims in the fields of investment, wages and pricing policies, employment and the location of its activities.

Public sector objectives
Within the public sector, objectives tend to be more clouded than in the private sector. They may embrace **commercial**, **economic** and **social** factors. The relative importance of such factors is likely to change not only with the government in power, but also over the life-span of the same government. This is because governments have difficulties in deciding whether public sector organisations should be concerned solely with providing a service in order to maximise welfare, whether they should break even and in doing so cover their costs, whether they should make a profit and run on commercial lines, or whether they should achieve the highest possible level of

profitability and administrative efficiency. Conflict often develops between these commercial, social or economic objectives.

An investment project, for example, by a public sector organisation such as British Rail, will have a purely commercial objective if it is concentrated upon those routes where it is likely to produce the highest return. Wider economic repercussions of the project, however, may have to be taken into account. A fuller analysis of the expenditure in the light of the current economic climate would include the extent to which the economy can cope with such an increase in expenditure without meeting a shortage of resources and the build-up of inflationary pressures. Again, investment plans would have to be modified if consideration had to be given to the social effects of decisions upon regional employment levels.

Investment funds are, after all, limited. Investment by the public sector National Coal Board, for example, in certain pits may be at the expense of other areas where high unemployment is of concern to the government. Similarly, a purely commercial decision by British Rail may involve the closure of certain routes, or reductions in the frequency of some services if losses are to be reduced and further investment programmes concentrated upon the more lucrative routes. British Rail may, however, be obliged to take heed of the effect upon rural areas where alternative means of transport may be limited and where cuts may reduce job opportunities for local residents.

An improved commercial return could be achieved by raising the price of the product or service in question. But this will involve questions of social justice if items like electricity, gas, coal and public passenger fares are increased, particularly if they are important items of expenditure for people on lower incomes.

The success or failure of any organisation, whether in the public or the private sector, can ultimately be measured against the extent to which it is able to achieve its objectives. Its ability to do this will depend upon its type, size, structure and degree of influence.

Types of organisation and their contribution to the mixed economy

This section is devoted to a description of the nature, functions and policies of private and public sector business organisations. Their different legal forms and the contributions they make to the workings of the mixed economy are examined. Public sector administrative organisations are considered in Book 2.

The private sector

The sole trader

The sole trader is the simplest and numerically by far the most commonly occurring form of business organisation in the UK. Basically, a single person provides the capital, takes the decisions and assumes the risks of the business. It is a type of organisation particularly well suited to local retail outlets and small local services such as hairdressers and window-cleaners, where customers value personal attention.

Legally the sole trader has unlimited liability. He/she is personally liable for all the debts of the business up to the limit of his/her personal estate. This may mean that in the case of insolvency even the sole trader's house and car could be taken in order to settle his/her debts.

There are no formal legal procedures to go through when setting up as a sole trader unless the business is being run under a name other than that of the owner. Then under the Business Names Act 1985 the name of the business must be disclosed. For example, if Mr Jones was to run a window-cleaning business called Sparkle, he would need to disclose this name so that those dealing with his business were aware of his true identity.

In the case of some business activities it may be necessary for the sole trader to obtain a licence, usually from the local authority, before he/she can lawfully trade. Some requirements are 'adoptive'; that is, the local authority may elect to license or not. Licensing requirements apply to such activities as pet shops, betting shops, bingo, hairdressers, taxi operators and street traders.

The sole trader may also be required under certain circumstances to register with or notify various government agencies about the business. He/she must supply information for tax purposes to the Inland Revenue, and if the annual turnover exceeds the VAT threshold he/she must register for VAT with the Customs and Excise Department. If the sole trader employs anybody then he/she will need to contact the Department of Health and Social Security for the purposes of national insurance and sick pay, and the careers office if the business employs people under the age of 18. The Factory Inspectorate is interested in any business using industrial premises, and the local authority's

Environmental Health Department in all shops and offices (concerning the health and safety of staff), in shops selling certain foods (for example, ice-cream or shellfish) and in businesses employing women or people under 18 on overtime.

The social and economic implications of sole traders are mixed. They represent the old idea of the free-enterprise economy, whereby the individual relied upon him/herself to make a living. The sole trader is his/her own boss, capable of implementing policies when he/she sees fit and answerable to no one apart from the customers. This last point means that the sole trader tends to survive against the competition of larger rivals by building up good personal relationships with customers and trying to ensure that the service is of the highest standard.

Another method of survival has been sought by many sole traders competing with the large multiples in the retail trade. By grouping together they have been able to enjoy some of the economies of scale associated with bulk purchasing. For example, the Spar (Society for the Protection of the Average Retailer) group of grocers' shops has formed its own purchasing and distribution system. Such associations are able to benefit from some of the other advantages of large-scale organisations, e.g. advertising and packaging.

Economically the sole trader suffers from a lack of finance. This is because he/she is largely dependent upon borrowing from the commercial banking system and is unable to command the same sort of credit as a larger organisation. This means that any expansion or modernisation which might lead to greater consumer choice or lower prices tends to be difficult to achieve.

However, it is often within small and simple organisations like that of the sole trader that new ideas may be nurtured, new industries bred and future industrial leaders trained. Potentially the sole trader may make a considerable and lasting contribution to the working of the mixed economy.

The partnership
A partnership may consist of any number between two and twenty people. However, as a result of the Companies Act 1985 there is no restriction on the number of partners making up a firm of solicitors, accountants or members of a recognised stock exchange. The partners provide the capital for the business and share the resulting profit or loss. This is an ideal form of organisation for a relatively small business requiring more capital than one person can

provide. It is particularly suitable for professionals such as doctors, dentists, accountants, architects and solicitors.

There are two types of partnership. The **ordinary** or **general partnership** was established by the Partnership Act 1890. The basis of this type of partnership is that, in the absence of any statement to the contrary, all partners should share profits and losses equally; all partners are subject to unlimited liability; and all partners have equal rights in the running of the firm. The ordinary partnership is dissolved either compulsorily or voluntarily in the event of:
1. the termination of the agreed period of its duration;
2. the completion of the venture for which the firm was founded;
3. the general agreement of the partners;
4. the death or bankruptcy of any partner;
5. the order of a court.

The second type of partnership is the **limited partnership**. This was established by the Act of the same name in 1907. The advantage of this type of partnership is that it allows for the formation of a partnership between an active partner and one or more 'sleeping' partners, who are not partners in the fullest sense as they take no part in the management of the firm. However, they enjoy the privilege of limited liability, which means that they are liable only for the debts of the business up to the extent of the capital they have put into the venture. Such partners are desired not for their expertise but rather for the capital they can put into the business.

Depending on the type of business involved or product sold a partnership has to abide by the same licensing, registration and notification requirements as the sole trader. It is also subject to similar checks from relevant local and central government departments.

The main contribution of this type of organisation to the working of the mixed economy is that like the sole trader it is a sufficiently small and flexible type of organisation to encourage the development of new ideas, processes and initiatives. It also has the advantage over the sole trader in that as a form of organisation its structure allows for the taking on of specialists, and for the provision of extra capital to finance an expansion where it is considered necessary.

The private joint stock company
The private joint stock company is one that has not stated in its memorandum of association that it is a

public company. It consists of an association of not less than two people who contribute towards a joint stock of capital through the ownership of shares for the purpose of carrying on business for profit. The term 'joint stock' refers to the total assets of the company and includes such items as plant, machinery, raw materials and stocks of finished goods. The ownership of these assets is vested in the shareholders who have put forward the finance with which the assets were acquired. In the case of many private firms the majority of the shares may be held by the members of one family or by one or two key directors in the business.

There are two main types of shares, referred to as **preference** and **ordinary**. The difference between these two types lies in the degree of risk associated with them. The ordinary share is the most risky, in that its return depends entirely upon the fortunes of the company. Although there is always the prospect of a higher dividend to compensate for the risk, there is also the danger of a *nil* return. As the fortunes of this type of shareholder are so bound up with the fortunes of the company, he/she has a right to elect the directors to manage it.

The preference share is less risky. It carries a fixed dividend which is paid before the ordinary dividend is established. However, even these shareholders may receive nothing if the company has done very badly. Many preference shares are issued with 'cumulative' rights, by which unpaid dividends may be carried forward to future years when the company's fortunes might have improved. Due to the smaller amount of risk involved in the holding of this type of share they very rarely carry any voting rights or say in the running of the company.

In all cases the transfer and taking up of shares must be conducted through private channels. The private company is an ideal form of business enterprise for family concerns and for the launching of new ideas or ventures. It is often a natural development from the partnership or sole trader.

There are a number of legal requirements based on the Companies Act 1985 that organisations must satisfy before they are able to operate as a private company. Under these it is necessary for the company to submit certain documents.

1. The **memorandum of association** must state the company's name, address of its registered office, objectives, amount of authorised capital and that the liability of its members is limited. This document must be signed by at least two people, who must declare that they wish to be formed into a company and promise to pay for the shares they have agreed to take.
2. The **articles of association** provide information on the proposed internal organisation of the company. They give details on such areas as the rights of shareholders, the procedure for private share transfer and the manner in which meetings are to be held.
3. A statement has to be made concerning the company's nominal capital.
4. Particulars have to be given concerning the nature of the directors and secretary.
5. A declaration has to be made that the Company Acts have been complied with.

Once these documents have been approved, the company will be issued by the Registrar of Companies with a **certificate of incorporation**. This means that it is accepted as a separate legal entity which gives its members the privilege of limited liability. The shareholders are therefore liable only up to the extent of the size of their holding in the company. The company also has continuity while there are shareholders alive and able to trade. The affairs of this type of organisation are more public than those of the partnership and sole trader because it is required to file its accounts with the Registrar of Companies.

The overall control and management of the private company is generally in the hands of the **directors**. They are elected by the shareholders and exercise their powers through a chief executive who may be a managing director or general manager. A private company need have only one director, and its directors may continue in office irrespective of their age. These factors combine to make it an attractive form of organisation for small family businesses. The voting powers of the company's shareholders at company meetings are generally proportionate to the number of shares that they hold.

The most important contribution this type of organisation makes to the working of the mixed economy is that it allows people to own a share in a business organisation whilst enjoying limited liability. This principle of **limited liability** means that each individual shareholder is liable only for the debts of the company up to the amount of capital that he/she has contributed or promised to contribute. Because this means that the degree of risk associated with any venture has been clearly expressed, individuals may be more willing to invest in the enterprise, and larger amounts of capital become easier to raise. Such a system means that many sole traders or partnerships are able, by forming themselves into private companies, to attract the type and amount of finance necessary to pursue new ventures, expand or modernise, which otherwise might have been impossible.

The contribution of the small firms sector

For classification purposes these first three types of business organisation are often bracketed together under the title 'small firms'. These are defined by the Department of Trade and Industry as firms in the manufacturing sector employing up to 200 people and firms in the service sector with annual turnovers below a specified maximum which varies from sector to sector.

Such firms may make a major contribution to the working of the mixed economy. They may provide a production outlet for the energies of enterprising people and thus they may act as a seed-bed for new entrepreneurial talent and a base for new large companies to grow and challenge established leaders. In certain cases the small firm may pioneer new enterprises until the size of the market and the potential economies of scale attract the interests of the larger firm and the use of mass production and distribution methods. For example, the revival of home wine- and beer-making was pioneered by small shops and later taken over by Boots and other chain stores.

Small businesses may also act as specialist suppliers to larger companies of parts, sub-assemblies or components. This is particularly true in the motor trade. There, the big companies may be supplied by many smaller businesses, which because of their small size and hence lower overheads may be able to produce the required component at a lower cost than the larger organisation is able to do.

The small firm sector may add to the variety of products and services flourishing in a limited or specialised market, such as rare books or freshly baked pies, bread and cakes. It may also act as a source of innovation in products, services and techniques, and in so doing new industries may be developed. Small firms make an additional major contribution to the mixed economy in the provision of jobs. In 1984 they accounted for an estimated six million jobs, which represented 36 per cent of private sector employment and 25 per cent of total employment.

The public limited joint stock company

This form of business organisation is essentially an extension of the private company. The main difference is that the public limited company must state in its memorandum of association that it is a public company. Also it may appeal to the general public for capital, and it must use in its name the words 'public limited company' or 'plc'. There must be a minimum authorised share capital of £50,000, a quarter of which must be paid up. The rules concerning directors are different. A public company must have at least two directors, and the directors of a public company must retire at seventy unless continuance in office is approved by the shareholders.

While in the private company many of the shareholders might be directly involved in the running and management of the business, in the public company there is an apparent divorce between ownership and management. Although the shareholders own the company, they have little opportunity of directly influencing company policy, with the possible exception of annual general meetings or extraordinary meetings. Their control is exercised through the elected board of directors, which then appoints the officials to run the business. This division is increased by the fact that people holding shares are always able to relinquish their ownership by freely selling them. When the shares are listed on the stock exchange the specialist facilities of this market may be used.

The public limited company is a form of organisation especially suitable for large-scale activities where a great deal of capital is required. It tends to dominate in such areas as car production, the chemical and petrochemical industries, and the tobacco industry.

In a similar manner to the private company, the public company has to fulfil certain legal requirements and issue similar documents in order to qualify for a certificate of incorporation. But then it has the added power to issue a prospectus in an attempt to persuade the public to invest in the firm. The prospectus must be drawn up in accordance with the Companies Act 1985, giving details of the company's operations, history, financial position and directors. The actual sale of the shares will generally be handled by an Issuing House.

The activities of public joint stock companies benefit the UK mixed economy considerably. As a form of business organisation they are relatively small in number, and yet they command a very significant portion of economic activity. The *Annual Abstract of Statistics* for 1982 reveals that in 1977 there were 975 quoted companies in the UK.

They had a combined gross trading income of £11,522 millions, and each employed on average 5564 people, with a combined employment representing just under 21 per cent of the total working population. Their fortunes may therefore be said to govern the livelihoods of many people in the UK.

The economic advantage public companies enjoy from being able to raise finance from the general public means that the scope and scale of their operations may be very large. They are able to achieve all the benefits of economies of scale, and move towards a size at which they are making the optimum use of resources. It also suggests that where this sector raises finance on the open market, resources should be allocated towards those projects which are economically most sound.

Probably one of the most significant implications of the existence of this type of organisation arises out of the ease with which the ownership of shares may be transferred. Many financial institutions – for instance, insurance companies, private pension funds and unit trusts – have thus been able to participate on behalf of their investors in the ownership of UK industry. This was revealed in the 1983 Stock Exchange Survey of Share Ownership, which showed that over 57 per cent of the ordinary shares of a sample of 222 companies in 1981 were held by institutions. This indicates that the ownership of industry is spread very far because the institutions themselves have two million shareholders; some of the institutions are pension funds with a total of thirteen and a quarter million members of occupational pension schemes; other institutions are assurance companies with fourteen million savers through life assurance.

The true ownership of public companies, therefore, is effectively in the hands of people who in many cases have little knowledge of the fact, since they rely on the financial institutions to handle their interests. This means, apart from the contribution of this type of organisation as an employer, that the nation as a whole has a tremendous vested financial interest in its affairs.

As a result of the ease with which the shares of the public company may be bought and sold, another form of business organisation has grown up. This is referred to as a **holding company**, which has achieved financial control over other companies through the acquisition of shares. In some cases these subsidiary companies, as they are termed, may provide the holding company's only source of income. Financial control is achieved by the acquisition of 51 per cent of the ordinary shares of the subsidiary, though often a holding of less than 50 per cent may give effective control. Each subsidiary retains its original name and continues to function as a separate entity. However, due to the majority shareholding of the holding company it may direct the policy of the subsidiary to fulfil its overall strategy.

Multinational companies
A multinational can be defined as an organisation in which all considerations related to its growth process and survival are based wholly on the interests of the organisation itself; national pressures have no influence except in that constraints may be imposed on the firm by any country in which it functions. In addition a multinational is defined as an enterprise that owns or controls producing facilities (i.e. factories, mines, oil refineries, distribution outlets, or offices) in more than one country.

Taken together, these two definitions conjure up a picture of a large world-wide organisation controlling many companies and outlets, whose pursuit of its own objectives comes before any national or even international considerations. This is, in fact, a fairly accurate description of some of the really large multinationals, such as Royal Dutch Shell or General Motors. They are truly internationally based organisations with a management team including many different nationalities. They have world-wide interests, often highly diversified, and in some cases they control larger resources than some of the governments with which they deal, even in northern Europe let alone those of developing countries.

Table 1.1 shows the world's leading multinationals. Their relative size may be appreciated when it is realised that Exxon's sales for 1983 of £83,634.6 m. were equivalent to approximately 31 per cent of the UK's GNP.

Multinationals operating in the UK are subject to the normal Company Acts, and are expected to abide by national economic, social and political policies. However, it is not always possible to make them fully accountable; for instance, due to their international nature, they may not reveal information on their operations abroad. This international nature may be appreciated by considering the activities of British Petroleum, the largest UK-based multinational concern. BP operates in more than seventy countries through 650 subsidiaries and associated companies.

Table 1.1: The world's leading multinationals

Rank	Company	Headquarters	Main activity	Sales (£ million)	Year-end
1	Exxon corporation	USA	Oil and gas industries	83,634·6	31.12.83
2	Shell Transport and Trading/Royal Dutch Petroleum	UK/Netherlands	Oil industry	61,027·0	31.12.83
3	General Motors	USA	Motor vehicles	55,092·6	31.12.83
4	American Telephone and Telegraph	USA	Telephone system operator	51,267·4	31.12.83
5	Mitsubishi	Japan	Sogo Shosha*	46,398·9	31.03.83
6	Mitsui & Co.	Japan	Sogo Shosha*	44,098·2	31.03.83
7	Mobil Corporation	USA	Oil and gas industries	42,841·0	31.12.83
8	C. Itoh & Co.	Japan	Sogo Shosha*	38,932·8	31.03.83
9	British Petroleum	UK	Oil industry	37,960·0	31.12.83
10	Marubeni	Japan	Sogo Shosha*	36,255·7	31.03.83

* An integrated trading company.
Source: *The Times 1000*, 1984–5.

Multinationals are undoubtedly the most significant of all the forms of business organisation. Because of their size, their impact is international rather than purely national. It is predicted that by the turn of the century the largest 250 multinationals will account for roughly half the world's output. Their contribution to the economy can be considerable. They may help to stimulate growth in a country by injecting capital, skill, enterprise and expertise into their operations in its economy. For example, the North Sea oil programme benefited from the experience and expertise that the large multinationals were able to bring in from abroad. Due to their size, the multinationals are able to spend a great deal of money and time on research and development; this has meant that they have contributed a considerable amount to the world's technological development.

Threat to national sovereignty
Multinationals have been criticised on the grounds that their activities may pose a threat to a country's national sovereignty. This is because, acting internationally, they may switch resources between countries to secure the best labour, location and tax advantages, and it may therefore be beyond the power of any one government to control them. Also, by a system of internal transfer pricing, they can minimise their tax burden. This is achieved by adjusting the price at which a product is transferred from a subsidiary in one country to that in another. This way the profits made on the product may be declared in the country with the most favourable tax rates. Such a situation is portrayed in Fig. 1.5, which shows the advantage to the multinational of declaring its profits in country B, thus minimising its total tax burden.

By switching sums of money from one country to another in anticipation of a devaluation or revaluation of the currency, multinationals may undermine national sovereignty still further. They may thus contribute to exchange-rate instability. Since about one-eighth of world trade is internal to multinationals, their activities may have a serious effect on the ability of a particular country to control its balance of payments. To a certain extent multinationals are able to ignore a country's financial, monetary, fiscal or prices and incomes policy because many of their activities take place abroad. Additionally, they may even attempt to influence a country's internal policies in order to ensure that a sympathetic government is in power to protect their trading and commercial interests.

Co-operatives
A co-operative is basically a 'self-help' organisation. It is a voluntary association of independent economic units such as households, workers, businesses or farms who join together to control and share the profits of production, or to achieve economies in buying or selling products, or for finance or insurance. The main types of co-

Intial Situation

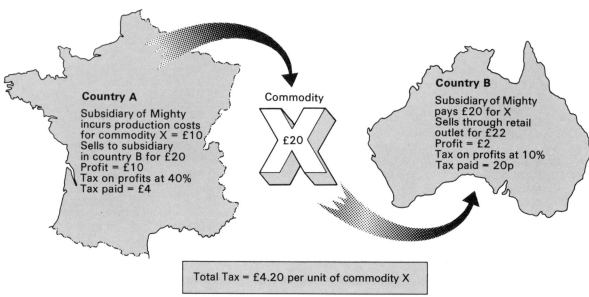

After Transfer Pricing

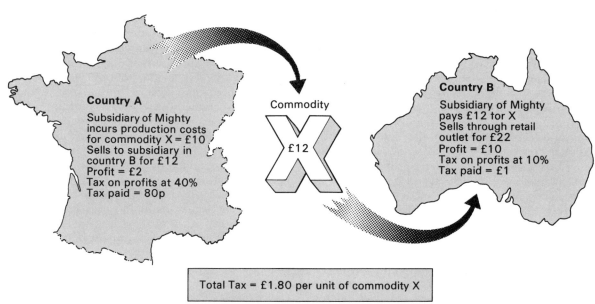

Fig. 1.5: Transfer pricing between subsidiaries of 'Mighty' multinational company

operative operating in the UK are shown in Fig. 1.6.

The **retail co-operative societies** are the ones with which most people are familiar. They have to be registered as self-governing bodies under the Industrial and Provident Societies Acts. The members of these societies are also the customers who use the shops. The society's shares are not quoted on the Stock Exchange and remain constant in value. Any number of shares may be issued. The return to the members on their shares is normally in the form of a payment of fixed interest on capital

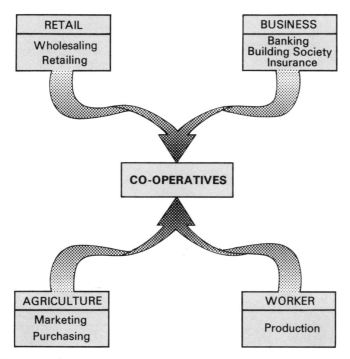

Fig. 1.6: Main types of co-operatives

and a dividend on purchases, in the form of either cash or trading stamps.

The shareholders have only one vote each, irrespective of the size of their investments in the society. This prevents any one member or group of members from taking control of the society. They elect a board of directors or a committee of management, who in turn employ officials to manage the day-to-day running of the business, and are responsible for its overall policy.

The retail societies are members of the Co-operative Wholesale Society (CWS), from whom they may purchase their stock. The CWS is managed by representatives elected from the retail societies and helps to provide, for the smaller societies in particular, some of the advantages of bulk purchasing which they would not otherwise be able to enjoy.

During the past twenty years the retail societies have tended to suffer as a result of the competition from the larger supermarkets such as Tesco, Sainsbury and Fine Fare. Their share of the total retail business fell from 10·9 per cent to 7·0 per cent between 1961 and 1984, whereas that of the larger multiples rose from 29·2 per cent to 48 per cent. This decline in business has contributed to a fall in the number of larger co-operative units. After the

Second World War there were well over 1000 separate societies in operation, whereas now there are less than 100, plus 30 branches of the Co-operative Retail Services. This is the largest society, with over two million members.

The main implication for the UK mixed economy of the existence of this type of organisation in retailing concerns the aspect of 'self-help'. By combining to form a retail co-operative, households should be capable of protecting themselves from unfair and dishonest trade practices and of ensuring that their needs as consumers are satisfied. This was the purpose of the first retail co-operative set up in Lancashire in 1844 by the 'Rochdale Pioneers'. They jointly provided the capital to open a small grocery warehouse to supply their needs. This was in order to fight against profiteering in the retail sector.

Apart from the retail societies there are a number of other co-operatives operating in the UK. In the field of commerce there is the Co-operative Bank, the Nationwide Building Society and the Co-operative Insurance Society. In agriculture, marketing and purchasing, co-operatives are formed. For example, farmers might find it advantageous to establish a co-operative for the purchase of fertilisers and foodstuffs, or for the marketing of fruit, livestock and grain. In each case larger quantities might be handled and consequently economies of scale enjoyed. In the field of production, a number of co-operatives exist producing such items as shoes, clothing and furniture.

A co-operative may adopt a formal constitution which will allow it to be a separate corporate body, thus enjoying limited liability. This may be achieved in one of two ways. Either by registering as an Industrial and Provident Society with the Registrar of Friendly Societies. Seven founder members are required to start and registration costs £300, although a reduction is given if the 'model rules' of a promoting body are used. Alternatively, it is possible to write co-operative principles into the memorandum and articles of association of a traditional company. Only two people are required to form a company, and the Registrar of Companies charges £50.

The Labour government of 1974–9 lent its support to the creation of more productive worker co-operatives where the purpose of establishing the co-operative was to save jobs. This was the case with Kirkby Manufacturing and Engineering, the Meriden Motor Cycles operation and the *Scottish Daily News*, all of which were threatened with closure and a resultant loss of jobs until the workers took over.

This type of organisation has tremendous social and economic implications for the UK mixed economy, because a co-operative represents a system based upon the philosophy of equality, equity and mutual self-help. The essential principles of co-operation are:

1. Membership is open and voluntary.
2. Control is democratic in that each member has one vote irrespective of capital or labour input.
3. Co-operatives accept that they have a social responsibility, although they still have to be run on commercially sound lines.
4. Profits are either ploughed back into the business or distributed to the members.

Such a philosophy should lead to less strife and conflict, because ultimately a co-operative is a business owned and controlled by the people working in it and run for their benefit.

In September 1978 the then Labour government established the Co-operative Development Agency in order to identify, promote and encourage viable projects to be undertaken on a co-operative basis. The Conservative government since its election in 1979 has supported the Co-operative Development Agency and as a result it has been able to encourage a number of co-operative ventures in such areas as building, printing and publishing.

The public sector

The nationalised industries
A nationalised industry may be described as an organisation created by Act of Parliament, owned by the general public, but directed by the government. The major UK nationalised industries are shown in Table 1.2. Their relative size and significance as employers of labour may be appreciated by considering that Imperial Chemical Industries, the fourth largest private sector industrial company in the UK, employed 117,900 people in 1983 and had a turnover of £8,256,000,000.

Table 1.2: The main UK nationalised industries, 1983–4

Industry	Turnover (£ thousands)	Number of employees
Electricity Council	9,128,400	141,385
British Gas	5,930,300	103,300
National Coal Board	4,932,000	268,000
British Steel	3,231,000	94,800
British Railways Board	3,188,800	200,789
Post Office	2,714,400	203,156

Source: *The Times 1000*, 1984–5.

Legally this type of organisation is vested not in a company but in a **public corporation**, which has been created by statute. The statute grants each corporation certain fixed financial and economic rights and duties. The corporation is created as a separate legal entity which can sue and be sued in the courts, and which can hire and fire its staff. Therefore, with the exception of matters specified in the statutes, a public corporation is free to conduct its business as it sees fit, and even its finances are treated separately from those of the government. The nationalised industries have no shareholders as such, as their equity is said to belong to the nation.

The nationalised industries are organised, controlled and run by four groups. (1) Parliament is responsible for general policy. (2) The minister assigned to the industry represents its interests in Parliament and is responsible for ensuring that its activities reflect the public interest. (3) Each nationalised industry has a board or council responsible for its day-to-day running. (4) The activities of the nationalised industry are observed by the consumer consultative council, which acts as a watchdog for the consumer and also as a sounding-board for new ideas or proposed changes put forward by the minister or board.

Arguments for and against nationalisation
The majority of nationalised industries were created as a result of the compulsory purchase by the government on behalf of the nation of the assets and ownership of an industry previously in the private sector. Opinions differ as to the contribution made by these organisations to the working of the economy.

The supporters of nationalisation see the process as the realisation of a natural monopoly. They claim that the very nature of such operations as rail, electricity and gas lend themselves to a large-scale form of organisation. This is because they have the potential to enjoy extensive economies of scale, and competition is deterred by the heavy initial costs of capital, research and advertising. Consequently they form a natural monopoly. In order to reduce any danger of consumer exploitation, supporters feel that this should be operated in the public sector.

Supporters also feel that nationalisation provides the state with the opportunity to control the allocation of some of the nation's key resources such as coal and steel. This is considered desirable because the private sector may sometimes fail through the market mechanism to recognise a particular need of society. Advocates of nationalisation also point out that it provides the state with the opportunity to control for strategic reasons those areas of economic activity, like transport, power and basic raw materials, which are crucial to national security.

Nationalised industries are responsible for 10 per cent of GDP in the UK. So it is possible for the government to use them as a balancing factor in the economy. For example, during periods of high unemployment, jobs may be maintained in the nationalised sector. During periods of inflation their prices and costs, especially incomes, can be carefully controlled.

People opposed to nationalisation feel that it has rather different implications. The greatest complaint is that the nationalised industry is totally insensitive to the needs of its consumers due to its centralised form of administration. The fact that it

is a state-run monopoly is felt to aggravate the situation still further. It is considered that, because the industry has been removed from the discipline of market forces, there is no way in which it can accurately gauge the needs of the consumer.

Another major criticism often levelled at the nationalised industry concerns the way it is controlled and administered. The administration of an individual industry or service is said to require an approach totally different from that employed in government administration. It is claimed, therefore, that the government personnel involved in running the nationalised industry are incapable of carrying out the task efficiently. Added to this is the point that the public sector lacks the spur to efficiency of the profit motive, which dominates in the private sector. Some opponents of nationalisation also feel that it will lead to an extension of state activities that may result in an infringement of private rights, in that private property is compulsorily taken into public control.

The structure of organisations

It has been shown that the type of business environment in which the organisation operates helps to determine its objectives. These objectives in turn lead to the establishment of a particular type of organisation. Both factors combine with technological change and the nature of the people involved to determine the organisation's structure.

The structure of any organisation essentially means the **network** or **pattern of relationships** between people both as individuals and as members of a working group. It reflects the relationships between the various groups, the way in which people **communicate** and are **co-ordinated**, the methods by which **authority** and **responsibility** are exercised by people within the organisation and their **roles** as managers, supervisors and employees. Every form of organisation is a method of co-ordinating a series of activities or tasks in order to carry out an operation and achieve set objectives. The structure will therefore help to determine the way in which the activity or task is completed.

Theoretical approach
There are three main theories (Fig. 1.7) that may be studied to find an explanation as to how different organisational structures have evolved or been planned. It is important to look at these theories

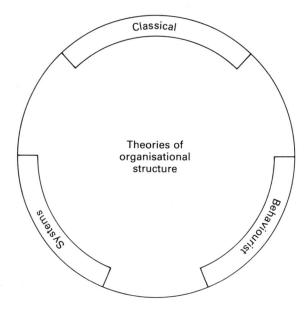

Fig. 1.7: Theories of organisational structure

because they help to provide a basis for the analysis and then possible modification and improvement of existing structures.

1. The *classical or traditional theory* provides a general set of principles concentrating on the way in which tasks should be grouped under departments or functional areas within the organisation. It states that if the organisation is to operate effectively then the grouping should be carried out on the following basis:

(a) The lines of responsibility for a particular functional area and the tasks relating to it should be clearly established and widely known.
(b) Authority should be delegated and derived from the position of the individual in relation to a particular functional area within the organisation.
(c) Each person in the organisation should be answerable to only one person.
(d) Lines of command should be as short as possible.
(e) Realistic limits should be placed on the extent of employees' managerial responsibilities.

2. The *behaviourist or human relations theory* concentrates on how people actually work together. It makes the point that it is possible to raise productivity in any organisation by improving human relations. The theory stems mainly from experiments carried out in the USA under the guidance of Professor Elton Mayo at the Hawthorne Works of the Western Electric Company near Chicago between 1923 and the early 1930s. Members of the workforce were found to be more effective and happy if they were made to feel what they were doing had some meaning and value, and if within the organisation their contribution was acknowledged and their position in the structure clearly defined.

This means that the organisation should be structured in such a way that there is the facility for **consultation** between management and the workforce, and the latter should then be able to **contribute to decision-making**. Every effort should also be made to create both satisfactory and contented working groups, which should receive **social** and **psychological rewards** as well as **economic** ones.

3. The *systems theory* concentrates on the fact that organisations are part of a system of taking resources from the environment, converting them into a good or service and then putting them back into the environment. This means that in a national context all organisations are interdependent; the output of one may be the input of another. For example, a school or college could not function without an input of books produced by publishers

and printers, writing-paper produced by paper manufacturers, and tables and chairs produced by the furniture industry. The theory acknowledges that the system must provide what is required. Otherwise it will cease to operate or will have to be radically altered. Each system is made up of a series of **sub-systems**.

The system actually functions according to the type of organisational structure – together with three other factors: (a) the background, qualities and motivation of the employees, (b) the level and stage of the technology employed and (c) the objectives of the organisation. Consequently the effectiveness of any organisational structure will depend upon ensuring that the other factors are correctly determined and where governed by their own sub-system that these are taken into account.

This point was taken up by researchers at the Tavistock Institute of Human Relations, which acknowledged the importance of considering both the social and technical sub-systems of any organisation when making changes. It is important to relate the people in the social sub-system to the tasks in the technical sub-system. Any technological change needs to be viewed alongside the social sub-system made up of the people who are going to implement it. For example, there is little point in mechanising a system of production if it destroys the social system of the people who are to operate it and in so doing eliminates any of the productivity advantages associated with the new system.

Formal and informal structures

Any organisational structure reflects both a formal and an informal set of relationships.

Formal structure

The formal set of relationships reflects the disposition of authority, span of control and chain of command and is often presented in the form of an **organisation chart**. An example is given in Fig. 1.8. This shows the Murphy Manufacturing Company, which has two divisions: one concerned with the manufacture and sale of plastic products, and the other concerned with making and selling paints.

The organisation chart in Fig. 1.8 reflects the concepts of line, staff and functional authority. **Line** authority stems from the ultimate or fundamental authority to command, act or decide on matters affecting others and to require them to act on any decisions made or orders given, which are directly concerned with achieving the

organisation's overall objectives. **Staff** authority is essentially advisory. A person in this position does not give orders to carry out line duties but rather gives assistance and makes recommendations for line managers to act upon. **Functional** authority is given to specialists in a particular area, who then have the right, unlike the staff managers, to give orders regarding matters appertaining to that function. This form of authority differs from the line in that its right to command is limited to a particular specialist area.

It is possible to identify these three concepts of authority within the network of relationships revealed in the chart (Fig. 1.8). The specific objectives of the Murphy Manufacturing Company are to stay in business and to make as much profit as possible through the manufacture and sale of plastic and paint products within its two divisions. Within each division the works manager is in charge of the manufacturing plant, the research manager is responsible for the improvement and modification of existing products or the development of new ones, and the marketing manager has responsibility for going out and selling the products. As they are so directly involved in achieving the organisation's objectives, these three managers are answerable on a *line* basis to the divisional manager. He/she in turn is answerable for the performance of the division through a direct line to the general manager.

Within each division the chief accountant and personnel manager advises the divisional manager on financial, industrial-relations and personnel matters. This is essentially a *staff* relationship. Similarly, at the company level the general manager would look to the chief accountant and to the personnel and public relations managers for advice. But the general manager would have more of a *line* relationship with the marketing, production, personnel and research managers, as they are more directly concerned with the overriding objectives of the organisation.

The relationship between the company and the divisions helps to explain functional relationships and authority. At company level each function may establish its own policies and procedures, and then these are carried out in the relevant divisional departments. For example, the company marketing manager may establish a particular advertising policy which also has to be adopted by the divisional marketing manager. This approach is known as **functional control**. It is important to recognise the particular position of the divisional

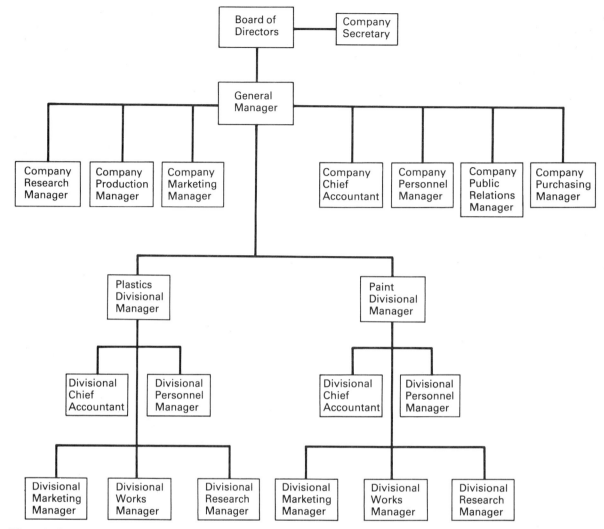

Fig. 1.8: Organisation chart

managers within this system of authority. Due to their *line* relationship with the general manager they may decide to go against the advice of, for example, the divisional chief accountant even though his/her advice may reflect the company financial policy. Under these circumstances the divisional chief accountant may refer the matter upwards on a line basis to his/her company functional head, who in turn may appeal to the general manager for a decision.

Within any formal structure some positions will involve both line and staff relationships. The people holding these positions need to be fully aware at any time whether they are acting in a line or staff capacity.

To secure a complete picture of the organisation's formal structure it would be necessary to show all the network of relationships operating within any function. For example, the company chief accountant might have line authority over a team comprising a management accountant, computer manager, wages manager and statistician. Similarly, the purchasing manager might have a chief buyer and stores manager working for him/her.

Informal structure

In reality the organisation does not function purely on the basis of a formal structure but may rely heavily on informally established relationships. This is because within the working environment a social system exists through people forming into social groups and developing informal and often unofficial methods of getting things done. This may be capitalised upon by managers and supervisors if they recognise the make-up of the informal groups and involve them in the decision-making process.

The particular value of giving recognition to the informal relationships is that it acknowledges the standards set by the social system in existence; failure to maintain those standards could result in exclusion from the social group, which might be felt to be far worse than any action that management might be prepared to take. Also the informal structure may take over from the formal if it is felt that the formal has become obsolete.

Environmental factors

The form of organisational structure that is established will be partly determined by the environmental circumstances, in terms of the nature of the market and the level of technological development of the product under which the organisation is to operate. It is possible to identify two contrasting forms of organisational structure that are relevant for different environmental circumstances: mechanistic and organic.

A **mechanistic** structure is one which reflects the classical theory with a precise definition of employees' tasks and the technical methods to be employed. It has a strong vertical system of communications and control, involving line relationships and an emphasis on the importance of loyalty to superiors. This form of structure is particularly suitable for an organisation operating in a stable market where the product is well established and technological developments are unlikely to render it obsolete, thus requiring rapid changes in design or function. This would probably be the form of organisation operating at Murphy Manufacturing if it was well established in the market with a successful range of plastic and paint products.

An **organic** structure is one where jobs are regularly redefined, where there is little specialisation and a network system of control, communication and authority. The employees emphasise the overall objectives of the organisation rather than the achievement of a particular task or function. This form of structure is suitable for a changing environment where modification and improvement are regularly made in the product or service and where the methods of production or operation are subject to technical change. This form of organisation would be particularly suitable for an organisation engaged in research and development work or in management consultancy, where the tasks and environment are constantly changing.

It may be concluded that an effective organisational structure requires (1) a degree of flexibility to allow for environmental change, (2) an acknowledgement of the value of the informal structure that may exist within an organisation, and (3) clear decisions regarding line and staff management.

The degree of mix within the business environment

This chapter has shown that the key features of the organisations making up the business environment are their objectives, their legal form and their structure. All of these features are directly influenced by the type of economy created by the government. UK organisations operate in a mixed economy, but governments of differing political persuasion will adjust the degree of mix within that economy. Since the Second World War successive Conservative governments have encouraged free enterprise and an expansion of the private sector, while Labour governments have promoted an expansion of state control and a larger public sector.

Such adjustments mean that organisations may find themselves in an economy where the degree of competition has changed, where government regulations and controls over the allocation and use of resources have altered, where the distribution of income and wealth has been adjusted, or even where the organisation itself may have been either placed under the direct control of the state or released into the private sector. The privatisation policy of the Conservative government elected in 1979 is a prime example of the kind of adjustment that may be made. A consideration of the different types of privatisation and the reactions of supporters and opponents to them should help to illustrate the implications for organisations of alterations in the degree of mix.

Privatisation involves the transfer of industries, assets and activities to the private sector and the extension of market forces throughout the economy. The newly elected Conservative government of 1979 had come in on a manifesto that contained many of the ingredients of the future policy of privatisation. For example, in the section on nationalisation it proposed, among other things, to sell back into private ownership the then recently nationalised aerospace and shipbuilding industries, with opportunities for employees to purchase shares. This heralded the gradual introduction by the Conservative government of a variety of different policy measures, all of which helped to open up the public sector to market forces.

The policies may be classified under three main headings. First, **liberalisation** which involves the promotion of competition, or competitive behaviour, in certain activities that were either reserved to statutory monopoly or subject to restricted entry. The Transport Act 1980, for example, allowed for the de-regulation of express coach services and the relaxation of other transport regulations, thus permitting the rapid development of private express coach services. Similarly, under the Telecommunications Act 1981 it became possible to connect approved equipment to the British Telecom network; the Act also allowed for the licensing of private competition. Under this provision in 1982 the Secretary of State for Industry granted a 25-year licence to Mercury to run an independent telecommunications system in competition with British Telecom.

The second type of privatisation involves the **transfer of the ownership of assets to the private sector**, through either the public issue of shares on the Stock Exchange or the sale of physical assets. The former was the approach taken with British Aerospace and Cable and Wireless, and the latter with the sale of British Rail's hotels. The third approach that has been taken to privatisation involves the **encouragement of the private provision of services** currently provided on a collective basis by the state. This generally involves contracting out services previously administered by government departments and local authorities. For example, local authorities such as Southend, Eastbourne and Peterborough have contracted out their refuse disposal services. Similarly some regional health authorities have contracted out the catering and laundry services operating in the hospitals.

The case for and against privatisation

The privatisation debate helps highlight the real issues involved for organisations of a change in the mix in the economy. The supporters of privatisation would agree with the view put forward by Nicholas Ridley, Financial Secretary to the Treasury, on 12 February 1982. He claimed:

> It must be right to press ahead with the transfer of ownership from the state to private enterprise of as many public sector businesses as possible. ... The introduction of competition must wherever possible be linked to a transfer of ownership to private citizens and away from the state. Real public ownership – that is, ownership by people – must be and is our ultimate role.

This statement illustrates the government's claim that privatisation should provide a major boost to wider share ownership through the sale of shares in public corporations to individual investors and private firms. The supporters of privatisation would also claim that it reduces the burden on the Exchequer: both through the receipts from sales of assets and through the removal from the Public Sector Borrowing Requirement of any further borrowing by the public body concerned.

Private ownership is often preferred because it is felt that it will result in lower costs; and the discipline of the market-place should result in better investment decisions. It is claimed that there is a danger that managers and employees in a nationalised industry may feel that the government as a banker is a 'softer touch' than a commercial bank. This is felt to result in a continuation of loss-making activities, resistance to any form of structural change or tight investment appraisal. The advocates of privatisation further claim that it should lead to a more efficient use of public resources, since industries not subject to competition may be subject to less pressure to achieve efficiency and to respond to consumer preferences.

The opponents of privatisation claim that it penalises the more successful public enterprise, because in reality the private sector will only buy profitable assets. Also this will mean that the Exchequer will lose the income from the profitable industries and will merely be left with the funding of the unprofitable ones.

Those opposed to privatisation claim that

liberalisation in particular is likely to break up an industry's network of services, thus hitting the ability of a nationalised industry to cross-subsidise the unprofitable parts of its service with the profitable. This could mean that some groups in the community might lose the service altogether or have to pay a much higher price for it. They highlight the case of rural transport and communication services. Arguments are also put forward against liberalisation on the grounds that it might result in 'cream skimming' as private companies in such industries as transport, aviation and telecommunications introduce new services only in the profitable sectors, which will then compound the problems for cross-subsidisation.

Finally, those opposed to privatisation claim that it may in many cases destroy what is really a natural monopoly, which would be damaged if competition was introduced; this in itself might result in wasteful duplication. They claim that this would be particularly true of a local telephone service.

2. Demographic, Social and Technological Change and the Organisation

A time of change

The past twenty-five years have been a time of rapid change. They have witnessed the growth of UK unemployment to above three million, the introduction of Value Added Tax, the commercial exploitation of North Sea oil, the acceptance of the UK into the European Community, the Falklands War, the change to a multi-racial and multi-cultural population, the passing of new laws to protect people at work in terms of safety, job security and equal opportunity, the election of the UK's first woman Prime Minister, the formation of the Social Democratic Party/Liberal Alliance, the reduction of the voting age to eighteen, a fivefold increase in the divorce rate, the introduction of production lines manned by robots, the appearance of video-recorders, microwave ovens and computers in our homes and of BMX bikes and turbo-charged cars on our roads. The Beatles and Rolling Stones, the Bay City Rollers, David Bowie, Queen and George Michael have all had their turn in the charts. Sainsbury, Tesco and Marks & Spencer have taken over in the high street, and McDonalds have taken a huge bite out of the rapidly expanding fast-food market.

Within this constantly changing environment individuals have had to live and public and private sector organisations have had to operate. To survive, an organisation has to be prepared to adapt to changing circumstances and to embrace new ideas and methods. This is necessary if it wishes to continue to meet the changing material and employment needs of the individual and the collective needs of society.

Economic, political and legal factors influence the general environment in which the organisation functions. Such factors will be reflected as a constant theme throughout both this and the second volume of the book. However, there are certain factors that have a more immediate impact on the organisation. These include demographic and social change, together with technological developments. The former involve changes in the total size and structure of the population and the make-up of society. These will create a different pattern of needs, which will cause organisations to adjust the scale and nature of activities. For example, central and local government departments have to adjust the provision of educational facilities according to the number of children of school age. Similarly, organisations involved in house-building have to take account of changes in the age at which people marry, the average household size and the geographical distribution of the population.

Technological developments allow organisations to make changes in the process by which a good or service is produced, or changes in the product itself. For example, technological change has enabled Fiat to establish one of the finest fully automated production lines, while at the same time it has led many firms to design and manufacture home computers.

Demographic change: population size and structure

In this section we consider the significance to the individual and organisation of changes in the total size and structure of the population.

The size of the total population

Table 2.1: UK population, 1931–2001

Year	Home population (thousands)
1931	46,038
1941	n.a.
1951	50,290
1961	52,807
1971	55,907
1981	56,379
1991 (projection)	56,912
2001 (projection)	57,968

Source: *Annual Abstract of Statistics* (HMSO, 1985).

The figures in Table 2.1 show how the population of the UK has increased since 1931. The growth rate in both absolute and percentage terms is analysed in Table 2.2. Because the figure for 1941 is not available, the period 1931–51 has been taken for comparison. The average rate of growth per decade during this period is 4.6 per cent.

Table 2.2: Growth rate of the population, 1931–2001

Period	Actual difference (thousands)	Percentage
1931–51	4252	9·2
1951–61	2517	5·0
1961–71	3100	5·8
1971–81	472	0·8
1981–91 (projection)	533	0·94
1991–2001 (projection)	1056	1·85

The analysis reveals that there was a fairly steady increase in the population of approximately 5 per cent for each decade up to 1971. There was a considerable fall in the rate of growth during the 1970s to around 0·8 per cent, which it is predicted will increase only slightly during the 1980s, but will then accelerate to 1·85 per cent for the final decade of the century.

Factors influencing the size of the population
The alteration in the total size of the UK population has been caused by changes in the **birth rate**, the **death rate** and the **rate of migration**. The birth and death rates are expressed as the number of births or deaths per year per 1000 of the population. Table 2.3 shows how these have altered during the period 1946–83 and also how they have contributed to the rate of population increase. The table shows that the variations in the rate of increase have been largely due to fluctuations in the birth rate rather than in the death rate, which has remained relatively constant.

The birth rate peaked in both 1946–51 and 1961–6. In the first case this was due to the very high marriage rates immediately after the war. In the second it was caused partly by the substantial increase in the number of immigrants coming from countries with high fertility rates and partly by the relative economic calm, which encouraged people to marry younger and have children earlier.

Since 1966 there has been a steady decline in the **birth rate**, and all of the signs seem to suggest that this is likely to continue. This has been due to a

Table 2.3: UK birth rate and death rate, 1946–83

Period	Birth rate (average annual figure)	Death rate (average annual figure)	Rate of increase %
1946–51	18·28	12·01	6·27
1951–6	15·68	11·78	3·9
1956–61	16·74	11·63	5·11
1961–6	18·34	11·81	6·53
1966–71	17·16	11·7	5·46
1971–6	14·14	11·9	2·24
1976–83	12·62	11·78	0·84

Source: Adapted from information supplied by the Office of Population Censuses and Surveys, the General Register Office (Scotland), the General Register Office (N. Ireland); and from *Annual Abstract of Statistics* (HMSO, 1985).

variety of factors. First, the average age of marriage has stopped falling, and people who have recently married are having fewer children in the first years of their married life than in the past. Secondly, the changes in the law concerning abortion and the spread of free contraceptives have tended to reduce the number of unwanted children. This is especially true amongst younger women; as is demonstrated in Fig. 2.1, there has been a significant reduction between 1971–83 of the number of births per 1000 for women under the age of 19.

The third factor that has contributed to the fall in the birth rate has been the changing role of women in society. More and more women have become active in the working population. This has meant that the immediate economic burden involved in having a child is greater than it used to be, since the

Fig. 2.1: Live birth rates by age of mother, 1971– 83

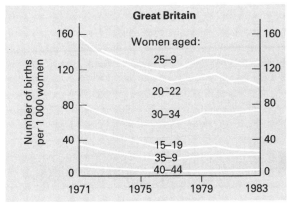

Source: *Social Trends*, no. 15 (HMSO, 1985)

mother's earnings have to be sacrificed at least during the final months of pregnancy, and in the majority of cases until the child is of school age or even older.

The long-term costs associated with bringing up children have also risen. Because of the raising of the school-leaving age and the increased provision of further and higher education places, children remain an economic burden to their families for a longer period of time. Inevitably these rising costs make potential parents think twice before embarking on a family, and as a result have contributed to the general decline in the birth rate.

The **death rate** has been relatively stable since the war. Mortality rates had already reached fairly low levels by 1945, and so there was very little chance of them improving.

Mortality in childhood and early adult life is very low. Of those who live until their first birthday, 95·1 per cent of the males and 96·8 per cent of the females survive until they are 45. Consequently, the loss of life in the child-bearing years up to 45 is so low that it is almost impossible for there to be any fundamental increase in the death rate that could significantly influence the size of the total population.

The main cause of death amongst the elderly has tended to be the degenerative diseases such as cancer and diseases of the circulatory system. Unless a significant breakthrough occurs in the treatment of these diseases, the pattern of death rate established since the war for this age group is likely to continue indefinitely. So the stable death rate experienced during the past thirty years is likely to continue into the foreseeable future, and the death rate is likely to continue to play a minor role in determining changes in the total size of the population.

Table 2.4: Net migration, 1941–2001

Period	Net migration (thousands)
1941–51	n.a.
1951–61	+57
1961–71	−428
1971–81	−346
1981–91 (projection)	−500
1991–2001 (projection)	−500

Source: Adapted from *Annual Abstract of Statistics* (HMSO, 1975 and 1982).

The total size of the UK population has been considerably influenced by alterations in the level of **net migration**. Table 2.4 shows that during the period 1951–61 there was almost equal emigration and immigration, with a net balance of 57,000. The majority of the immigrants during this period were from the 'old Commonwealth' countries and Ireland. In the 1960s outward migration exceeded inward by 428,000. This change was brought about initially by the Commonwealth Immigrants Act 1962 and then perpetuated by subsequent restrictive measures imposed on immigrants. This situation continued in the 1970s, and the projected net migration figures indicate that it is likely to continue in the future, running at about 500,000 each decade.

It is not only the numbers involved in net migration that are important but also the demographic characteristics of the population involved. During the past thirty years the majority of the immigrants entering the UK have been relatively young. This is because most immigration has been of people coming to work in the UK, and their families. Consequently, they have increased the size of the population of child-bearing age and hence account for a fairly high number of births. The immigrant population has also tended to produce families slightly larger than the national average. Due to their relative youth, the death rate amongst the immigrants has been comparatively low.

In general the emigrants leaving the UK have been older than their counterparts entering the country. The term 'brain drain' has often been applied to these emigrants, as many of them have been highly qualified people attracted by high salaries and better opportunities abroad. Many people have gone to the United States of America and Canada, although more recently there has been a flood of people to the Arab states, where it is possible to earn three times the equivalent UK salary as a doctor, scientist, technician, engineer or football coach. The loss of such talented people must reduce the ability of the UK to satisfy all its collective and material needs.

The significance of changes in the total population size
The increase in the size of the UK population since the war, and the projected increase until the turn of the century, is significant in terms of the availability of resources to support it. A study of this relationship between population size and the available resources may be approached in two

ways: either by considering the amount of food necessary to sustain a larger population; or by looking at the effect of population growth on the level of national output.

The **Malthusian approach**, so called because it was originally described by the Reverend Thomas Robert Malthus in his *Essay on Population* in 1798, is that the size of the population grows geometrically, whilst the food supply, the means of sustaining that population, grows only arithmetically. This suggests that an ever-increasing population will eventually outrun its means of subsistence.

On the evidence available to him, Malthus was justified in his fears. However, he had not foreseen the Industrial Revolution, which would enable the UK and other industrial countries to improve production to such an extent that an ever-increasing population could be supported by exporting surplus production of manufactured goods in exchange for imported foodstuffs. But although the UK and other developed countries have been able to operate under this system, there is still a large proportion of the world that has not been so fortunate and suffers from serious malnutrition and famine. Perhaps the developed world has been able to survive only because of the uneven distribution of world resources, which has enabled industrial countries to satisfy their needs while others have not.

Can this uneven distribution continue to be tolerated if, as is predicted, the world's population doubles during the next thirty years? If it is not, then countries like the UK could be in a vulnerable and potentially dangerous position. This has already been shown in the early 1970s in the case of the UK's dependence on imported oil. If a similar situation arose in the case of food, then the Malthusian fear of the eighteenth century might become the reality of the twenty-first. To ensure that such a situation does not arise, and that such a basic material need as food is available for the UK citizen, the government will either have to move the country towards greater self-sufficiency in food, or encourage collective self-sufficiency within Europe.

The concept of **optimum population** relates the size of the population to its output. An optimum population, given the amounts of human and physical resources available to a community, is such as to maximise output per head in that community. This means that if the population were smaller, production would be smaller per head; and if it were larger, production would also

be less per head and therefore there would be a problem of overpopulation. This is a more satisfactory approach than that taken by Malthus because it acknowledges that both population and output are dynamic factors, and so a country's optimum is constantly changing. Changes in the total size of the population may be caused by alterations in any of the three factors already considered, whereas changes in the level of output might be caused by developments in technology, productivity or trade. By attempting to control and influence these factors, it is possible for the government to move the population towards its optimum size.

It is generally considered that the UK's population is already near to its optimum size. However, for reasons already indicated, this does not mean that the country will be capable of supporting the projected population for 2001 of 57,968,000. The experience of the UK in the past has been that output and resources have expanded in line with the population increase. For example, people living a century ago would never have thought it possible that the country would ever have been able to support the population of 56,379,000 in 1981.

However, it would be foolish to believe that countries like the UK will be able to go on maintaining output per head indefinitely by merely improving production as the population increases, or that such adjustments in output will not have implications on other aspects of the life of the community. In fact, there are three fundamental problems associated with the continual increase in the population and resultant adjustment in the level of output:

1. Any adjustment will inevitably affect the distribution of the fruits of production amongst the population. Continual change would provide the opportunity for the creation of either greater equality or greater inequality.
2. There are certain goods which rely on scarce resources whose supply is very difficult or expensive to increase. This is because the resources necessary for this output are in relatively fixed supply. For instance, the quantity of land is fixed so that there is a limit to the area which can be used for agriculture, especially when you consider that land is also needed for housing and recreational uses.
3. Social problems such as excessive noise, pollution and urban congestion are often

associated with an expanding population unless adequate plans are made by government organisations to deal with these a long time in advance. Even then, plans may prove inadequate; an example recently is the UK motorway network, which was built in the 1950s and 1960s to standards that seemed adequate given the forecasts made then of traffic growth. As it turned out, traffic has grown much more quickly than forecast, so that the motorways are now inadequate for present needs.

Declining population

Consideration should also be given to the significance of a **declining population**. Although it is unlikely that such a situation would arise in the UK in the foreseeable future, it is important to consider its implications in order to secure a complete picture of the significance of changes in the total population. There are four main implications to consider:

1. From the point of view of the optimum concept, output per head will expand if the country was originally overpopulated and contract if it was underpopulated, or at the optimum.
2. A declining population is usually accompanied by an older population, since the birth rate will be lower. This older population is likely to be less receptive to new ideas. Such attitudes may tend to hold back the development of the economy. The older population, especially the relatively high number of pensioners, will make greater demands on the welfare services, which in turn will impose a larger burden in terms of taxation on the already declining numbers making up the working population.
3. Levels of production of consumer goods and investment would need to be fundamentally altered to meet the smaller requirements of the declining population.
4. The major advantage associated with a smaller population is that it would be likely to lead to a reduction in congestion and pressure on the fixed supplies of resources such as land.

The sex structure of the population

The population's sex structure refers to the relationship between the number of males and the number of females in the total population. Table 2.5 indicates that, since the war, the UK population has always contained a larger number of females than males. This is shown by comparing the total figure for all ages of both males and females. Since 1941 this gap between the sexes has become increasingly smaller, though the projections suggest that it will continue.

Numerical female dominance has persisted in spite of the larger number of male births. The larger number of male births is revealed by the fact that, for each of the years shown, the 0–4 total of males has been larger than that for females. This male dominance continues up until middle age. Then the situation is completely reversed, as is shown by all the classifications over 45, which indicate a considerably larger number of females than males in the population. The reason for this reversal is the longer life-expectancy of women over men, and the loss of predominantly male lives in the two world wars.

These differences in the numbers of each sex are also revealed in the make-up of the population by marital status. For example, *Social Trends* for 1985 reveals that in 1982 among those aged 65 and above there were nearly five times as many widows as widowers. This had a significant effect on the pattern of demand from this age group for sheltered accommodation and health and social care. Organisations involved in meeting these needs would have had to make allowances for the larger population of females who might have preferred single-sex accommodation and would be likely to suffer from different health and social problems than their male counterparts.

The long-term projection in the table may have to be revised if the activity rate of women in the working population continues to increase. In 1951 the activity rate stood at 34.7 per cent; by 1983 it had grown to 47.6 per cent, and it is likely to continue increasing. This will mean that a growing number of women will be exposed during their lives to both the rigours of child-rearing and the additional stresses associated with employment that have traditionally shortened male life-expectancy. It is possible that the life-expectancy of women may be reduced by the shouldering of these additional pressures.

The age structure of the population

The significance of the changes that have taken place in the age structure of the UK population since 1941 becomes apparent if they are viewed as percentage changes – see Fig. 2.2. The figure shows that the percentage in the youngest age group (0–4) expanded for the first two decades, started to drop

Table 2.5: The sex and age structure of the UK population

(millions)

Ages:	0–4	5–14	15–29	30–44	45–59	60–64	65–74	75–84	85+	All ages
Males										
Mid-year estimates:										
1941	1·7	3·4	3·5	4·6	3·9	1·1	1·4	0·5		20·0
1951	2·2	3·6	5·0	5·5	4·5	1·1	1·6	0·7		24·2
1961	2·2	4·1	5·2	5·2	5·1	1·2	1·6	0·7	0·1	25·5
1971	2·3	4·6	6·0	4·9	5·0	1·5	2·0	0·7	0·1	27·2
1976	1·9	4·7	6·3	5·1	4·8	1·5	2·2	0·8	0·1	27·4
1980	1·7	4·3	6·5	5·5	4·8	1·3	2·3	0·9	0·1	27·4
1981	1·8	4·2	6·5	5·5	4·7	1·4	2·3	0·9	0·1	27·4
1982	1·8	3·9	6·7	5·6	4·6	1·5	2·2	1·0	0·1	27·4
1984	1·8	3·9	6·7	5·6	4·6	1·5	2·2	1·0	0·1	27·4
Projections:										
1986	1·8	3·6	6·8	5·7	4·6	1·5	2·2	1·1	0·2	27·4
1991	2·0	3·6	6·5	6·0	4·7	1·4	2·2	1·1	0·2	27·6
1996	2·1	3·8	5·8	6·2	5·1	1·3	2·2	1·1	0·3	27·9
2001	2·0	4·1	5·4	6·5	5·3	1·3	2·1	1·1	0·3	28·2
Females										
Mid-year estimates:										
1941	1·7	3·3	5·7	5·7	4·6	1·3	1·7	0·8		24·8
1951	2·1	3·5	5·2	5·7	5·1	1·4	2·1	1·1		26·1
1961	2·1	3·9	5·1	5·3	5·5	1·5	2·4	1·2	0·2	27·3
1971	2·2	4·3	5·8	4·9	5·2	1·7	2·8	1·4	0·4	28·7
1976	1.8	4·5	6·1	4·9	5·0	1·7	2·9	1·6	0·4	28.8
1980	1·7	4·1	6·2	5·4	4·9	1·5	3·0	1·7	0·4	28·9
1981	1·7	4·0	6·3	5·4	4·8	1·6	2·9	1·8	0·5	29·0
1982	1·7	3·8	6·4	5·5	4·8	1·6	2·9	1·8	0·5	28·9
1983	1·7	3·7	6·5	5·5	4·7	1·7	2·8	1·8	0·5	28·9
Projections:										
1986	1·7	3·4	6·6	5·7	4·6	1·6	2·8	1·9	0·5	28·9
1991	1·9	3·4	6·2	6·0	4·8	1·5	2·8	1·9	0·6	29·1
1996	2·0	3·6	5·6	6·2	5·2	1·4	2·7	1·9	0·7	29·3
2001	1·9	3·9	5·1	6·4	5·5	1·4	2·6	1·9	0·8	29·4

Source: *Social Trends*, no. 15 (HMSO, 1985).

towards the end of the 1960s and then fell sharply throughout the 1970s. This decline was due largely to the fall in the birth rate. However, in the 1980s the increase is likely to be restored.

One of the most significant changes in the age distribution of the population since 1941 has been the increase in the elderly, both in absolute numbers and as a proportion of the population. The number of people aged 65 or over represented 14.9 per cent of the population in 1983 compared with 9.8 per cent in 1941. This involved an absolute increase of four million people during the period.

Fig. 2.2: Population by age group Source: *Social Trends*, no. 15 (HMSO, 1985)

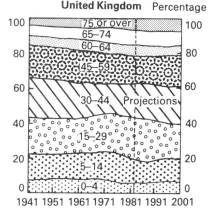

United Kingdom   Percentage

This rate of expansion is not predicted to continue to the end of the century because of the effects of the low birth rates in the late 1920s and 1930s. However, it is expected that within the over-65 group the proportion of people who are more than 75 will continue to increase. These changes will place more demands on those organisations providing health, social and housing facilities, since it is the oldest people who tend to need these services, rather than the more active young elderly aged 65–74.

The dependent population – made up of children under school-leaving age, women aged 60 or over and men aged 65 or over – expanded until the early 1970s. This was caused by two factors: first, the low inter-war birth rate, which resulted in a relative decline in the number of middle-aged people; secondly, the slightly higher birth rate of the 1950s and 1960s. Thus since the war the population tended to become top- and bottom-heavy. This meant that the proportion of the population of approximately working age (the middle group) became increasingly smaller, and was required to support an ever-larger number of dependants in terms of children and the elderly.

This situation had serious economic and social effects. The larger number of dependants required an ever-expanding education, health and social-service system. To finance such an expansion, taxes had to be increased on those who worked, which had an adverse effect on 'work effort' and encouraged demands for inflationary wage increases to compensate for the higher proportion of income being taken in taxes. Social factors, such as the decline of the extended family, aggravated the situation still further, because the state had to accept a larger responsibility towards the elderly. In the past this might have been partly shouldered by the immediate family. It became the acknowledged responsibility of the state to provide adequate properly heated and supervised accommodation for senior citizens, and to ensure that old people were properly fed and received appropriate medical treatment.

Even though the size of the middle group grew in the 1970s, and this trend has been predicted to continue in the 1980s, projections for the final decade of the century suggest that the burden of dependants will continue to reappear for many years to come. The proportion of dependants could be expanded still further as a result of the growth of unemployment since the late 1970s. Increased support has been needed for those people who do not have jobs, and unemployment has also encouraged young people to stay longer in education and people to retire at an earlier age.

The working population and its occupational distribution

The **total working population** is made up of all those people who are willing and able to work. It consists of people in employment, those in HM Forces and women's services, those who are self-employed and those who are registered as unemployed. Table 2.6 reveals that between 1961 and 1971 *the working population declined as a proportion of the total population*, but in the 1970s this trend was reversed.

Three main factors contributed to these changes:

1. Adjustments in the birth and death rates caused changes in the number of people of working age, that is, the 16–65 age group.
2. Due to greater provision of pension and welfare facilities for the elderly, there was a widespread acceptance of a retirement age of 65 for men and 60 for women. This meant, for example, that the activity rate of the 65+ group fell from 15·9 per cent in 1951 to 5·2 per cent in 1980.

Table 2.6: The working population and activity rates in the UK, 1951–80

Year	Population (thousands) Total	Working	All ages	15+	15–19	20–4	25–44	45–64	65+	20–4	25–44	45–64
						Males and Females					Females	
1951	50,225	23,809	47·4	59·6	81·3	79·7	66·7	59·5	15·9	65·4	36·1	28·7
1961	52,807	25,345	47·9	60·5	72·9	76·8	69·4	66·0	12·7	62·0	40·8	37·1
1966	54,643	26,174	47·9	62·1	68·6	77·2	72·6	60·6	13·1	61·6	47·1	46·1
1971	55,907	25,421	45·5	61·1	58·4	75·1	74·4	71·5	11·3	60·1	50·6	50·2
1980	56,314	26,819	47·6	59·8	53·8	78·0	79·7	71·0	5·2	68·5	61·0	53·0

Source: Adapted from *British Labour Statistics: Historical Abstract 1886–1968*, Department of Employment; *Department of Employment Gazette*, November 1973 and April 1981; *Annual Abstract of Statistics* (HMSO, 1982).

3. The activity rate of the 15–19 group fell from 81.3 per cent in 1951 to 53.8 per cent in 1980. This was caused by the progressive raising of the school-leaving age to 16 and an increase in the number of young people continuing their education after this minimum school-leaving age.

Table 2.6 also reveals that *female employment has played an increasingly important role in the size of the total working population*. In particular, there has been a large and continuous increase in the number of women aged between 25–64 in the workforce. The majority of the women in this age group are married, and they have been able to increase their activity rate for a number of reasons:

1. The recent decline in the birth rate and the wider availability of crèche facilities have reduced the number of women who either want or have to fulfil the traditional full-time role of wife and mother.
2. The greater application of technology to housework has allowed women to devote far more time to activities outside the home.
3. There are more jobs available that are suitable for women with young children, such as those with flexible hours, those in the service sector and those of a light industrial nature.
4. There has been a general change in attitude towards the role of women in society and their right to be treated equally in the jobs market. This has been supported by such legislation as the Equal Pay Act 1970. This was later amended when the Sex Discrimination Act 1975 was introduced, and in the same year the Employment Protection Act came into force, further extending a woman's right to return to work after having a child.

If the government is to meet the employment needs of the population it must try to stimulate the economy to a level of activity that will satisfy the requirements of the working population. It must also acknowledge and make provision for the larger number of women in the total working population.

Occupational distribution
The occupational distribution of the population may be categorised under four main headings. First, those working in the **primary** industries, which refers to the activities of agriculture, forestry, fishing, mining and quarrying. Secondly, those employed in **manufacturing and construction**. Thirdly, those people who operate all the various **services** in the country, such as the public utilities, distribution, commerce, transport and communications, professional and scientific services, catering and hotels, and national and local government. Fourthly, those people who are members of the **armed forces**.

Table 2.7 shows that since 1951 there has been a large proportionate movement of people out of the primary sector, and gradual movement out of manufacturing, construction and the armed forces, into the service industries. This has been caused by a number of factors. Increased mechanisation has tended to reduce the numbers working on the land and in the extractive industries. Similarly, the numbers employed in the manufacturing and construction sector have been reduced by the introduction of new technology, which has resulted in higher productivity and the loss of jobs in this sector. The increased number of people employed in the services reflects the growing expertise and reputation of the UK in such fields as insurance, banking, finance, business services and the professional and scientific services. These activities have become very large contributors to the invisible earnings side of the UK balance of payments. The growth in the service sector also reflects the increasing number of people who were taken on in the 1970s by central and local government, which undertook at that time to expand the scope and level of public services. This is a trend that has been arrested to some extent in the 1980s by a policy designed to increase efficiency and productivity, and hence to provide such services with a smaller workforce.

What the figures fail to reveal is the growing

Table 2.7: Occupational distribution of employees in the UK, 1951 and 1980

	Estimated proportion (%)	
	1951	1980
Primary	8·5	3·1
Manufacturing and construction	44·4	35·4
Services	44·8	60·1
Armed forces	2·3	1·4

Source: Adapted from *British Labour Statistics: Historical Abstract 1886–1968*, Department of Employment; *Social Trends*, no. 12 (HMSO, 1982).

occupational mobility of the nation. It is now considered likely that the average person will have to change his/her occupation at least three times during his/her working life. This will be necessary because of the ever-changing collective and material needs of society in its demand for goods and services, and the tremendous technological changes that have brought these about. For example, the electronics industry, producing a wide range of goods from televisions to computers, has grown up since the war, mainly because technological advances have made possible new products, and hence have created new jobs. This essentially dynamic situation in the needs of the labour market has encouraged the government to introduce a number of measures to increase occupational mobility. Through the Manpower Services Commission it has provided advice for firms on training programmes and tried to promote the development of certain required skills and crafts. It has also set up retraining programmes in its own Skillcentres and local colleges, and made a special provision for pre-vocational training through the Youth Training Scheme (YTS), which is open to all young people after they have completed their compulsory secondary education.

Geographical distribution of the population
Table 2.8 shows that since 1951 there has been a drift of population away from Scotland, Northern Ireland, Wales and the whole of the North of England. This has been largely due to the relative

economic decline in these less prosperous areas. People have moved into those regions where there have been better employment opportunities, housing and general amenities, such as the whole of the South of England and the Midlands. Governments have tried to stem this migration of people away from the depressed areas of high unemployment. They have attempted to increase employment in these areas by a variety of regional policy measures such as the offer of grants, tax incentives and other inducements to firms to move to areas of high unemployment.

These shifts in the geographical distribution of the population have also made it necessary for organisations concerned with satisfying collective and material needs to alter their scale of operations to take account of the changes in the demand for housing, education, entertainment and transport.

Social change

The social structure of the population
Fig. 2.3 provides a picture of the adult population according to social class as determined by occupation. This system of **social classification** was used by the Office of Population Censuses and Surveys when carrying out its 1981 population census. The 1985 edition of *Social Trends* identified that when these figures are compared with those for 1971 it can be seen that there has been an increase in the professional and intermediate classes

Table 2.8: Geographical distribution of the UK population, 1951 and 1983

Area	1951 (%)	1983 (%)
North	6·2	5·5
Yorkshire and Humberside	9·0	8·7
East Midlands	5·7	6·9
East Anglia	2·8	3·4
South East	30·0	30·2
South West	6·4	7·8
West Midlands	8·8	9·2
North West	12·8	11·3
Wales	5·2	5·0
Scotland	10·1	9·2
N. Ireland	3·0	2·8

Source: Office of Population Censuses and Surveys; General Register Office (Scotland); General Register Office (N. Ireland); *Regional Trends*, 1982, and *Social Trends*, no. 15 (HMSO, 1985).

Fig. 2.3: Social class of adult population, 1981
Source: Adapted from *Social Trends*, no. 15 (HMSO, 1985)

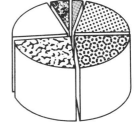

Professional 3.8%
Intermediate 21.8%
Skilled non-manual 22.2%
Skilled manual 25.8%
Semi-skilled manual 19.5%
Unskilled manual 6.9%

– such as doctors, solicitors, teachers, nurses, engineers, designers and technicians – and a fall in the number of people in the manual social classes.

Information such as this has been of particular value to organisations when assessing the potential market for a new product or service. If their market research has suggested that a certain class of person is likely to buy the new product or service, then the organisation has been able to use the figures in order to gauge the potential size of the market and then aim the advertising at this group. This has been of special value for products or services appealing to a particular social class such as types of holiday, forms of entertainment and publications (books, magazines and newspapers). For example, newspapers like *The Times*, the *Telegraph* and the *Guardian* draw their readership mainly from the professional and intermediate social groups. The increase during the 1970s of the numbers in these groups encouraged the circulation managers of these newspapers to step up their advertising in order to secure a slice of this expanding market.

This type of information regarding social class has also been widely used by companies operating in the home computer market. Their market research has revealed that a large proportion of their sales have been to the middle two social groups – the skilled non-manual and skilled manual workers. The advertising of the software to accompany these computers has therefore been placed in the type of newspaper that these groups are most likely to read; and the size of the potential market is clearly indicated by the social class figures.

Types of household

Table 2.9 shows the different types of household into which the population is formed. These are classified as people living within a traditional family situation and those living outside such an arrangement. The most noticeable change since 1961 has been the **increase in the total number of households**. This has grown over a twenty-year period by about 20 per cent, whereas the total population has expanded by only about 6·8 per cent.

The reasons for this change can be largely found in the more than proportionate increase in the number of people living on their own or in a single-parent family. Between 1961 and 1983 the latter has risen from 2 to 5 per cent and the former from 11 to 24 per cent. The increase in the number of people living alone can be largely attributed to the greater number of people surviving into old age as widows and widowers, and partly by young people choosing to live alone before getting married.

The **increase in the proportion of one-parent families** reflects the rise in the divorce rate, the increasing number of births outside marriage and a reduction in the number of adoptions of illegitimate children than in the 1960s. Because of this and the changes highlighted above, there has been a marked reduction in the number of households composed of married couples with dependent children. All of these changes suggest both an increase in the number of households and a general fall in the size of households.

This information is of considerable value to organisations in both the public and private sectors. Government departments involved in the administration of social services or benefits have studied the changes in household formation in order to ensure that adequate support and suitable housing have been available for elderly people living alone or for people trying to bring up a family on their own. Schools have needed to take account of the type of household formation in order to prepare for hardship cases that may arise amongst one-parent families, or to adjust to the differing role that the child might have within the household.

Private sector organisations have taken account of such changes in household type when deciding upon the sort of housing units to build. For example, due to the increasing number of people living on their own, many more single or small units have been constructed in the form of maisonettes, flats or one-bedroom houses. Similarly, the food-processing industry has responded to this trend by offering food products in smaller portions in order to cater for the person cooking alone. A certain sensitivity to such trends has also been apparent amongst advertising agencies. They have recognised that when promoting a particular product they should not exclude any household group. For example, an advertisement should not suggest that a certain brand of cereal is eaten only by the traditional family with two children, otherwise this may exclude other household types from trying it.

The distribution of income and wealth

The distribution of income of wealth between individual members of society determines the standard of living that individuals can secure and maintain.

Table 2.9: The types of household making up the population, 1983

Great Britain

	(Percentages)						(Thousands)		
	1961	*1971*	*1976*	*1981*	*1982*	*1983*	*1961*	*1971*	*1981*
No family									
One person:									
Under retirement age	4	6	6	8	8	8	726	1122	1469
Over retirement age	7	12	15	14	15	16	1193	2198	2771
Two or more people:									
One or more over retirement age	3	2	2	2	1	1	536	444	387
All under retirement age	2	2	1	3	2	2	268	304	535
One family									
Married couple only	26	27	27	26	27	27	4147	4890	4989
Married couple with 1 or 2 dependent children	30	26	26	25	24	24	4835	4723	4850
Married couple with 3 or more dependent children	8	9	8	6	6	6	1282	1587	1100
Married couple with independent child(ren) only	10	8	7	8	8	8	1673	1565	1586
Lone parent with at least 1 dependent child	2	3	4	5	4	5	367	515	916
Lone parent with independent child(ren) only	4	4	4	4	4	4	721	712	720
Two or more families	3	1	1	1	1	1	439	263	170
Total households	100	100	100	100	100	100	16,189	18,317	19,493

Source: *Social Trends*, no. 15 (HMSO, 1985).

Income

Fig. 2.4 shows the **distribution of pre-tax income** by selected groups of incomes. It reveals that for the lowest 50 per cent there has been little variation since 1949, while at the top end of the scale the share of the top 1 per cent declined steadily over the period from 11 per cent in 1949 to 6 per cent in 1981–2. The middle two groups absorbed this downward redistribution.

This sort of data relating to change has been of particular value to government departments when forming their taxation and benefits system. Although the achievement of a fairer distribution of income is not the main aim of this process, it is still one of its results. The flow chart in Fig. 2.5 on page 36 shows how the system operates. It demonstrates how individuals receive income from many sources, with the most important being earnings from employment and social security benefits. Tax is paid on both earned and unearned income, and individuals also pay national insurance contributions. This then leaves disposable income, which should also be viewed alongside the 'benefits in kind' that individuals receive in the form, for example, of education and health care.

Government departments attempt to ensure that there is a fair distribution of income to households

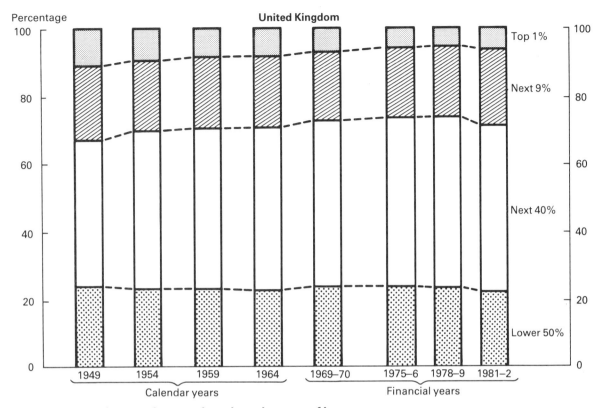

Fig. 2.4: Shares of pre-tax income: by selected groups of incomes
Source: *Social Trends*, no. 15 (HMSO, 1985)

in order that they can maintain an 'acceptable' standard of living. This represents something of a balancing act. The government weighs the achievement of an acceptable standard of living against the disadvantages of high tax and national insurance rates, which could reduce the incentive for individuals to work or for organisations to invest.

These changes and adjustments have also been of significance to private sector organisations, because they have a direct impact on patterns of demand. A gradual movement towards greater equality has widened the base of those demanding to own their own home, to go on foreign holidays and to acquire such consumer goods as cars, washing-machines, and stereo systems.

Table 2.10: UK distribution of wealth

	1971	1976	1978	1979	1980	1981	1982
Marketable wealth plus occupational and state pension rights Percentage of wealth owned by:							
Most wealthy 1% of population	21	14	13	13	12	12	11
Most wealthy 2% of population	27	18	17	17	16	16	16
Most wealthy 5% of population	37	27	25	25	24	24	24
Most wealthy 10% of population	49	37	36	35	33	33	34
Most wealthy 25% of population	69–72	58–61	57–60	56–9	55–8	56–9	56–9
Most wealthy 50% of population	85–9	80–5	79–83	79–83	78–82	78–82	78–82

Source: *Social Trends*, no. 15 (HMSO, 1985).

Wealth

A further indication as to the relative position of individuals within society has been the **distribution of wealth**.

Table 2.10 shows the changes that have occurred in the distribution of wealth between 1971 and 1982. Wealth is taken to include both fixed and financial assets which could be sold, together with any rights that individuals might have towards

occupational or state pensions. The table illustrates that during the early and mid-1970s there was a movement towards greater equality, although since 1977 there has been very little change.

As in the case of changes in the distribution of income, this information has been important to the government when framing taxation and benefits policies. It was used in particular in 1974 when the then Labour government issued a Green Paper on a proposed wealth tax.

Technological change

The previous sections of this chapter have shown that demographic and social change causes alterations in the material, social and employment needs of society. This means that organisations in the public and private sectors have to adjust the type, range and quantity of goods and services that they offer. Technology helps such organisations to make these adjustments, while at the same time it may also help them to improve upon existing services and products.

Technology involves the application of scientific and other organised knowledge to the advancement of techniques and systems for making and doing things. These techniques and systems generally involve people, organisations, living things and machines. There are therefore two aspects to technology: the **organisational** and the **technical**. The latter aspect involves the harnessing of machines, techniques and knowledge – the essential activity of making things work. The former aspect represents the many facets of administration and public policy; it relates to the activities of designers, engineers, technicians and production workers and also concerns the users and consumers of what is produced.

These two aspects are reflected throughout this section. We will consider the relationship between the organisation, its technology and processes, and the implications of changes in technology on organisations, employees and the environment.

The organisation, its technology and processes

The use that is made of modern technological methods by organisations depends upon the type of good or service that is to be produced, the variety and quantities required and the amount of capital available for the investment in new and existing technologies.

Production processes associated with very large quantities usually involve a massive investment in a

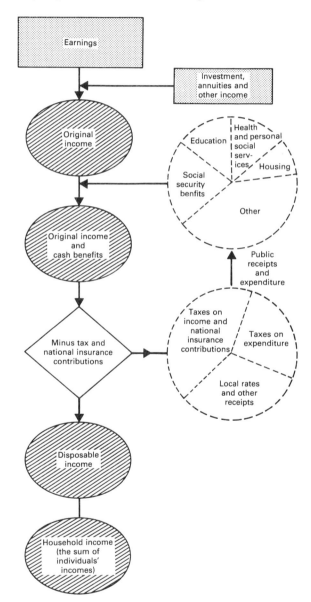

Fig. 2.5: How disposable income is influenced by taxation and benefits
Source: *Social Trends*, no. 10 (HMSO, 1980)

highly **automated** plant. The adoption of such mechanised methods allows for **specialisation** and the formation of a partnership between people and the machine. This is the case for cars, washing-machines, dish-washers and televisions. **Manual methods**, on the other hand, are likely to be used when producing one-off items such as furniture, leatherwork or pottery. Under these circumstances there will be a greater scope for variations in the product, although due to the higher labour content it is possible that the product will be more expensive.

The processes carried out by different organisations fall into three main categories: changing the composition and nature of materials, changing the shape of materials, or assembling components into a finished product. In each case relevant technology may be applied to improve and advance the process.

1. *Changing the composition and nature of materials.* This type of process generally involves the application of heat and/or chemical techniques. It includes such treatments as washing, crushing, grinding, milling, boiling, mixing with other ingredients, applying chemicals, sorting, grading, heating, blanching, freezing, canning, drying or smoking. The purpose is to change the composition, form, nature or appearance of something in order that it can be either consumed directly by households – as with frozen or canned foods – or worked upon further and then used – as with, say, board for the manufacture of kitchen units or the metals for car components.

Many of these processes are **highly mechanised** and embrace the very latest technologies. For example, the processing of iron into steel involves a sophisticated technical system making use of oxygen. A mixture of 70 per cent molten iron and 30 per cent scrap is put in an oxygen furnace. A water-cooled oxygen lance is lowered into the furnace, and high-purity oxygen is then blown on to the metal at very great speed. This has the effect of removing the impurities from the molten charge because the oxygen joins with the carbon and other unwanted elements. At the same time lime is added to act as a flux in order to carry off the oxidised impurities as a floating layer of slag. This then leaves the steel, which can be tapped off.

Similarly the application of high technology to the processing of food has made it possible to ensure that through canning, freezing, drying, smoking or treating with preservatives it is possible to stop the action of bacteria on food. As a result certain foods are on sale throughout the year even though they may be out of season. For example, the refining of sugar is carried out by a series of specially controlled **separation processes** in order to remove all impurities. These processes include boiling, washing, filtering with lime and bone charcoal, boiling in large vacuum pans, drying and finally compressing into moulds if lump sugar is required.

2. *Changing the shape of materials.* Because of the variety of different materials used for making parts or components a wide range of techniques have been developed for the shaping of those materials. In general, such techniques involve either forming or machining. The technology involved in these techniques depends in the case of the former on the application of heat and pressure, and in the case of the latter on the use of sophisticated cutting machines.

Forming involves the distortion of the shape of the original raw material. This is sometimes carried out by pressing, panel beating, bending or cold forging. Heat is applied during glass-blowing, forging hot metals, vacuum-forming plastics and rolling steel. For example, at a steel-rolling mill, hot metal billets are passed through a series of rollers until they become the right shape and thickness. Some other techniques of forming involve melting and then allowing materials to cool. For example, in the sand casting of shapes for components or parts, molten iron is panned into a mould and allowed to cool. When the sand is removed the iron remains in the shape of the original mould cavity.

Molten materials can also be shaped by forcing them into a cavity under high pressure. This technique is known as **pressure die-casting** when it is used with metals, and **injection moulding** when either plastics or rubber are used. Different types of pipes are produced by a process called **extrusion**, where the molten material is forced through a die to give long sections.

The **machining** process involves taking the rough shape that has been formed and then working on it to create the final required shape. A number of sophisticated machines are used in carrying out this process. For example, the **milling machine** may be employed in order to make flat surfaces by means of a rotary cutter and also flat surfaces cut at different angles. Holes may be made by the use of a **drilling machine**, and then threads may be added by a process known as **tapping**. Excess material can be removed, and a shape can be made by turning the work on a **lathe**. The lathe is a machine that rotates the work against some kind of cutting tool. A **grinding** machine may be used to finish the part very accurately and also for making cutting tools to be used on other machines.

3. *Assembling components into a finished product.* Assembly involves putting parts and components together in order to make a finished product. Many sophisticated techniques and systems are employed in carrying out these operations.

The method by which components and parts are joined together depends upon the type of material that they are made of. Metals may be welded, soldered or held together by nuts, bolts, screws and rivets. Plastics are generally welded; wood, paper and cloth are often stuck with adhesives. The people employed in putting together many engineering products require considerable skills. This is because for safety reasons such products must be assembled correctly and the best match of components made.

The efficiency of any assembly system depends heavily upon organisational skills. It is necessary to ensure that all the components making up a product are available so that assembly may take place. The shortage of any particular component can cause serious delays.

All the points outlined above have led to a great deal of research into the systems of organising and carrying out the assembly of products. In many cases this has resulted in the creation of large **assembly lines** where each worker is required to carry out a relatively small number of tasks. This form of **division of labour**, or **specialisation**, means that each individual worker becomes highly skilled at his/her part of the assembly process, which should improve the standard of the assembled finished product.

Research has also taken matters a stage further by encouraging organisations to make use of **robotics**. This involves using machines to carry out the majority of the assembly operations. For example, increasingly cars are being produced on a fully automated production line, which involves holding the car body components in jigs and then spot-welding them automatically.

Implications of technological change

The period since the Second World War has witnessed the steady march of technological progress. It has seen the harnessing of nuclear energy, the introduction of the gas turbine and the development and introduction into many types of automobiles of the Wankel engine. It has also seen the development and exploitation of new materials such as plastics and glass fibre, which has been moulded into car and boat bodies. Some of the new materials have special properties; carbon fibre, for instance, is suitable for high-temperature turbine blades; certain types of ceramic material are resistant to high temperatures and are particularly suitable for heat shields on spacecraft. Civil engineering has seen the further development of highly sophisticated machinery, used for heavy earth-moving and excavation.

In transport and communications the automobile has become firmly established, the aeroplane has become increasingly more sophisticated, and the down-blast hovercraft has taken off. With the introduction of space satellites television broadcasting has become truly world-wide. LASERS (light amplification by stimulated emission of radiation) have helped to provide a means of communicating over a very long distance. Space exploration has truly blasted off from the first Sputnik in 1957 to the threshold of extraterrestrial exploration in the 1980s.

Information technology, which combines computing and telecommunications, now features in every aspect of our working and domestic lives. In science and engineering, computers are now used to push back the boundaries of technology itself. For example, some pharmaceutical companies now attempt to design new drugs on the computer rather than in the laboratory. Aerospace and auto companies now simulate the aerodynamic behaviour of their products with a computer instead of building a costly prototype and putting it in an expensive wind-tunnel.

The technological advances highlighted above generally result in one of two types of change: **process innovation** and **product innovation**.

Process innovation

This involves the use of new technologies to make existing products more efficiently and hence more cheaply. For example, the microchip has been used to make industrial robots which are then employed to make washing-machines, dish-washers and cars. At the same time use may be made of computers to simplify and improve on the design of the products. Fig. 2.6 illustrates how computers have been used in manufacturing industry both for

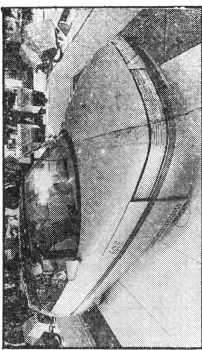

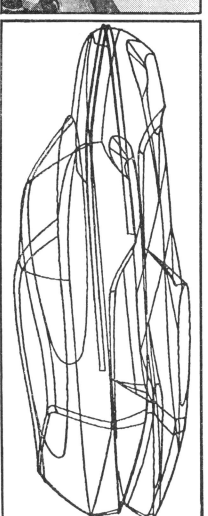

Auto engineering: modern software allows quick innovative car designs, such as this Citroen Eole prototype

Design at the touch of a button

The fastest-growing and most rapidly changing use of computers in manufacturing industry is for designing products and for controlling the production process.

CAD/CAM/CAE (computer aided design, manufacturing and engineering) is revolutionizing industrial practices in a way undreamt of a decade ago. To some it is as important a step as the invention of the motor car – opening up new vistas of freedom from traditional, time-consuming methods, and allowing the creative process to transcend the drudgery of repetitive physical operations.

The new systems have rendered the drawing office, equipped with banks of draughtsmen using rulers, pens and pencils and vast sheets of paper, obsolete overnight. Today's designers call up stock measurements and parts from a computer memory and create

new products with a light pen on a screen.

Powerful software allows the resulting two-dimensional "drawing", to be turned into a 3D model on the screen which can be twisted and turned, and even subjected to expected stresses and strains.

The systems do not stop at individual products – whole factories can be designed using CAD/CAM techniques.

McDonnell Douglas, the US aerospace corporation and a pioneer of CAD/CAM, has developed through its new information systems group a system called PLACE which enables an entire production cell to be created by computer simulation.

The screen shows robots, machine tools, assembly conveyor belts and so on, all of which are manoeuvrable

around the factory floor. The robots can then be programmed to perform the allotted tasks, and the whole concoction can be viewed from every angle.

This is the type of highly sophisticated CAD/CAM system that clearly is going to be in increasing demand throughout Europe as the growth of computer – integrated manufacture, still in its infancy, accelerates in competitive industries such as motors.

CAD began to take off in Europe only five or six years ago, but has been growing at a phenomenal rate. According to the London market research company Frost & Sullivan, European revenues from CAD were $100 million in 1979, but by 1983 totalled $750 million. This year's figure is estimated at $1,225 million, rising to $2,300 million by 1987, indicating a

growth rate twice that for computers themselves.

Frost & Sullivan says that the largest user of CAD is the mechanical and electrical engineering sector, with expected purchases of $635 million this year in Europe, followed by electronic printed circuit board design and integrated circuits.

In the UK, according to some estimates, just 4 per cent of the CAD market has been satisfied.

As part of its overall IT programme, the Department of Trade and Industry has put considerable effort and expense into promoting CAD/CAM in the past three years. It claims success particularly in making industry more aware of what CAD/CAM can do and its advantages to businesses.

The DTI's main thrust has now changed in emphasis from the specific to the all-embrac-

ing. Advanced Manufacturing Technology (AMT) is now the key to the future; it incorporates not only CAD/CAM/CAE but also advanced robotics and whole-factory computerisation and automation. Thus, the original aim of making businessmen aware of the new technology has shifted into a broader policy of encouraging companies to develop a whole new manufacturing strategy.

The commitment of the Government to the computer revolution in manufacturing is demonstrated by the numerous schemes and, not least, the money devoted in the past to making industrial managers aware of how quickly their world is changing.

Excluding capital aid, the DTI has devoted £16 million to its various CAD/CAM and associated schemes.

Edward Townsend
Industrial Correspondent

Fig. 2.6:
Source: *The Times*, 25 March 1985

designing products and also for controlling the production process. Computer-aided design is known as CAD, and computer-aided manufacturing CAM.

Product innovation
This involves the development of new markets and finding new goods and services to sell to existing markets. For example, the application of technology in the home led to the development of the 'white goods industry', which includes washing-machines, driers, fridges, freezers and dish-washers. This has resulted in the development of the materials and services associated with these goods, for example special types of paints, metals and plastics and appropriate detergents to use in the machines.

The research and development departments of many companies are constantly striving for new ideas that can eventually be turned into innovative products and services. At present a number of organisations are engaged in research into the design of a system for the automatic centralised monitoring and control of the whole range of household functions like heating, lighting and safety. In the transport–communications area research is taking place to make 'armchair shopping' a reality for everyone. In the industrial field considerable research is undertaken; for example, Shell UK is in the process of developing laser technology to measure the level of liquids stored in bulk tanks. The same company is seeking to develop a microprocessor cut-off device, which can be used to avoid the over-filling of fuel tanks in vehicles powered by liquefied petroleum gas.

One area of research that has led to an innovative service is that described in Fig. 2.7. The new Flydacraft is a driverless vehicle that is essentially a cross between a monorail and a train. It incorporates the latest ideas in transport and computer technology. If the service proves to be successful in Cardiff then it is likely to lead to sales overseas.

Reactions to technological change
Countries may react very differently to the kind of technological development described in this section. Even within countries, opinions differ. Generally the **less developed countries** focus on the positive side of technological development. They acknowledge that technology has helped to increase and stabilise the food supply. This may be achieved by the application of machinery and

power, fertilisers and pesticides and processing techniques. They recognise that technology has contributed to the improvements in medicine, pharmacy and sanitation that have caused a resultant reduction in mortality rates and an increase in life-expectancy. They also feel that technology might contribute to a general raising of their nation's standard of living. This might be achieved by organisations adopting new processing methods, which would help to raise productivity and in so doing reduce costs, increase output and make a wider range of products available to the population.

However, people active in international aid and development agencies insist on the need for **appropriate technology**. Rapid, wide-scale technological innovation in agriculture or transport sometimes has disastrous effects on people's lives in the developing countries.

Problems arising from technology in the industrial world
For the **developed countries** most material needs are already satisfied; so they are not looking for improvements in technology in order to provide for the fundamentals of life. Technology may instead lead to a worsening of certain undesirable economic, social and environmental side-effects.

This may be particularly true when countries are unable to control the rate of application of new technologies and the resultant increase in apparent economic growth. For example, CAD and CAM may make it possible to produce more sophisticated cars at a lower cost. However, such automation is likely to reduce job opportunities, which in turn would create more unemployment. Society would then have to support the families of those who have lost their jobs, and the unemployed people involved would have to cope with the social stresses associated with not working. The availability of a cheaper and more sophisticated car would also probably cause an increase in the number of vehicles on the road, with a resultant increase in the costs associated with accidents and pollution.

People in the developed world sometimes express concern in particular over the effect that developments in technology may have on the environment. There are a number of problems. The first is that of **controlling the application of technology**. This is particularly true of **nuclear armaments**, where the political difficulty exists of controlling the deployment of the nuclear capability held by independent nation states.

Tracking a winner with the low-flying train

by Philip Beresford
Transport Correspondent

A REVOLUTIONARY British transport system with an exciting export potential is planned for the Welsh capital, Cardiff. Next week, South Glamorgan county council will offer a test site to a driverless vehicle which is a cross between a train and monorail. And the performance of the system, Flyda, will be closely monitored by American and Australian transport experts, who are considering placing orders.

Flyda is the brainchild of Francis Perrott, a former Royal Navy engineer. For the past three years he has been working on the project full time from his manor house outside Cirencester. But the idea goes back over 20 years when Perrott "became interested in ultra-light trains in a semi-hobby way".

Within four years, Cardiff will have a 3-mile network capable of carrying 5,000 passengers an hour. It will cost £20m. The electrically-powered Flydacraft will travel on special elevated track for over half the route. Each Flydacraft will be capable of carrying 20 passengers.

The vehicles have four conventional wheels underneath the carriage, as well as wheels on the roof. When they travel on the elevated sections, the track grips the wheels top and bottom on one side only (see illustration). When travelling at ground level, the Flydacraft runs like an ordinary train on the four wheels underneath the carriage.

Automated trains consisting of six Flyacraft coupled together will serve city-centre passengers every minute, reaching a maximum speed of 35mph. According to Perrott, a computerised device on board every Flyacraft will allow each one to be routed to an individual destination. In practice, that would mean any train leaving the city centre could split into two or three individual Flydacraft heading up the three or four branch lines that Carfdiff is planning.

The great advantage of the system is the cheapness of its construction. Perrott claims that the elevated track costs about 5% of the price of underground tunnelling. And being small – just 3m high and 2m wide – erecting it would envolve little demolition.

South Glamorgan council sees a "lot of attractions" in Flyda, according to a spokesman at the authority's economic development unit. The project is moving ahead rapidly. Even before the 200m test track is ready in six months' time on council-owned land, planning permission will have been granted for a larger 1¼-mile development track in a dockland re-development area. Perrott says that should be ready by the end of the year.

Within four years, the complete system should be operational, with plans being prepared for extensions into the depressed valleys outside Cardiff. "One of the keys to new employment is really first-class travel from the valleys to Cardiff," says Perrott.

Australia and America are showing an interest in Flyda. Dallas, which is planning a huge conventional public transport system costing $4.5b is considering the system as a cheaper option. "If they used Flyda, they could save at least $2.5b in construction costs," says Perrott.

Fig. 2.7:
Source: *The Sunday Times,* 17 February 1986

The second problem concerns the **population explosion** in which technology has so far played an almost neutral role. This is because it provided the new drugs and medical techniques that encouraged the increase in the first place, while at the same time also provided the means for effecting control through the development of more efficient methods of contraception.

The developed world has also expressed concern over the **social impact** of technology on life in both the town and the countryside, which has caused an upheaval in the traditional social order. Undesirable effects include 'urban blight' and inner-city decay; people no longer wish to live in city centres, and so such areas have been deserted by the middle classes and left to the socially disfavoured. The development of communications and the wider ownership of cars have contributed to the destruction of the countryside, as rural communities have been overwhelmed by the number of vehicles.

Ecological problems – perhaps the gravest dangers – have been caused by the application of advanced technological methods. They have resulted in the pollution of the environment and disturbance of the balance of the natural forces of regeneration. This has been caused in particular by the over-cutting of trees, the use of chemical-intensive farming methods, and the uncontrolled emission of toxic waste products.

Society, organisations and governments, especially in the developed world, need to monitor and control the application and development of technology very carefully. In that way it will be possible to maximise the benefits while minimising the costs associated with technological development.

The effect of technological change on work patterns

At the beginning of this century a full-time employee worked on average about 54 hours per week. He/she was unlikely to have a paid holiday, and his/her maximum working life-expectancy was 58 years (12–70). By 1983 the average number of hours worked was 40 (including overtime); 93 per cent of workers had four or more weeks of holiday; since 1974 the working life-expectancy has been 49 years (16–65). These improvements enjoyed by the worker in his/her pattern of work have been largely caused by technological change, in the form of automation, computerisation and the use of robotics.

The rate of this change has been accelerated in recent years by the application and development of **information technology**, which combines computing and telecommunications. It allows organisations to acquire, process, transmit and present information in all forms: audio, video, text and graphics. This has resulted in workers being increasingly involved in handling information about operations rather than having to carry out the operation themselves.

Here we will consider the impact these changes have had, and will have in the future, on the pattern of organised work.

Productivity

The application of new technology usually helps to improve the performance of any organisation's plant by making it more productive. For example, when Rolls-Royce introduced a new automated production line in Derby it both increased productivity by 200 per cent and reduced unit labour costs by 20 per cent. A three-person shift was able to produce what used to take thirty workers. However, improvements in productivity also depend upon the type of product, the combination of resources employed, the style of management and the morale of the workforce. These factors all have a direct impact upon the effectiveness of the new technology in practice, and hence on productivity.

Pattern of the working week

As we saw there has been a gradual reduction in the length of the working week. This is likely to be reinforced still further if workers seek to compensate for higher productivity through a reduction in hours rather than through higher earnings. This may be achieved in a variety of different ways. Longer annual holidays may be taken. A fixed reduction may be made in the length of each working day. Or a round-the-clock shift-work system might be divided between five or even six working crews.

One company that has moved strongly in this direction is Volvo in Sweden. The firm has introduced arrangements in one of its plants whereby workers can select from six different shift patterns, some of which comprise six-hour shifts and involve working between 29 and 40 hours per week.

Greater flexibility in the pattern of work may also be introduced by the adoption of **personal flexibility schemes**, which are the shift-worker's version of flexitime. They allow for flexible hand-over times between shifts and, in some systems, the same kind of accumulated debit and credit hours as operated with flexitime. It is also possible for a **time flexibility scheme** to be operated, as has been introduced in some organisations in West Germany. This is based on net working hours and allows employees to arrange their working times to accommodate the rest of their lives – for instance, longer hours in the winter and shorter hours in the summer, or working mothers opting to work only during the term time.

Improvements in industrial relations

If the flexible schemes described above were to be widely introduced they would provide employees with far more say in the arrangement of their working day. This should help to improve their motivation and attitude towards work.

The wider application of information technology might improve industrial relations still further, because it could help to break down the barriers between the shop-floor and management. As a result of the introduction of information technology the people carrying out the production

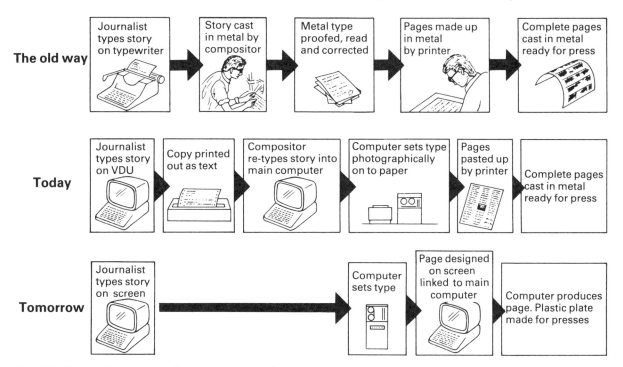

Fig. 2.8: New technology and newspaper printing

operation will be controlling the process by the use of visual display units (VDUs), and keyboards, which have traditionally been the tools of white-collar office and management staff. As blue-collar workers increasingly work on such units the distinction between white- and blue-collar workers is likely to be forgotten.

Unemployment

It was always felt that technological change would have the effect of freeing human beings from soul-destroying routine tasks. Due to the changes in the patterns of work described above, people would be able to engage in more fulfilling creative tasks and leisure activities. Unfortunately this has not always been the case. Although technological developments may lead to improvements in productivity, unless these are matched by a corresponding increase in demand or by a more flexible attitude towards the pattern of work, there may be a net loss of jobs and hence an increase in unemployment.

This situation may be made worse if home industries are unable to compete successfully with foreign companies in the fight to provide the new information technology systems. Also the rate of technological change may speed up the rate at which many existing products become obsolete, thus throwing even more people out of work.

Fig. 2.8 demonstrates how new technology is leading to a loss of jobs in the newspaper industry. It relates to a new production method which has been introduced by a number of newspapers. It moves from a system, which relied heavily upon labour for the setting up and printing of the newspaper pages, to one that gradually introduces computers to take over some of these tasks, culminating in the operation of a direct-input system. This allows the journalists writing stories and the staff taking advertisements by telephone to type them straight into a computer terminal, which automatically sets them into type. This bypasses the traditional typesetting and cutting, reduces labour costs and speeds up production.

Even if the new technologies do not lead to a loss of jobs they will undoubtedly have an impact upon the tasks making up a particular job. It is feared that as production systems are designed the methodology will either consciously or unconsciously seek to eliminate human intelligence and judgement from the process. This will have the effect of reducing the level of skill required to carry out a particular job and in so doing will make it less satisfactory to the individual worker.

3. The Recruitment of Labour

Manpower planning

The response of an organisation to the ever-changing environment in which it operates will be reflected in the statement of its objectives and its overall corporate strategy. The organisation's objectives in relation to its level, pattern and method of production will then form the basis for making forecasts concerning its future labour requirements in terms of both the number of employees and their respective skills. These labour requirements are then related to the size and nature of the organisation's existing labour force in order to determine the extent to which they can be met from existing manpower resources.

All those activities designed to balance the company's demand for labour with an appropriate supply contribute to what is known as manpower planning. The means by which the company seeks to meet its labour requirements will be expressed in a manpower plan covering anything from one to five years. However, manpower planning is an ongoing process, because the dynamic nature of the economic, social, political, legal and technological environment will tend to cause the company to alter its objectives in the light of such changes.

The organisation will also be obliged to respond to changes in competitive pressures, while objectives may also be altered to take account of any mergers or take-overs in which it may become involved. Any such changes in its objectives will require an updating of the manpower plan. The possibility also exists that the manpower planning itself may identify certain limitations in relation to the future labour supply that seriously question whether the company's objectives are in fact attainable. The end result may be that objectives have to be modified in the light, for example, of a skill shortage that even the most ambitious training schemes could not satisfactorily overcome.

Similarly, changes in the legislation relating to employment or the government's policy on such matters as pay and training schemes may bring about a change in the manpower plan. Such developments may in turn cause the organisation to review its objectives. Legislative or policy changes will not automatically oblige the company to scale down its objectives, since the government's new strategy may be aimed at lowering the costs of employing certain types of labour as well as raising its quality. In this case the organisation may then be able to embark upon a set of more ambitious objectives. It is essential therefore that both the manpower plan and the organisation's objectives are worked out together rather than in isolation and monitored continuously to ensure that they complement each other.

Existing manpower resources

The first step in manpower planning is to obtain detailed information about the current labour force in order to gain a comprehensive picture of the supply of labour from internal sources. This involves producing a **manpower inventory**. The collection and interpretation of the resulting data is now more readily and accurately achieved with the use of computers and software specifically designed to meet the needs of manpower planning. The inventory will need to cover not only the number of employees and their working hours but also such matters as their skills and potential for transfer and/or promotion.

In making forecasts of the supply of labour available from internal sources, allowance must be made for any overtime or short-time working, absenteeism, the usual internal transfers and promotions, labour turnover and changes in working hours, holidays and other conditions of employment.

A typical manpower inventory will collect information under the following headings:

- Age, sex and marital status.
- Date employment commenced.
- The means by which the employee first learnt of the vacancy.
- Job title.
- Department, section and job location.
- Previous job titles, departments, etc. within the organisation.
- Status: hourly (full-time, part-time, shift, etc.), weekly, monthly, managerial, etc.

- Date of leaving and reason.
- Qualifications.
- Work experience.
- Previous work experience.
- Type and level of skill attainment.
- Training and development.
- Potential for transfer and/or promotion.

All the information from the manpower inventory can then be analysed not only to determine what labour resources the organisation currently possesses but also to identify important trends that may have implications for its future labour requirements. The data will provide an opportunity for measuring and analysing labour turnover in order to forecast future wastage. This analysis will attempt to establish a correlation between labour turnover and such factors as age, type of job, length of service, commuting distances, improved pay and career prospects elsewhere and the avoidance of stress or conflict with other employees. It may then be possible to introduce measures designed to reduce labour turnover and to plan for losses that are generally unavoidable. Similarly absenteeism can be subject to analysis.

The information on the age structure of the various categories of employees will highlight problems such as those associated with a large number of employees all reaching retirement age during a relatively short period of time in the near future. Alternatively the existence of another age group that dominates certain positions in the company may frustrate the promotion aspirations of other employees.

The manpower inventory will also allow plans to be made which cater for the effects of promotions and transfers arising from retirement or possible resignation among supervisory or managerial staff. This gives rise to what are known as **succession requirements** and calls for information on employees that can be lined up as potential replacements. Some may already display the qualities necessary for promotion and can therefore fill positions arising in the immediate future, while others may have been identified as replacements after undergoing further training and development and, in this case, can fill positions arising over the next few years.

The succession requirements will also have to take account of the additional transfers and promotions arising from the downward chain reaction caused by a single replacement further up the organisation's hierarchy. If, for example, an employee is promoted to fill a vacancy arising from the retirement or resignation of a regional sales manager then this will have a knock-on effect, with the result that several other promotions and/or transfers will have to be planned for.

This type of analysis will help to identify those managerial and supervisory posts that face a weak replacement position, and for this reason the assessment of staff must be a continuous process. Moreover changes in the organisation structure itself arising from the centralisation or decentralisation of certain activities and decision-making also require that manpower planning is an ongoing part of personnel management.

Improving the productivity of manpower

Another part of manpower planning is to assess the opportunities for making a more effective use of the labour force. The present manning arrangements and working practices may be such that certain parts of the labour force are not fully utilised. In this case it may be possible to introduce improved working methods and to change the way in which the work is currently distributed between the existing employees.

Through no fault of their own some employees may find that they are not kept fully occupied during their working day while during other periods they are not able to cope with their workload, and the company may then be obliged to introduce overtime working. In this case measures that raise the productivity of employees may allow the company to raise its output with a less than proportionate increase in the input of labour.

The manpower plan will also have to take account of the anticipated increase in productivity associated with any improvements in technology embodied in new capital equipment. Improvements in productivity rely primarily upon making a more intelligent use of the manpower resources rather than simply stipulating that employees should put more physical effort into their jobs. Organisations that do rely upon such an approach will soon find their scope for improvements in productivity severely limited when compared with those that are prepared to introduce new working methods into a better organised workforce using improved plant, machinery and equipment. The latter may also actually reduce the amount of physical effort associated with certain tasks or reduce the mental strain connected with routine administrative procedures.

External manpower resources

As well as the continuous analysis of internal labour resources, manpower planning must also be supported by monitoring the availability of labour from external resources. If the organisation fails to identify trends in the working population at both local and national level then it runs the risk of not being able to satisfy any additional manpower requirements from external sources. For example, incorrect assumptions may have been made concerning the relative ease with which the organisation expected to recruit certain types of employee, only to discover that specific skills are in very short supply and can command a much higher reward than was anticipated in the manpower plan. The repercussions of this may be that the organisation's objectives then have to be reviewed and modified.

Manpower planning must take account of the following factors when assessing the extent to which future manpower requirements can be satisfied from local external sources:

1. Local demographic trends with particular reference to the size and age structure of the working population.
2. Developments in the local transport system that will affect the catchment area for labour.
3. Housing schemes and the future availability of various types of accommodation.
4. Environmental developments that will influence the attractiveness of the area as a place in which to live.
5. The effect upon the area of any changes in the government's policies on regional and urban development.
6. The pattern of employment/unemployment and the availability of workers with certain skills, qualifications and experience, and the situation in relation to part-time and casual labour.
7. Local competition for various types of labour and its effect upon rates of pay and fringe benefits, for example.
8. The effect of educational and training establishments upon the quality of new entrants to the labour force and the skills of retrained workers.

In addition to this assessment of likely developments in the local labour force, the organisation must also consider the extent to which manpower requirements may be influenced by factors operating at a national level. Such developments are likely to affect the ability of the organisation to recruit certain types of labour, as well as its cost and other important matters such as conditions of employment. Manpower planning must therefore also take account of the following factors:

1. National demographic trends and the implications for the growth of the working population.
2. Developments in the economy as a whole reflecting the application of new technology and changes in the pattern of demand. These, in turn, will affect the relative strengths of the demands for different types of labour. There may, for example, be a greater demand for people skilled in the use of computer-aided design techniques or those with the specialist management skills required to meet the needs of the rapidly growing fast food industry.
3. Central government measures designed to change the emphasis and structure of university and polytechnic courses and the provision of technical and pre-vocational education in schools and colleges.
4. Changes in the scope, structure and content of training and retraining courses administered by the government's Manpower Services Commission and any changes in the role of the industrial training boards.
5. Government policies that will influence the determination of wages and salaries, the role of trade unions and any changes in such Acts as those dealing with equal pay, sex discrimination, employment protection, wages councils, trade unions and industrial relations and more' recently the Employment Acts 1980 and 1982.

The manpower plan

Having completed a manpower inventory and used the data and information to produce a comprehensive analysis of the organisation's strengths and weaknesses, a manpower plan can then be devised. This plan relates the future availability of labour to the future demand for labour. This manpower plan must deal with the following areas:

1. Recruitment

A schedule must be produced that deals with the timing of the recruitment programme for the various types and levels of labour and the approach to tackling any difficulties that earlier investigations have identified as likely to affect the recruitment of certain kinds of labour.

2. *Transfers*

This part of the plan involves the future redeployment of existing employees between various jobs, departments, sections and locations. The latter covers not only relocations within the existing premises but also transfers involving the proposed movement of employees to different geographical locations where the organisation operates.

3. *Redundancy*

Jobs that have become obsolete or a reduction in certain areas of the organisation's activities will require a programme for redundancies. This must cover the timetable and selection procedure for redundancies and/or early retirements and the determination of redundancy payments or pensions. The plan may also specify how the organisation intends to assist redundant employees in their search for alternative employment.

4. *Training*

This will deal with the duration, structure and content of training and apprenticeship courses to be completed by the specified number of young recruits, and the training and retraining courses for existing employees. Details will also be provided on how existing and new courses will take account of changes in technology, working methods and other developments that will require the acquisition of new skills and techniques. The plan will also deal with the ways in which the training programme is to be adjusted to take account of developments in courses associated with the Manpower Services Commission and the appropriate industrial training board.

5. *Productivity*

Measures designed to ensure that existing and future positions are filled by the best possible people must be supported by action so that they can work more productively. There are different ways of measuring productivity depending upon the nature of the organisation's activities. For example, in a manufacturing organisation the aim may be to reduce labour costs per unit of output by a minimum of 5 per cent whereas in a fast-food outlet the objective may be to raise the value of sales per head by 8 per cent. The plan will therefore describe those changes that will contribute higher productivity in the various parts of the organisation and will deal with the following potential sources of greater efficiency:

(a) The combined effect of the application of new technology and the introduction of increased mechanisation/automation to production methods and administrative procedures.
(b) Measures designed to reduce labour costs through the reorganisation of working methods that make a fuller utilisation of manpower resources.
(c) The role of the training and retraining programme in raising productivity through the development of new and existing skills and techniques.
(d) The use of incentive schemes whereby higher productivity will raise an employee's earnings, e.g. bonus payments when certain output targets are achieved, a fixed rate per unit of output, sales commission or a scheme allowing employees to share in some of the extra profit generated by higher productivity.
(e) Productivity can also be raised by measures aimed at improving industrial and human relations within the organisation so that favourable changes in the attitude and behaviour of employees produce a more satisfied and better-motivated workforce.

6. *Labour turnover*

A high labour turnover is bound to affect the quality and level of output as well as raising the manpower costs associated with the recruitment and training of labour. Having identified the avoidable causes of manpower wastage, the plan may include the following remedies:

(a) An improvement in earnings for employees who might otherwise be enticed to join organisations offering higher pay to attract a type of labour that is in short supply.
(b) A productivity scheme whereby an employee's effort and attitude are more closely reflected in their earnings. An updating of the pay and salary structure so that differentials are also more in line with changes in the generally accepted view of the value and importance attached to different jobs.

(c) Improving career and promotion prospects and ensuring that the criteria used are seen by employees to be fair, and that effort and excellence are suitably rewarded. Such measures will not only improve incentives but also remove the frustrations that cause employees to leave an organisation.

(d) The identification of sources of stress and conflict between employees, and between employees, management and supervisory staff, will involve the introduction of measures designed to improve industrial and human relations. Some employees may be leaving the company because of disputes that they believe have been unfairly handled, and this will require improvements in disciplinary and grievance procedures. Stressful situations may also have been produced by the inconsiderate action or comments of other employees and by shortcomings in the communications skills of management and supervisory staff.

(e) Improvements in the recruitment, induction and training programmes and in the promotion and transfer procedures will help to reduce wastage. This is because the respective qualities and abilities of employees will be more accurately matched to their jobs, thus reducing the possibility of stress when employees cannot cope with their duties or a sense of under-achieving because of the status and responsibilities attached to their jobs.

Having produced a manpower plan, every effort must be made to ensure that it is continually updated in the light of both internal and external developments that will affect the organisation's demand for labour and its availability. The objectives of the measures introduced will also have to be compared with their results. This monitoring process will allow adjustments to be implemented smoothly rather than suffering the dislocation when wholesale changes are required to deal with problems that have reached crisis proportions.

Consultation
Since manpower planning is concerned with the overall structure and uses of the workforce it is essential that trade unions and employee representatives are regularly consulted during the formulation and implementation of the manpower plan. In recent years social, political and legal developments have led to increased participation by workers so that their views can be taken into account when their interests are affected by the company's decisions.

Apart from the fact that it is an important principle of good industrial relations to involve employees in matters affecting them, the provision of relevant information and the mechanism for consultation are now supported by the Employment Act 1982. A failure to involve employees in such decisions is likely to increase the possibility of resistance to the changes contained in the manpower plan, as they may interpret them as being solely a threat to their skills and security of employment.

The selection and recruitment of labour

No matter how sophisticated the technical means of production, the ultimate success of an organisation depends upon the quality and contribution of its workforce. It follows that an organisation must have both an efficient recruitment policy and an efficient selection procedure in order to ensure that it has a workforce of the highest possible quality (Fig. 3.1). This is as important for the highly capital-intensive industries as it is for the more labour-intensive sector of the economy providing both commercial and personal services. In the case of the former a failure to obtain certain standards in terms of either skill or attitudes from a relatively small workforce can have repercussions upon the level and quality of output as severe as in places where labour is the dominant input.

Investigating and planning
It is essential to establish that there is in fact a need to recruit somebody. A common response to a change in working methods, staffing levels or the introduction of new technology is to assume that another member of staff is required. A closer investigation may reveal that this is not so. Perhaps the component tasks could be shared by other members of the department, incorporating job enhancement, job redesign or job enlargement. Maybe some elements of the job could be dispensed with altogether.

In the case of new equipment or the introduction of new technology, it may be possible and even preferable to retrain existing members of staff, rather than recruit new ones who already possess the skills or knowledge required. So it may not be necessary to recruit anyone at all.

Fig. 3.1: The recruitment of labour

Let us assume, however, that a need has been established. A member of the personnel department will then perform a job analysis and prepare a job description unless a current and relevant one exists. A job description explains the dimensions, duties and responsibilities involved in a job and, where appropriate, lists the tasks to be performed. The personnel officer will need this document in order to know what the person recruited will be expected to do.

A 'person specification' will then be prepared, which details the qualification, experience and personal attributes required in the person who is appointed. There are various designs for this form; some list requirements under 'essential' or 'desired' headings, while others give a long comprehensive list under such categories as intelligence, disposition and interests. Care must be taken to prevent this list becoming very long or too specific; it should not rule out the possibility of recruiting someone who meets some but not all of the requirements, but who in the event will do the job satisfactorily. As far as possible the manager of the department that has the vacancy will work closely with the personnel officer in the preparation of this document, so that it will be as accurate as possible.

Search

The first labour market to be addressed is right on the doorstep: the people already employed by the organisation.

A notice of the vacancy may be posted on company notice-boards, and internal candidates would be encouraged to apply. It may be company policy to fill a vacancy from within wherever possible, and there are several advantages to doing so:

- The company already knows the applicant, his/her standard of work and personality.
- The applicant is familiar with the nature of the organisation.
- People working for the company are likely to have more realistic expectations of what the job entails.
- It is good for morale for people to be seen progressing through the company, developing their potential and gaining broader work experience. Repeated external appointments lead to frustrated career aspirations.
- It is cheaper and quicker than recruiting externally.
- The recruitment policy is seen to be based on sound and fair principles.

The main disadvantage is that no 'new blood' comes into the company, and this could be detrimental to the growth of the organisation in the long term.

It may be possible to fill a vacancy by transferring, promoting or training an existing member of staff. This may, in time, lead to a subsequent job vacancy in another area of the organisation's operations. If there are no suitable internal applicants, then recruitment will have to be from external sources.

Sources of recruitment

1. **Recommendations** – from present employees, friends, family members, professional colleagues.

2. **Unsolicited applications** – from people who write in or phone the company as a casual enquiry. Some companies have such a good reputation as employers that they receive a constant stream of such applications and very rarely need to advertise. Staff applications received in this way can be stored and referred to when required.

3. **Colleges and universities**. At one time an annual recruitment drive in which teams from personnel departments visited colleges and universities to recruit graduates was a common feature. 'The milkround', as it was known, is less common today as it is a costly and time-consuming way to recruit people who, on average, stay with the companies for less than five years.

4. **School-leavers** – may be suitable for those vacancies where experience is not essential and the organisation is willing to provide training.

5. **Trade unions** – maintain a register of members and in the case of craft unions this will help to ensure that people recruited from them have the skill or knowledge that the job requires.

6. **Professional bodies** – often publish journals in which companies may advertise. Some professional institutes and associations run an employment register for members seeking jobs. Companies can make use of their employment service. For companies wishing to fill a vacancy that requires a particular qualification (an accountant or mechanical engineer, for example) this may prove to be a useful source of recruitment, since the magazines and journals allow them to reach specialist areas of the labour market.

7. **Government bodies** – such as PER (the Professional and Executive Register), the Jobcentre and Career Advice Centres offer a service, either free or relatively inexpensive, that attempts to help those who are unemployed or due to be made redundant to find suitable work.

8. **Recruitment bureau** – usually staffed by specialist consultants and dealing specifically with one field or type of appointment, usually at a senior level. Such bureaus provide a personnel service tailored to the recruiting company's needs, from initial search through to selection. Results are usually good, but the service is expensive and a charge is usually made for consultation even if a candidate is not appointed.

9. **Employment agencies**. These deal mainly with secretarial and clerical positions. They have a wide catchment area, usually test secretarial skills and interview applicants before recommending them for a position. They charge a percentage of salary as a fee.

10. **Temporary staff**. Used for recruiting labour on a short-term contract basis, and some may then be offered a permanent appointment if a vacancy occurs or when the temporary employee has proved to be suitable.

11. **Advertisements**. These are by far the most popular method of making people aware of a vacancy. Recruitment advertising in the national press has become a sophisticated and expensive business, and many companies now leave it to their advertising department to design advertisements or hand the job over to a recruitment advertising agency. Such agencies can usually be relied upon to know the best style of advertisement for the job and the most suitable publication. They do, of course, have a vested interest in the advice they give.

An advertisement is more than just a way of getting in touch with potential applicants. It creates an impression of the company. The sort of language used will give an indication of the culture and climate of the organisation. The size of advertisement, quality of artwork, plus the salary and benefits package give an impression of the financial standing of the company. It is also a way of giving visibility to the company logo and of indirectly advertising the company's service or products.

The personnel department will need to monitor the means by which it approaches the potential sources of recruitment. This can be a costly exercise, and the results need to be analysed to discover if the current approach produces the desired volume of response from the calibre of people required – i.e. is it cost effective?

The application form
This document is extremely useful as it gives all the essential personal and career information about each candidate.

When sending out the application form it may be accompanied by some information about the company, the job vacancy and type of person who will be recruited for it. This would not include the 'person specification' itself; but some indication of what is required will allow people to pre-select themselves – they perform the first stage of the selection process. It is important, therefore, that only absolutely essential requirements are stated in this way so as not to deter suitable borderline applicants.

Completed application forms are then compared against the person specification and the job description. They are sorted into batches of potential candidates, possibles and unsuitable applicants.

As an alternative to an application form, candidates may be asked to submit a c.v. (*curriculum vitae*). This is a career history presented in narrative form and is becoming increasingly popular amongst applicants for senior management positions.

At the point where completed application forms or c.v's are considered alongside a person specification and job description, then the recruitment phase has given way to selection. With the sifting out of unsuitable applicants the selection process has begun.

The interview
Depending upon the nature of the vacancy and size of the organisation, applicants may be interviewed just once on a one-to-one basis. Or they may be seen by a succession of people or by a panel made up of people from the organisation who are likely to be involved to varying degrees with the person who eventually fills the vacancy. In the case of larger organisations it is usual for an applicant to be interviewed by a member of the personnel department, and by the manager of the department in which he/she will work if selected. It may be considered important for others within the organisation to be included in the selection procedure, such as supervisors, directors or heads of departments, and this to some extent may govern the type of interview chosen. In the case of a small organisation that does not have a specialist personnel department, the interview may be conducted by a senior member of the staff whose department has the vacancy needing to be filled.

The purpose of the interview is to find the right person for the job. This is done by achieving two main objectives:

- assessing the suitability of the candidate for the position;
- providing information about the job and the company.

It is important that the interview is considered as a two-way process. The applicant is assessing the suitability of the job and the company just as much as the company is assessing the suitability of the applicant. Neglect of this consideration may lead to a job offer being refused by a potentially suitable candidate, who gains the wrong impression of the company, its activities and what the vacancy requires in terms of skills, knowledge, responsibility and attitudes, for example. In human relation terms the interview is an interaction between people. The applicant behaves in response to the environment and the behaviour of the interviewer. It is thus worth spending some time creating an atmosphere in which the interviewee feels at ease and free to talk.

For this reason a different impression of the person may be gained by successive different interviewers from the organisation. No single impression is necessarily all right or all wrong, and some might say that the interview itself is an artificial and unreliable way to form an opinion on personality. Perhaps it could be more accurately described as forming a personal impression of observed behaviour. It is nevertheless possible, and necessary, for line managers with no qualifications in psychology or interviewing techniques to judge whether an applicant has the right sort of personality and temperament to 'fit in' with others in the department.

Assessing suitability

Assessment procedures should seek to cover seven essential areas. Depending upon the nature of the vacancy the organisation will attach different degrees of emphasis to them. These areas are as follows:

1. **Physical make-up**. General health, physical characteristics and the attention that an applicant gives to his/her personal appearance.
2. **Attainment**. This includes not only educational achievements and those associated with the skills and/or knowledge needed for employment but also the level of attainment reached in activities connected with the applicant's outside interests, where some form of diploma or certificate may have been awarded.
3. **General intelligence**. This recognises that formal qualifications, or a lack of them, do not necessarily reflect the applicant's general level of intelligence.
4. **Interests**. These may be intellectual, sporting, recreational, social, artistic or a hobby of some kind.
5. **Disposition**. This deals with the natural characteristics of an individual in terms of the impression he/she makes upon other people. This aspect of assessment will therefore cover such areas as the extent to which the candidate is likely to prove acceptable to other people, and what sort of impression he/she will make upon them. The general disposition might, for example, be friendly, outgoing or introverted, confident or hesitant, emotionally stable, influential or easily influenced by others, or steady and self-reliant.
6. **Circumstances**. This is a difficult area to assess as it covers aspects that may be of a very personal nature, such as a candidate's domestic circumstances. But some information may be important in assessing the extent to which personal circumstances may either contribute to or detract from an individual's ability to carry out the prospective duties and responsibilities to a satisfactory standard.

Tests

In some instances a more sophisticated filtering technique than the interview is called for, and here tests are used. There are various types. Whilst experience has shown that tests do not provide an adequate guide to selecting the right person for a job, they are all in their way good indicators of those applicants who will *not* be good at the job.

1. **Aptitude tests**. These are used to discover the mental and physical capabilities of people who have no formal qualifications, or perhaps to establish whether someone has the potential to do a particular job before a costly training programme is embarked upon.
2. **Achievement tests**. In contrast to aptitude tests, which seek to measure potential ability, achievement tests measure the skills and knowledge a candidate has already acquired. Shorthand, typing, fork-lift truck driving and translating are examples of skills that can be tested in this way.
3. **Psychological tests**. These are effective only if administered and evaluated by properly trained and qualified staff. Such tests are designed to produce a profile of the main features of a person's personality and temperament.
4. **Assessment centres**. These have been adopted by several large organisations and are used most widely today in the testing and selection of potential managers. The applicants spend time together working on a problem and exercises they have been set. Their behaviour is closely monitored during this time, and personality traits and leadership qualities are identified.

Once an applicant has been appointed, then successful personnel management requires that policies are pursued so that the new employee stays with the organisation, does well in the job, and their full potential is realised. The workforce is, after all, the organisation's most valuable asset.

4. The Employment of Labour

Training and development

An important part of manpower planning concerns itself with the training of employees and the development of management and supervisory skills. An organisation must continually review, modify and update its training and development programmes in response to both internal and external factors that affect the competitiveness of the organisation and the welfare of the workforce. The following factors may stimulate changes in training and development programmes:

1. An investment project that involves new plant, machinery or equipment and the application of new technology.
2. A deterioration in productivity levels and a fall-off in quality that also produces an increase in scrapped work.
3. New working methods that seek to trim down the number of employees in certain areas of work and require the remaining employees to adopt additional skills and generally become more flexible in their work.
4. Alterations to the end product or service or diversification that affects working methods.
5. An increase in the skill levels of existing employees because a labour shortage inhibits their recruitment from outside the organisation.
6. The promotion or transfer of management and supervisory staff and the development of their potential.
7. A need to increase job satisfaction and motivation as part of measures to reduce labour turnover and absenteeism.
8. The need to improve upon working practices and methods in order to reduce the number of accidents..

The resources devoted to training can give rise to substantial costs. So it is important that the training needs are correctly identified, the desired standard of skill is established, the training programme is administered efficiently and the results achieved by the employees undergoing the training are then compared with the standard of performance it was hoped to achieve.

Training needs
In the case of improving the existing skills of operators or craft workers, or of programmes for new employees, it is necessary to carry out a skills analysis. This analysis produces a job description covering the physical and mental activities involved in the various tasks, the knowledge required and the necessary standard of work in terms of quality and quantity. A machine-tool operator, for example, will require certain manual skills, an ability to read drawings, a knowledge of the machine, its controls and measuring instruments, and an ability to make certain judgements. Thus the job analysis covers not only physical movements but also other aspects of the employee's behaviour relevant to the job. As the description of manpower planning indicated it is also necessary to establish longer-term skill requirements because an anticipated shortage of highly skilled employees will require apprenticeship schemes up to five years in advance.

The design of the training programme
The structure and content of the programme is designed to ensure that the employee acquires the necessary skills and knowledge and develops the appropriate attitudes and behavioural aspects of the job. The degree of success however will depend heavily upon a programme design that takes account of the need to motivate the employee to complete the course and reach the required standard. **Motivation** may be generated by a pay increase, promotion or the status and satisfaction associated with possessing a new skill and using the most up-to-date machinery or equipment. The employee must also see the relevance of the training, and the methods used must sustain his/her interest.

Motivation will be adversely affected if the employee develops a sense of failure or frustration at making only slow progress. In the case of a complex task, therefore, it is advantageous to break it down into a series of simpler operations so that the employee can learn and practise each stage separately, until a level of proficiency is achieved. The employee then moves on to the next stage, and such progress will generate a sense of achievement and satisfaction. A series of stages can then be practised so that standards achieved in earlier ones are maintained, and the employee can also see the relevance of each part of the training as the whole task is put together. Any theoretical content of the training should also be dealt with in a manner that demonstrates its relevance to the skills being acquired or helps explain the reasons for developing certain attitudes or behaviour.

Depending upon the method of training to be given, a decision must then be taken whether the employee will be given on-the-job or off-the-job training.

On-the-job training

This is a common form of training where the task involved is not too complex and the relevant skills are not too difficult to acquire. The trainee is placed in the actual working environment and uses the same kinds of machinery, tools, equipment and materials as the fully productive worker (Fig. 4.1). On-the-job training is also possible for certain types of clerical and administrative jobs where the trainee will immediately handle the relevant

paperwork or carry out certain procedures. This is a relatively inexpensive form of training as it does not require specialist facilities, and the job is learnt on the equipment to be used when the training period is completed. The trainee will not experience the problems that can arise when transferred from the artificial environment of a training establishment where the skills and knowledge may have been developed on different machinery and equipment.

The success of on-the-job training, however, depends heavily upon the teaching skills of the instructor, who may be a supervisor or an experienced employee, and the amount of time he/she can devote to the trainee. There is also a risk that the trainee will pick up bad habits and 'cut corners'; and although such practices may not put at risk the efficiency and welfare of existing workers, they may be inappropriate to the efficiency, health and safety of inexperienced trainees. A lack of supervision and instruction may produce a high proportion of scrapped work and damage to machinery and equipment. Apart from the cost involved, workers may make remarks, humorous or otherwise, that make the trainee hesitant or nervous, and this potentially stressful situation will affect the rate of progress.

Fig. 4.1: On-the-job training

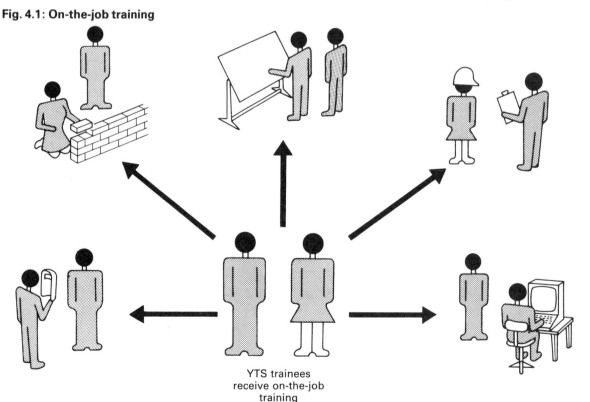

YTS trainees
receive on-the-job
training

On-the-job training will be more successful as a means of teaching what are mainly visible skills if the supervisor has completed a government-sponsored instructor's training course. In this case the supervisor will have acquired instruction techniques such as the ability to break a job down into separate stages and to indicate which of them requires special attention or where precautions must be taken. The supervisor will demonstrate each stage to the trainee, who is also given the opportunity to raise any questions about equipment or materials or the reasoning behind certain aspects of the job. The supervisor will also have been trained in the communications skills that are of great importance when dealing with trainees. This is the case, for example, when explaining methods or procedures, giving encouragement or correcting mistakes and generally motivating the trainee. A trained supervisor will also be aware of the degree of supervision that a particular trainee requires and how to build up his/her confidence.

Off-the-job training
Small organisations generally have to depend upon on-the-job training, since the intake of new employees is usually too small to justify expenditure on specialist training facilities and full-time instructors. They may allocate on-the-job training to a supervisor or an experienced worker, and an employee may be persuaded to take up such a role if provided with a financial incentive, a job title that raises his/her status or adequate time to carry out such responsibilities.

However, where the skill analysis of a job indicates the need for a much higher level of manual dexterity, the co-ordination of senses, powers of judgement and knowledge, then small organisations are able to use off-the-job training facilities provided by local colleges or government training and skill centres. Colleges and polytechnics between them offer a wide range of part-time and block-release courses that industry and commerce can take advantage of for different types and levels of training. In some areas the courses in educational establishments reflect the specialist skill and knowledge requirements of those organisations that account for a large part of the local employment.

Large organisations may use such external courses for a part of their off-the-job training programmes. But the size of their labour force, their annual intake of new workers and their financial resources generally make it viable for

them to set up their own specialist training facilities staffed by trained instructors. Off-the-job training means that it is possible to provide more lengthy courses of instruction dealing with higher-level skills; trainees can systematically work through the various stages to develop the appropriate manual skills, knowledge, attitudes and behaviour.

Off-the-job training should avoid some of the problems associated with on-the-job training described earlier, and the return on this type of investment will be seen in higher productivity and quality of output. There is a possibility, however, that trainees could experience some difficulty when they leave the college or training-school environment, where they use special machinery and equipment, and move into their work-place. Off-the-job training therefore may be supported by a period of on-the-job training so that trainees can gradually adapt to the specific needs of a job when they become productive workers.

Before passing on to a description of supervisor and management training, it is important to emphasise the important role played by various types and levels of training in all organisations. There is perhaps a tendency to relate training to the more visible skill requirements of the industrial and manufacturing sectors of the economy, which employ a large number of operatives, craft workers and technicians. The reader will find it a worthwhile exercise therefore to consider the various skill requirements in terms of manual dexterity, knowledge, attitudes and behaviour for people employed in such areas as horticulture, retailing, hotel and catering, health care, marketing, banking, public administration, transport and secretarial work.

Management and supervisory development
As described earlier, an essential aspect of manpower planning is the need to ensure that there is always a ready supply of trained and experienced people who can be promoted to supervisory positions and higher levels of management. In addition to the succession requirements, however, it is also essential to the efficiency and success of an organisation that the potential of people holding existing positions of authority and responsibility is developed as fully as possible.

The techniques used in the development of management and supervisory staff are less clear-cut than those used for other categories of employees, where for example the manual skills and knowledge requirements can be clearly identified and then incorporated into a training programme. An individual may be regarded as a good manager because of his/her success in initiating, controlling, co-ordinating and organising certain activities within the organisation, identifying the sources of any problems, introducing successful remedies and generally improving the performance of the area of work for which he/she is responsible. The problem, however, is in identifying and assessing what exactly are the personal qualities and skills that help to make someone a successful manager and then devising the appropriate techniques for developing similar qualities and skills in others who are likely to benefit from a management development programme.

As far as any formal qualifications are concerned, the employee can be encouraged to study for the award of the relevant professional or institutional body. It is useful for an employee singled out for his/her first management or supervisory position to increase his/her knowledge of the specialist area of work in which he/she is involved; but in the case of appointments to much higher positions of authority and responsibility, less attention is generally paid to formal qualifications. This is because these more experienced employees will already have demonstrated their in-depth knowledge in their specialist area of work even though it may not be reflected in a formal qualification.

Formal qualifications in management itself are increasingly provided by universities, polytechnics, business schools and private management centres, and these are valuable in so far as they can provide training in the clearly identifiable tools of management employed in organisations. These tools include forecasting techniques and methods of cost analysis, work study and project management, in addition to the specialist areas such as marketing, accountancy, personnel and production and an appreciation of the overall environment within which organisations operate.

These management courses aim to provide a solid foundation for the further development of management skills and to introduce techniques aimed at developing analytical, planning, creative, decision-making, problem-solving and communications skills. These techniques include case studies, business and role-playing exercises, which attempt as far as possible to simulate the situations arising in the working environment.

Management courses are increasingly meeting the need to establish direct and close links with employers in terms of their structure, content and the training techniques used. This is reflected in the trend towards part-time and sandwich courses and the provision of intensive post-experience courses for mature managers. This enables people to relate their knowledge and newly acquired management skills to the real-life situations they confront in their own organisation. The relevance of management development is further strengthened by meeting the specific needs of an industry or an organisation that indicates its own particular requirements with respect to its management development programme. Closer links with employers have also led to the practice whereby they seek the assistance of people on management courses in tackling real-life problems arising within their organisation; this has the advantage that real situations are dealt with and the results can be analysed in the light of the management techniques and skills applied to a problem.

Despite the progress being made in the development of external management courses, organisations still tend to favour an approach that relies essentially upon internal methods. To some extent this may be due to the increase in the size of organisations, as they can justify the employment of specialist training staff and the use of management development consultants. Internal programmes allow the participants to become more familiar with various features of the organisation, such as its particular structure and systems, while gaining experience in a wide range of activities where management skills can be developed.

Any knowledge requirements may involve the use of external courses, while a combination of the following internal methods may be used to develop practical management skills:

1. *Job rotation*
This involves moving people to new jobs, which may also be in different sections or departments and generally carry the same level of authority and responsibility. An individual will gain the experience that may be necessary before being promoted. He/she can increase his/her understanding of what is involved in various jobs while also appreciating more fully their respective contributions to the organisation's objectives.

2. *Projects*
A manager may be given a special assignment that involves tackling a problem which has arisen

within the organisation and will take him/her beyond the scope of their existing job. The manager will investigate the problem and put forward recommendations for dealing with it. Alternatively the assignment may be based upon an investigation into the proposed introduction of changes in connection with methods of production, technology, management techniques, the organisational structure or the administrative system.

This project or assignment approach can also be used in conjunction with a group of junior managers who are brought together to form a board to handle such matters or to investigate ways of improving efficiency in their own departments. When employees are brought together in this way they will learn to appreciate more fully what is involved in other people's jobs and the factors that influence their view on the issues being dealt with. Whether acting individually or as a group they may be given the authority to put their recommendations into practice; and this form of internal management or supervisory development will introduce the element of reality into their decision-making, as they will be responsible for the results of the action to be taken.

3. *Action learning*

This technique is based upon the view that the skills of senior managers in particular are best sharpened and enhanced if they face new challenges and problems. Managers are said to benefit from taking over different jobs within the same organisation or from being seconded to another organisation for perhaps up to a year where they will face different circumstances and problems. Action learning is perhaps the strongest reflection of the view that, although knowledge, theory and simulated exercises can be of use in some areas of management development, there is no real substitute for the experience and learning derived from actually doing a job.

To some extent this also recognises the view that some people are naturally gifted in terms of the abilities that are required to become a good manager, but their full potential will be exploited only if they are continually stretched by a realistic and challenging environment that makes greater demands upon them as managers. The result will be that existing skills are improved upon and latent skills are stimulated.

The importance attached to action learning can be seen in the growth of programmes in business schools and management centres providing opportunity for managers to discuss the action they have taken at work in regular group meetings. A group may be comprised of managers from different organisations and areas of responsibility, so that there is an exchange of views and a discussion of any alternative action that could be taken.

4 *Coaching*

This involves regular informal meetings between a manager and a subordinate to discuss the latter's performance in relation to any objectives or targets. These sessions allow the manager to identify an individual's strengths and weaknesses, but care must be taken to ensure that the subordinate does not come to see such meetings as solely the means of bringing him/her to task for mistakes or a lack of progress.

The subordinate should be encouraged to discuss any current problems and to explain the reasoning behind any solutions he/she proposes to use. The manager can then offer advice and use the situation as a means of encouraging the subordinate to analyse the proposed course of action or consider ways of improving performance in the area of work for which he/she is responsible. The subordinate may be delegated extra authority and responsibility and perhaps given a project or assignment to further extend and test his/her potential for promotion.

These coaching or counselling sessions should be properly structured and regarded by both parties as part of a development programme during which the subordinate is also encouraged to express a view on his/her future with the organisation and career ambitions.

The success of coaching depends heavily upon the skills of the manager. He/she in turn should be encouraged to acquire and develop coaching and counselling skills. Without such training a manager may unwittingly simply be giving instructions and making decisions on behalf of the subordinate without adequate explanation. This will adversely affect the employee's confidence and motivation.

Performance appraisal

An appraisal system is a method used to review the standard of work being done by people within an organisation. It centres upon the appraisal interview, which is an opportunity for a manager to meet on an individual basis those people who work for him/her to assess their performance, identify any particular strengths or weaknesses and propose suitable action to be taken.

Most companies appraise management performance either formally or informally; many appraise clerical staff, but in a recent survey conducted by the Institute of Personnel Management it was found that only 2 per cent of the 236 companies surveyed had formal appraisal schemes for shop-floor workers.

The appraisal is usually performed by a job-holder's immediate manager, who will use whatever information is available to enable him/her to take an accurate view of the employee's work.

During the course of this interview the employee's standard of work is discussed, taking into account past and present performance and plans for the future. The level of success with which he/she has met objectives set and performed tasks required will be examined in depth. Proposals or recommendations are then put forward, where possible, for improvement in job performance. This might take the form of further training, or the acquisition of different skills, knowledge or equipment.

Performance appraisal forms
As he/she goes through the interview, the appraising manager will make notes on a performance appraisal form. This document is stored by the departmental manager or more usually the personnel department as a permanent record of employee performance.

If the appraisal is to be purely objective, the form used will be of a simple design; it may even be a blank sheet of paper. A more systematic appraisal form would give the appraising manager a series of tasks or categories into which the total job can be divided. He/she would then consider each area of work in turn and discuss it with the job-holder. The appraising manager's aim at all times should be to foster an atmosphere of trust in which both parties to the interview feel at liberty to express views and comment upon any difficulties that have prevented a task being performed to satisfaction. The job-holder should be able to raise problems or areas of concern without feeling that this is an admission of failure for which he/she will be penalised. The theme should be one of objective problem-solving, not fault-finding or criticism of a person's character.

On a highly structured appraisal form the manager may be required to use a rating scale by awarding marks out of five based upon questions relating to the employee's personal characteristics and other factors that indicate levels of performance. To ensure that managers adopt a uniform approach as to what justifies a certain mark out of five, each part of the appraisal form may list a series of words describing the level of competence from which the manager must make a choice.

When, for example, the manager is appraising the initiative of a subordinate this particular section may include a description of those characteristics the organisation regards as representing initiative. This description may cover such factors as an ability to work without constant and detailed supervision and instruction, the inventiveness and enterprise displayed by an employee in using his/her own resources to tackle problems, and his/her willingness to put forward ideas on improved working methods. The manager will then be faced with five possible views; these could range from one that places the subordinate in a category of needing constant supervision and instruction (for which one mark is awarded) to a category describing the subordinate as always able to work without supervision while also displaying resourcefulness and originality in dealing with problems and suggesting new working methods (for which the maximum five marks are awarded).

One of the problems with appraisal scores is that the majority of marks tend to cluster in the 'above average' area. Reasons for this are human rather than statistical. It is generally accepted that appraisal forms should be shown to the people being appraised – in fact that appraisees should help to write them. Most people who work hard and who want to succeed do not like to see their job performance described as 'average', 'satisfactory' or '3/5'. Although such comments mean that the job is being done to an acceptable standard, they are often taken as an implied criticism by appraisees, and may cause defensiveness and resentment. Managers are aware of the harmful effects on employee motivation, job performance and working relationships by marking a person's performance as average or lower than average. So they may mark higher than they would otherwise, because they know the employee will see the form. A manager may also mark high because he/she wants to help a member of staff gain promotion or may simply like the person or need to rely upon their support.

If the appraisal scheme is linked to a company's

salary structure the accuracy with which a manager rates members of staff can be even more suspect. Again there is the potential problem of demotivation and possible alienation from the department's goals experienced by those people who receive a lower-than-expected salary increase. Furthermore, the department manager may consider that all those people working for him/her deserve a higher-than-average increase because they have worked hard, worked extra hours or managed to complete a project before the deadline date. This could be considered a misuse of the appraisal system and needs to be closely monitored. It is generally considered wiser to operate an appraisal system that is not directly linked to a salary structure, and to space the appraisal interview and salary review several months apart.

The appraisal interview

A successful appraisal interview, then, is much more than a straightforward form-filling exercise. An appraising manager who has been trained to do the job properly will appreciate the significance of the human-relations aspect of the interview and will try to perfect a style of interview that is best for the person he/she is appraising. This begins with adequate preparation, ensuring that all the relevant information is to hand, and that everyone knows what performance appraisal is and appreciates its importance and value.

Scene-setting is psychologically important, and the appraising manager should select a location for the interview in which the employee being appraised will feel comfortable and free from interruptions. It is often better to get away from the office altogether and use a spare conference room or training room. There should be some time set aside at the beginning of the interview for putting the employee at ease and establishing a rapport.

At all times the interview should be conducted with care and sensitivity. Consideration should be given to the feelings and emotional needs of the person being appraised. Many people associate so closely with the work they do that it becomes the image they hold of themselves. We often hear someone say, 'I am an accountant', rather than, 'I work as an accountant'. They derive their identity and prestige, in the family, in the peer group and in society as a whole, from the work they do.

There is a school of thought that we all have needs which can be ordered into the kind of hierarchy shown here:

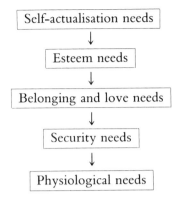

It is generally accepted that employees seek the satisfaction of these needs, to a greater or lesser extent, from their experiences at work. We need to earn money, to feel relatively secure, to belong to a group with whose aims we identify, to do a worthwhile job, to feel that we are doing well.

It follows that any criticism of an aspect of job performance will have a deeper significance to the job-holder than to his/her manager. Care should be taken to avoid emotive language. Constructive suggestions for solutions to problems identified should be invited and proffered wherever possible.

Consideration should also be given to those factors and influences beyond a job-holder's control that affect the level of performance. Such influencing factors might be the job-holder's dependence on others within the organisation, budget levels, freedom to act and scope within the job for improvement.

Attitudes towards appraisal

The introduction of an appraisal scheme can often meet with considerable resistance from line managers. Some perceive their role as manager in purely task-oriented terms. They do not agree that the personnel function within an organisation is a responsibility shared by everyone who has people reporting to them. Such managers see the appraisal system, and particularly the interview, as a job that should be done by the personnel department. Some complain that the system takes a disproportionate amount of time to the benefits gained from using it. Some argue that they have a close working relationship with members of their staff, they know who is doing well or who needs further training, so the appraisal interview as such is superfluous. Others use the appraisal interview as a time to counsel or discipline staff informally, or to sell a new idea to them.

It is important that such attitudes are taken into account during the training session for those who are to perform appraisal interviews. If there is no tangible change or outcome in the form of follow-up action then the process will be seen by all those who take part as a waste of time. The information gathered from appraisal interviews can be used in manpower planning, to identify training needs and develop an individual's potential; to find ways to increase output, quality and safety; to improve morale, motivation, communication and relationships; and to find more efficient methods of working.

From a manager's point of view this is a good way of monitoring the work being done by the people for whom he/she is responsible. The appraisal interview gives the manager a chance to talk with each member of staff individually and to give that one person sole attention for a designated period of time. Depending upon the size of the department and the management style adopted by the appraising manager, this may be the only opportunity for considering the career aspirations, training and development needs, and expectations of each person. The manager should take this chance to offer praise where it is due and to reinforce a sense of loyalty towards all those who belong to the work group. The employee should be made to feel that he/she makes a worthwhile contribution and is of value as a person and as a member of the organisation.

After interviewing each person the manager can gather together all the performance appraisal forms and consider his/her staff and the work being performed. It enables the manager to take an overview of his/her area of responsibility and look for ways to improve methods of working. This aids future planning and identifies strengths and weaknesses in business systems, methods and organisation structure.

To the manager or company committed to **management by objectives** (usually shortened to MBO) the appraisal interview is an opportunity for the measurement of the success with which objectives set jointly by manager and subordinate have been met. This system attempts to improve company performance and to motivate, assess and train employees by integrating their personal goals with the objectives of the company. It is likely that a manager using this system would have frequent meetings with staff at which work performance would be appraised.

For the person being appraised the interview should provide an opportunity to talk about career development with his/her manager; to highlight areas of concern and to participate actively in objective problem-solving; to be consulted on future plans and to help set targets; to feel that the company knows which of its employees works hard and does a job well, and values those employees.

Organisation and methods (O and M)

This is the means by which organisations seek to improve the efficiency of those employees involved in office work and administrative and financial procedures. O and M is therefore concerned with investigating the existing procedures in these areas of work from the point of view of why they are needed, how they are organised and the methods currently used. Such investigations are necessary because over a period of time the nature of an organisation will change in terms of size, the degree of integration, the production methods and the type of goods and services supplied. These developments may mean that the clerical, administrative and financial procedures have to be reviewed and more effectively geared towards the needs of the organisation (Fig. 4.2).

Even in the absence of those developments that alter the character of an organisation, there is still a need periodically to investigate procedures in order to make them more efficient and to minimise the costs incurred. The benefits of O and M studies may be seen through improvements in the following areas:

1. A simplification of procedures, documentation and forms and a general reduction in paperwork.
2. Fewer errors and the provision of more accurate data and information.
3. An office layout and the introduction of equipment that reduces the movement of people and documents.
4. More efficient communications.
5. Staff efficiency, job satisfaction, morale and reduced labour turnover.

O and M studies may lead to the simplification of procedures or even the installation of totally new systems that seek to make full use of new technology in secretarial, clerical, administrative

Fig. 4.2: Organisation and methods in practice

and financial work. Many organisations employ the services of O and M consultants who are highly trained and experienced in such work and are able to undertake a detailed scientific analysis. They are also able to make recommendations that are free from the bias or vested interest that may influence the investigations and recommendations of a departmental manager who is given an O and M assignment involving an area of work for which he/she is responsible.

The O and M consultant will liaise with senior management and will become familiar with the climate of the organisation. This is likely to produce recommendations that are more acceptable to the senior management. The O and M team will understand the limitations within which it has to work and can thus avoid suggestions that may conflict, for example, with the organisation's policy on redundancies, transfers, recruitment or capital expenditure on expensive equipment. The latter might be part of proposals aimed at bringing about more fundamental changes in the existing organisation and methods. Another advantage of a consultant when compared with making a department manager responsible for such work is that the former is more likely to see a problem in an organisational context and to offer a centralised solution also of benefit to other departments.

Having established the procedures to be studied and the parameters within which they must operate, the O and M team will then conduct a detailed analysis that will cover the following points:

1. The purpose of the procedure.
2. The methods used.
3. The staff involved.
4. The skills involved.
5. The equipment.
6. When the procedures are carried out.
7. Where the work is located.
8. The degree of supervision.
9. The volume of work.
10. The time taken.
11. The costs.

Consideration will be given to alternative ways of performing the work, and this will give rise to recommendations concerning a more efficient and cost-effective system. The new procedures will then be explained to senior management. The O and M team will also provide a description of what is to be done by those who will be using the new procedures, along with details concerning their purpose and scope, any new forms or documentation to be used and the date by which the new procedures will become effective.

Apart from introducing changes that make procedures quicker, easier and more efficient, and that cut down on red tape and bureaucracy, the O and M consultants may advise on the best choice of hardware and software in any proposals concerning the use of computerised systems and other technological developments that assist both internal and external communications. Their investigations may also cover aspects of the physical environment in which procedures are carried out, such as office design and layout, colour schemes, general décor and ergonomically designed furniture.

Work study

The aim of work study is to provide a service to management that will assist it in its aim of making the most efficient use of labour, materials, machines, equipment and space (Fig. 4.3). Work study is concerned with the methods used on the factory floor but an increasing part of O and M studies now also uses clerical work study as part of its techniques to raise efficiency. Work study involves making a detailed examination of a task and the environment in which it is carried out in order to achieve the following objectives:

1. An improvement in the way an operation or process is carried out.
2. A more efficient manning of plant, machinery and equipment in order to make the most productive use of such items of capital.
3. The improved handling of materials and components.
4. A more efficient shop-floor layout.

5. Improvements to the individual work-places in terms of the layout of tools, materials, components and controls and the design and measurements of the employee's seating and workbench.
6. A reduction in the effort and fatigue associated with the movement of hands and feet.
7. An improvement to the physical working conditions such as heating, ventilation, lighting and noise.
8. The provision of accurate and detailed information concerning the time required to perform particular tasks in order to assist production planning and control, costing, and the design of bonus and productivity schemes to act as financial incentives for employees performing the various tasks.

Method and motion study

The investigations and analysis undertaken by the work study team will be conducted in two phases. The first phase will involve **method study**. This covers the observation, recording, analysis and critical examination of the existing or proposed methods of working. A great deal of attention will also be paid to the physical movements made by the workers in handling tools, equipment, materials and components and in using and operating items of plant and machinery. This aspect of the investigation involves what is known as **motion study**; it seeks to reduce fatigue and to increase the

Fig. 4.3: Work study in a factory

efficiency of the workers' movements. It is generally accepted, for example, that where possible both hands should be used and moved simultaneously in carrying out a task. Arm movements should be curved and continuous and avoid frequent directional changes.

Motion study recognises that effort and fatigue can be reduced if certain hand and arm movements are avoided. This can be assisted by a work-place where the positioning of tools, materials, components and controls take account of such factors and of the need for the worker to operate using smooth rhythmical movements.

Work measurement

Having completed the method and motion study and decided upon the new methods, the next stage covers **work measurement**. This seeks to determine the time required to perform a particular task. Work measurement provides the means by which standard times for jobs can be established, and this information is used for the purposes of production planning, assessing the utilisation of machines, costing and designing financial incentives for the employees.

The standard time can be used to devise an incentive scheme based upon piecework, whereby the worker is paid a fixed amount for each piece produced, or a bonus scheme, whereby the worker receives a fixed amount per hour plus a share of the saving obtained by completing the work in less than the time allowed, i.e. the standard time. These schemes not only help to raise the productivity of labour but also contribute to a more efficient utilisation of machinery and equipment. Higher productivity should not be achieved at the expense of the quality of the work, however. So the extra earnings of a worker may also be adjusted to take account of the extent to which the work rejected by the inspection or quality-control department exceeds a certain percentage of the accepted work.

The need for work study

It can be seen then that work study plays an important part in improving the efficiency of an organisation. The contribution it makes towards the minimisation of costs will be particularly useful for organisations that sell their goods or services in competitive markets. Work study will help such organisations keep unit costs as low as possible, thus enabling them to offer attractive prices and at the same time to protect their profit margins.

An organisation may be able to boast a highly skilled workforce and the use of the latest technology, but such resources will be used to their maximum advantage only if they are periodically subjected to work study techniques. Over a period of time some workers may develop working practices that lead to a deterioration in efficiency or quality, while other workers may never have been instructed in the best way to do a job. Management and supervisory staff may also be guilty of not having given sufficient consideration to what may be more efficient methods. This may be because they are too busy or lack the training to appreciate the cumulative effects of what may have been a gradual and piecemeal development in methods, shop-floor layout and work-places; for these reasons they may not recognise the implications of these fragmented and *ad hoc* changes for the efficiency with which tasks are carried out.

A failure to carry out work study may eventually lead to a situation where output is affected by bottlenecks in certain parts of the organisation's operations. There may be a deterioration in quality and an increase in scrapped output, an increase in overtime working to meet production targets and a general rise in costs affecting competitiveness and profits. Work study should therefore be practised continuously rather than resorted to only when faults and deficiencies are reflected in a disproportionate increase in costs, lower profits and declining market share.

In some companies departmental managers are expected to share the responsibility for improving performance and the quality of the work. The striving to improve is not seen just as an ideal but rather as a task they are expected to perform as an ongoing process to make maximum use of the resources available to them. An attitude of constantly wanting to improve and looking for better ways to work can be fostered in all parts of the workforce. It makes coping with change less stressful and also creates the right atmosphere for changes to occur. An environment in which actions, methods, systems and procedures are questioned and improved upon rather than adhered to for their own sake helps produce a more flexible, creative and efficient workforce and avoids the penalties that arise from complacency.

Employee participation and co-operation are invaluable in problem-solving and looking for better ways to work. Very often the person actually doing the job is the best 'expert' to ask how it could be done more efficiently. Any such suggestions can be analysed in the context of how the proposed changes might affect the efficiency of operations elsewhere in the organisation. Some companies offer financial rewards for ideas received through suggestion schemes. Profit-sharing schemes are also used to stimulate the interest and the co-operation of the workforce in raising productivity by adopting new methods and adjusting their working practices to accommodate the introduction of new technology.

Attitudes to work study

Both shop-floor workers and departmental managers themselves may be suspicious of the purpose of work study, and this may promote concern about possible redundancies. Every effort must therefore be made to gain the confidence of the workforce by giving a full explanation of the purpose of the work study. This may be assisted by appointing a trade union representative to a works study committee set up to select the areas that are to be subjected to study, and to discuss the reports that cover the subsequent investigations, analysis and recommendations.

If the workforce gains a greater understanding of work study, it is more likely to view the technique as a means of improving methods, rather than as a device used by management to find fault in what the workers do and then to use the information to criticise them and to support their claims that they should be working harder. If the fears of workers concerning redundancies can be allayed, this will lead to their co-operation in the introduction of any new technology that may be associated with new methods. The workers should also be given an early indication as to how they may benefit financially from any incentive schemes that may be linked to the new methods and how the payments are likely to be determined.

The work study team therefore needs to possess skills that go beyond those that are purely technical in nature. The team should be trained in those aspects of the work that rely heavily upon good communications skills and an understanding of how human nature is likely to influence the immediate reaction of a worker whose every movement is being observed, recorded and timed. Work study is likely to be treated with greater suspicion during a period of high unemployment and a generally depressed economy. In conditions such as these management has the difficult task of demonstrating the role that work study can play in discovering the more efficient methods that will help the organisation to survive such difficult times, and of showing how the effect upon competitiveness will help to secure jobs in the future.

In more buoyant times, however, the workforce is likely to be more appreciative of the purposes of work study. The organisation can use this greater feeling of job security to create a more flexible workforce. Work study can thus be a source of positive attitudes towards the introduction of new working methods, attitudes that recognise the importance of adapting skills to match the changes brought about by scientific and technological advance.

Job evaluation

Job evaluation schemes are used to establish the relative worth within an organisation of each job in terms of seniority and pay. They are concerned with the demands and characteristics of a job rather than who occupies the job.

The need for job evaluation

Without such a scheme there would eventually be levels of seniority, because over a period of time a natural 'pecking order' would establish itself; also, the forces of demand and supply operating in the labour market would produce pay differentials that reflected the relative scarcity of different types of labour. The outcome of these developments, however, could be a pay structure that would not necessarily be fair or desirable.

Employees are concerned less with their pay in relation to the economics of the labour market but rather with earning an income that they believe to be fair and that allows them to maintain and perhaps improve upon their living standards. They will also view their income in terms of how it compares with pay in other parts of their organisation and with the income received by people with similar jobs in other organisations.

The element of fairness was a major influence upon the trend in pay claims in the 1960s and 1970s. Pay claims were submitted that firstly sought to compensate for the previous rise in the cost of living with an amount to provide at least some protection against the anticipated rise in the general level of prices. These pay claims were also intended to achieve an increase that in percentage terms was at least comparable to the rises obtained by other groups of workers.

This was one way of interpreting fairness in the

determination of pay levels. However, this overall approach tends to produce a continuous upward acceleration in the size of pay increases. This is because a price–wage spiral can add to inflationary pressures in the economy, while some settlements may distort what some workers regard as traditional pay differentials between themselves and other groups of workers. Each new round of pay claims is therefore influenced by the further rise in the cost of living and by the attempt by some workers to restore the differentials between themselves and those who have traditionally been above or below them in terms of pay or salary scales.

It is against this background that an organisation must seek to design a wage or salary structure that is considered fair by its own particular employees. The organisation must also consider its pay and salary structure from the point of view of how its operating costs will be affected and how new pay differentials may be needed to ensure that it can continue to retain and recruit the skills required to meet its manpower requirements. Job evaluation is the means by which an organisation can arrange, in order of relative values, the jobs held by its employees. The implementation of a job evaluation scheme shows that an organisation is making a concerted effort to assess the value of jobs in a fair and systematic way and that the pay and grading system is not the result of arbitrary decisions or of the personal influence or choice of certain individuals.

Large organisations tend to use the more comprehensive and detailed job evaluation techniques because they have the specialist staff to design and administer them. They also have a greater need for more sophisticated job evaluation techniques because of the wide range of jobs held by their employees when compared to smaller organisations. The pay and salary structure of large organisations may be one of the factors taken into account by the smaller organisations that are seeking a relatively simple method of arriving at a pay structure.

All forms of job evaluation will involve an element of subjective judgement, in that the opinions of the evaluators will to varying degrees influence the value attached to a particular job. Job evaluation does not lend itself to a system of assessment that is totally free of subjective judgements, even if the system is highly complex. This is because personal opinions will be involved in the design of the system itself, for example in initial decisions on what factors are to be taken into account in measuring the worth of a job.

How job evaluation works

A job evaluation scheme used by a large organisation may seek to value a job by considering the following factors:

1. The experience required.
2. The complexity of the job.
3. The range and levels of skill and knowledge demanded by the job.
4. The degree of initiative, discretion and judgement, for example, involved in decision-making.
5. The degree to which the decisions taken have a direct impact on the organisation's profits, and the potential size of that impact.
6. The number of people who have to be supervised, and the nature of the work carried out by the subordinates.
7. The number of people with whom direct contact is made, and the positions held by such people.
8. The amount of physical effort involved.

Each of these factors will be considered against the information contained in the job description. Points will be allocated to each job factor out of a maximum of perhaps five. The individual scores will then give a total score for that job. The job values can then be used to help design a wage or salary structure, and the total for any particular job will then allow it to be placed at a certain point in that structure.

A system of **weighting** may also be used, as the organisation may decide that not all the job factors have the same degree of importance. The organisation may decide to give a greater weighting to those factors it believes more closely associated with the successful achievement of its objectives. The nature of its business may, for example, cause it to allocate a greater weighting to the decision-making factor rather than supervision responsibilities.

It is also unlikely that the same system will be used for all types of job in the organisation, since the job factors will be different, and any weighting system used may also have to be adjusted. There may, for example, be schemes for such categories as manual workers, clerical staff and management positions. Each of these categories may then be broken down into sub-groups, but the further this process is taken the more complex the system becomes and the greater the likelihood of subjective values being involved in justifying why so many schemes are required.

To be effective a job evaluation scheme should seek to take into account the following factors:

1. It should provide acceptable and consistent results.
2. Evaluators should be provided with defined yardsticks to help them achieve a greater degree of objectivity and consistency.
3. It should include an appeals procedure for those employees who believe that their job has been incorrectly evaluated.
4. The system must be capable of demonstrating to employees who appeal against their position in the pay structure why their particular job was given a value lower down the scale.
5. It should be capable of being used as a basis for pay negotiations with trade unions or other employee organisations.
6. The hierarchy of jobs produced by the job evaluation should be used to support the promotion system and the training and management development programmes.
7. The factors considered in the job evaluation scheme should complement the job enrichment or job enlargement schemes being operated by the organisation in order to raise the status or prestige attached to a job or to widen the range of activities associated with a job.
8. It should be capable of dealing with changes in job specification and of indicating the new position of a job and the appropriate level of pay within the wage or salary structure.

Job evaluation and pay

Job evaluation produces a hierarchy of jobs but does not itself determine the wages and salaries the organisation is prepared to pay to its employees. The evaluation will indicate the ranking of jobs in terms of their levels of pay and therefore their positions within the wage or salary structure decided upon by the organisation. The actual pay for jobs may then differ from the level suggested by the job evaluation and by the wage and salary structure adopted by the organisation, because several other factors may then have to be taken into account:

1. Employees may receive extra payment for length of service with the organisation.

2. A merit award may be paid.
3. An allowance may be paid for unsocial hours or dirty work.
4. The market rate for a job may be higher than the wage or salary allocated to it in the hierarchy of jobs, so that recruitment and retention of staff would be difficult if the pay were not made more attractive.
5. The need to consider the position of trade unions and other employee organisations may affect individuals' pay.

In making these adjustments the organisation must ensure that it does not duplicate the work undertaken during the job evaluation. It could find itself in a position of having granted an allowance for length of service, for example, and this may already have been allocated a certain weighting under the job factor of experience with the organisation as part of total experience.

It is useful for organisations to have some information relating to the pay levels and structures and job evaluation schemes operated by others, and to monitor current trends in connection with recent pay awards. Information on national earnings and movements in pay in different sectors of the economy is available from government publications such as the *Department of Employment Gazette*. Salary surveys are also published by the British Institute of Management and the British Institute of Administrative Management. In addition, some organisations contribute to local salary surveys or provide each other with information on a quid pro quo basis. Advertisements in the local and national press and in professional and institute journals are other useful indicators of current rates of pay.

In making comparisons and using this information as part of the establishment of its own pay structure, an organisation will need to consider the following factors:

1. Jobs in different organisations with the same title do not necessarily carry the same level of responsibility.
2. Some jobs have greater relative value in one industry than another.
3. There may be differences in fringe benefits.
4. The status, prestige and security attached to the job will differ between organisations.
5. The local labour market faced by different organisations may moderate or accelerate local pay rates.

6. The real value of pay in terms of purchasing power will differ between various parts of the country because the cost of living will not inflate evenly all over the country.
7. The bargaining strength as influenced by the activity of local trade unions or other employee organisations will not be the same in all places of employment.
8. Earnings in terms of take-home pay will not be a useful guide if different bonus or productivity schemes are in operation or if there is a profit-sharing scheme.

The introduction of a new job evaluation scheme
Because such schemes deal with the sensitive areas of pay and status they must be introduced with great care. The method of evaluation should be clearly explained to employees and their representatives, who should be consulted in the planning stages. It is also advisable for an employee representative to be a member of the job evaluation committee. It is the usual practice to agree that no loss of pay or status will be incurred as a result of the evaluation and that any resulting anomalies will be ironed out over a given period of time.

One of the problems of mergers and take-overs is dealing with the different personnel systems and practices of the organisations involved. Identical job evaluation schemes are unlikely to exist, and employees are unlikely to have been receiving the same wage rates or salaries even if the job descriptions were fairly similar and if each scheme had identified and used the same job factors. Differences may still arise as a result of the job factors being allocated different weightings and the two evaluations being influenced by the respective cultures of the organisation.

In this situation a great deal of attention will have to be given to standardising the personnel policies and procedures in the light of what may be changes in the overall objectives of the newly formed and larger organisation. This may involve accepting that anomalies exist and agreeing to introduce changes over a period of time rather than more immediate changes that may produce long-term human and industrial-relations problems.

A new job evaluation may also be required as a result of changes in working methods and the introduction of new technology. The job evaluation techniques will have to be re-examined in the light of the new skills and working practices associated with the introduction of more sophisticated plant, machinery and equipment and how this requires greater flexibility and co-operation on the part of employees.

The way in which work will be done in the future with the increased use of computers, robots and other technological developments will require that organisations will have to assess their employees with job evaluation techniques that are continually being updated. The 'one person, one job' concept is giving way to more integrated work-flows. Improved communications and the ability to provide, assimilate and transmit information rapidly are having a profound effect upon the role of managers, for example. It is becoming increasingly difficult to establish where one person's 'territory' ends, in terms of work performed and decisions taken, and where another's begins.

Information and work efficiency

Organisations need a management information system. Management needs information in order to support its decision-making, to control the organisation and to plan for the future. The system itself is the means by which various kinds of business data are processed and converted into information that relates to the organisation's operations. Much of this information may then be subjected to further processing.

For example, data may be processed in order to establish the performance of each of the sales representatives employed by an organisation. This information may then act as the data that can be processed to provide further information on what is happening to total sales. This information, along with other data, may then be used to obtain information relating to how the total costs of employing the sales representatives may have changed in relation to the total sales achieved by the sales force. Thus what is information relating to one aspect of the organisation's operations may then be used as the raw data for obtaining additional information connected with another aspect.

Where information is needed
Data must be processed into the information required at the various levels of the organisation's activities. Information is required at three levels:

1. At the **operational level**, whether it is on the factory floor or in an office, there will be foremen and supervisors, for example, responsible for

ensuring that certain aspects of the work are planned and undertaken efficiently. In the case of a factory, a foreman may need the following information in relation to the item that must pass through the section for which he is responsible:

(a) the quantity to be handled;
(b) the completion date;
(c) the availability of plant and machine capacity;
(d) the tasks to be performed;
(e) the labour available;
(f) material and component requirements.

This kind of information will assist the foreman in planning and controlling the work over a period of time and is essential for decision-making at an operational level. This level of the organisation will then give rise to data that will be processed to provide much of the information required by middle management.

2. The information required by **middle management** will cover those areas that are concerned with the efficiency with which operations are carried out and the extent to which the resources under their control are being used to achieve the organisation's objectives. Much of this information will therefore be concerned with the productivity of labour and machinery and with the rate at which materials and other inputs are used up. Middle management will need a great deal of information of a financial nature. This data is used to monitor and take decisions relating to the control of the factors contributing to costs, revenues, profits and the achievement of objectives.

3. So far the acquisition of information has relied essentially upon processing data generated from within the organisation. But at the level of **senior management** some important information will be derived from external sources. Planning and decision-making in relation to the organisation's objectives and strategies will require information relating to broad areas of its business rather than the more specific and perhaps detailed information needed for decision-making at the lower levels of planning and control. Senior management will therefore require information about (a) overall profitability and the contribution that each part of its business makes to the total profits; (b) capital requirements and the position in relation to internally generated capital and the availability and cost of external sources of finance; (c) manpower requirements; and (d) forecasts concerning the future levels of demand in the markets where its output is sold.

Information obtained by processing internally generated data will therefore have to be supported by information derived from processing data collected from external sources. In the case of future competitiveness and market prospects, information will be required in connection with (a) developments in internal costs and sales trends; (b) changes in the markets where the organisation acquires its labour, capital and other inputs; (c) the strategies adopted by its competitors; and (d) the likely repercussions upon the organisation itself and its markets of economic, social, political and legal changes.

A characteristic common to all the three levels of an organisation is that they all require information that will allow them to allocate the resources under their control to achieve their objectives. This is as true of senior management taking decisions concerning the allocation of capital between various projects as it is of foremen or supervisors concerned with allocating labour, equipment and machine time to a particular operation for which they are responsible. Having taken such decisions, they will then need information on the progress being made and on how efficiently the project is being carried out. In this way further control is exerted over the activities which stemmed from the original decisions relating to the use of resources.

Communication methods and channels

There are many channels available for the communication of information. The choice will depend upon a combination of the following factors:

1. The need for an immediate feedback or response.
2. Cost.
3. Speed and urgency.
4. Accuracy.
5. The number of people who need the information.
6. Confidentiality.
7. The desired degree of formality/informality.
8. Convenience.
9. Complexity and amount of detail.
10. The type of information, e.g. financial, statistical, plans, drawings, rules, regulations, job description.
11. The need to maintain a record of the information supplied.

The media used for communicating the information can be selected from the following:

1. Written reports.
2. Manuals containing the instructions connected with certain procedures, operations or methods of production.
3. Letters with any necessary enclosures.
4. Circulars and memoranda.
5. Notice-boards.
6. The organisation's own magazine or newspaper.
7. Sheets of figures or standard forms containing numerical or other types of information under specific headings.
8. Graphs, charts, drawings, photographs, video-tapes, closed-circuit television, films and other visual techniques.
9. Meetings and interviews.
10. The telephone.
11. Informal discussions.
12. A Tannoy system.
13. The use of computerised systems for the acquisition and communication of data and information.

Regardless of the media selected the information provided should be entirely relevant to the needs of the recipient and avoid superfluous comments and unnecessary detail. Thus the information required by a foreman or supervisor may need to be concise yet very accurate in terms of the operations to be completed and the numerical values relevant to it. This is in contrast to the much broader information supplied to middle and senior management. The latter may require only broad indicators and a general description of both the internal and external developments that must be considered when assessing the organisation's performance and determining objectives and strategies.

Exception reporting
To ensure that the information provided to management is relevant, clear and concise and makes effective use of their time, such information may be restricted to that which relates to 'exceptional' developments. Middle management, for example, may require only information connected with those measurements of performance that deviate by more than a certain percentage from the targets established for them. The information dealing with either an exceptionally good or bad performance in connection with a particular measurement should also be supported by clear and concise statements of the internal or external factors that may have contributed to such developments. If the principle of exception reporting is used then this will make a more effective use of the time and skills middle management devotes to decision-making and controlling action.

Vertical information flow
This refers to the direction of the communication channel. A **downward information flow** describes the provision of information by a superior to an immediate subordinate and can cover the following areas:

1. The issuing of instructions; the delegation of work and information concerning the objectives and targets to be achieved by the subordinate.
2. Procedures, working methods and practices and the rules and regulations that have been established by the organisation.
3. Information in connection with how the subordinate's job and performance will contribute to the efficient conduct of other aspects of the organisation's activities; hence the overall objectives of the organisation.
4. An assessment of the subordinate's performance.

Some of this information may not necessarily come directly from a subordinate's immediate superior. This may be the case with general information dealing with the structure of the organisation, its goals and the kind of information provided by the personnel department when the employee first starts work. In the case of information that relates to the work undertaken by the subordinate, however, then the communication channel will be from superior to immediate subordinate.

An **upward information flow** is from a subordinate to a superior. This may be the feedback from a downward flow or it may originate from the subordinate him/herself. An upward flow can deal with the following areas:

1. The provision of information required by a superior.
2. Information on the subordinate's own performance, problems and aspirations.
3. Information on other employees in the subordinate's section and relations with sections with which there is a direct link.
4. Ideas on improved working methods and practices and possible solutions to any problems that have been identified.

In the interests of good and effective working relationships it is unusual for an information system to provide a *formal* upward communication channel. This allows a subordinate to initiate information, which is then supplied to someone above the subordinate's immediate supervisor. This is the case in particular with information relating to the subordinate's own work or section and for which the immediate superior is responsible. In the case of a grievance procedure, however, a subordinate may at some stage be able to take a complaint to someone at a higher level other than his/her immediate supervisor.

Horizontal information flow
This describes the passing of information between people who are of the same status. The interdependence that characterises many of the operations within an organisation means that formal arrangements must exist for the exchange of information to promote the highest degree of co-operation and efficiency between the different sections and departments. In the case of the production department, for example, there will have to be close contact with the purchasing department on such matters as changes in material and component requirements and the potential use of more advanced and efficient machinery and equipment. Similarly there will have to be close contact between the various activities that contribute to marketing, such as advertising, market research, and transport and distribution.

Frequency
Some information, such as that relating to industrial or manufacturing operations, may be required many times during the course of a single working day to ensure that work is carried out smoothly and efficiently. Much of the information required by middle management may be prepared on a weekly or monthly basis, and this is often the case with accounting information that is used for measuring performance and control purposes. Senior management, however, may often need information that reports on both internal and external developments arising over a longer period of time. More frequent information relating to much shorter periods of time would not depict trends or problems and would also be a waste of the resources devoted to its collection and analysis.

An essential feature of information that concerns the aspect of how often it should be provided is that it must be timed to meet the different needs of the various levels of management and control. Operational information required by foremen and supervisors must be updated and communicated on a very regular basis. Middle management will not be able to function efficiently if the information reported to it is either premature or too late to be used for the purposes of management control – because the subsequent decisions based upon the information may then prove inappropriate in the light of more recent developments.

The quality of information
Many of the essential characteristics of good information and an efficient information system can be summarised in terms of the following factors:

1. The right people receive the correct information at the right time. It is entirely relevant to the recipient's needs.
2. The information must be accurate and concise yet sufficiently comprehensive to avoid a time-consuming request for extra information that the sender should have foreseen and included in the original communication.
3. The information should be presented and communicated without ambiguity or possible misunderstanding.
4. The recipient of the information must have confidence in the ability of the sender and hence in the contents of the communication.
5. The sender must have confidence in the ability of the recipient to understand, use and take effective decisions based upon the information supplied.
6. The information must be relevant and hence of value. It must assist the recipient in taking decisions that make the most effective use of the organisation's resources, that lead to the possible introduction of new and improved working methods and practices to raise productivity, or that leads to other action producing an improvement in profitability via its impact upon costs or sales revenue.
7. The information system, the communications media and the kind of information provided should be periodically reviewed and adjusted in the light of actual and potential developments within the organisation itself and in response to external trends and changes. This is particularly necessary in connection with further advances in information technology.

8. Vertical and horizontal flows should be clearly defined. Confusion, combined perhaps with a lack of confidence in either the sender or recipient, may lead to the *ad hoc* growth of informal and uncoordinated information systems. These can result in alternative sources of information and a situation whereby the different levels of management may receive inconsistent, inaccurate or even conflicting information.

Computers and information
Advances in technology have led to computers being used for storing, processing, retrieving and analysing large volumes of a great variety of data. Technology has also had a revolutionary impact upon the means by which data and information are communicated. Information systems have been increasingly influenced by the fact that computers are becoming cheaper, smaller and faster. Computers are now used in all types of systems from the largest mainframes down to the smallest personal computers located on desk-tops or work-benches.

Low cost
In recent years labour costs in the UK have been increasing by an average of about 8 per cent per annum, while computer-processing costs have fallen by more than 20 per cent per annum. The cumulative effect of the new technology means that relative to the cost of computer-processing power people are now at least twenty times more expensive than they were ten years ago.

The size of computer components is also decreasing dramatically. A megabyte of memory in one computer manufactured in 1976 would have occupied 512 cubic inches; but by 1985 a computer from the same manufacturer had reduced storage requirements to 0·5 cubic inch per megabyte. The price of memory is also falling. In 1971 the same manufacturer costed a megabyte at over £250,000. Today the price has dropped to about £6000, while the cost of a megabyte of storage on a microcomputer is down to about £1500.

Computer software has become increasingly sophisticated and can be designed specifically to meet the needs of the organisation. Or it can be purchased from a great variety of ready-made packages. This latter type of software is particularly useful for small businesses using microcomputers.

Speed and efficiency
In a competitive environment, information is an important asset. Efficient production, marketing, distribution and cost control depend upon the availability of timely and reliable information. Managers require information about the performance of the organisation as a whole, its component parts and perhaps also individual employees in key positions. Strategic planning needs information on competition, the economy, technology and other factors likely to affect markets. Computers provide the means to store, summarise, and analyse all these details in a way that best suits the needs of managers and the problems they deal with.

The organisation that can react quickly to changes in the economy and the market environment will strengthen its competitive position. Reaction time can be reduced by cutting down time lost through slow communications, lost messages, time-consuming searches through traditional filing systems, and the manual production of documents that require both the numerical and pictorial presentation of statistical information. Higher productivity can be achieved by using such techniques as **electronic mailing** and **filing** and **word-processing**. These all reduce the time it takes the organisation to react to changes and to develop and supply new products or services where computers have also helped to identify market opportunities.

Job satisfaction
A paper-based information system, particularly in a large organisation, will involve such a quantity of data that individual employees will tend to be involved in repetitive and routine processes. No individual will be able to handle effectively or have access to all the data or information required to complete the whole job of which their particular task is only a part. Computer technology, however, allows individuals to be responsible for an entire job since all the data and information which they require can be provided at their fingertips. This will contribute to greater job satisfaction and a sense of improved status among the employees using the new technology. The overall improvement in morale may then be reflected in a further rise in productivity.

Convenience
Computers also allow information to be collected close to the source of the operation or transaction.

A great variety of information can be obtained by processing the data recorded and stored by the electronic cash-registers used at a supermarket's check-outs, for example. This will be communicated not only to the supermarket manager but also directly to the warehouse that supplies the supermarket and to the organisation's head office. Portable terminals and personal computers now mean that salespeople, engineers and construction workers can enquire into a central office database, enter transactions and receive work schedules or sales leads at the place where they happen to be operating at the time.

Terminals can also be put into the hands of customers or other organisations likely to be a source of business. Airlines, for example, have terminals in travel agents in order to attract reservations. Distribution and manufacturing organisations can install terminals on the premises of their major customers.

5. The Acquisition and Use of Capital

Fixed capital formation

Importance for the organisation

The acquisition of new fixed assets by organisations in both the private and public sectors plays an important role in ensuring that they can continue to meet the future demand for their goods and services. If an organisation does not make any provision for the fact that its fixed assets – plant, machinery, equipment and premises – will eventually wear out or become outdated and obsolete, then both its efficiency and its capacity to produce will be impaired (Fig. 5.1). An organisation needs funds not only when it is first set up, therefore, but also to make sure that it stays in business and remains competitive.

This is not just a question of an organisation being prepared to undertake **capital investment** programmes, which replace items of capital as they wear out. Businesses must also be prepared to install items of capital with operating capacities that will allow them to meet **anticipated increases in demand** for their output.

In addition to safeguarding or raising its productive capacity, an organisation must consider introducing items of capital or production techniques that reflect the application of recent advances in science and technology. Some organisations undertake investment programmes that involve allocating part of their capital to finance **research and development ('R and D')** projects. Such R and D is aimed at new products, materials or processes or the means by which advances in science and technology can be applied to various parts of its operations. Capital expenditure is therefore also the way in which an

Fig. 5.1: Fixed capital formation can cover a wide range of spending on such areas as plant, machinery, equipment and premises

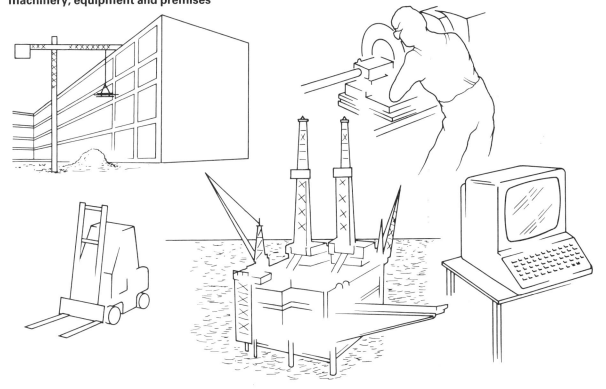

organisation will improve its competitive position, because more efficient items of capital will increase its productivity and so help to keep its unit costs low. Thus the firm can offer competitive prices in the markets where it operates.

Research and development projects will also strengthen an organisation's position because of possible improvements in non-price factors such as design, quality and reliability and the introduction of new products or services. Improved competitiveness will ensure the survival of the organisation, raise profitability and from the point of view of the workforce make jobs more secure; this is particularly so if the organisation faces competition from imported products.

Investment expenditure can also make some jobs less tiring by reducing the amount of physical effort involved as well as increasing the level of automation or mechanisation in areas of unpleasant work. The most dramatic improvements in the productivity of workers do not come from continual exhortations for them to work harder but by allowing them to use more productive plant and equipment. The most successful organisations are those that make the most intelligent use of their workforce and are prepared to achieve this by committing themselves to **capital expenditure programmes.**

Tables 5.1 and 5.2 indicate both the level and distribution of fixed capital formation in the UK during the early 1980s.

Importance for other parts of the economy and community

Fixed capital formation by organisations will enable **households** to obtain goods and services at prices that allow them to increase their total consumption of many items. It also provides them with a wider range of goods and services upon which to spend their incomes. Spending on capital projects will also mean **employment** in those sectors of the economy that produce the plant, machinery and equipment. Employment in the construction industry will benefit from the capital spending of organisations upon factories, offices and warehouses, for example.

If our organisations fail to invest, they will become less competitive. This has repercussions not only for employment in the capital goods industries; it also means less employment in the organisations themselves because they will lose their markets to foreign competitors. In addition, if the producers of capital goods suffer a loss of

orders, then the scale of their operations may contract; so they too will find it increasingly difficult to maintain a competitive position in their export markets.

Thus a general failure on the part of organisations to invest will eventually lead to growing unemployment and lower living standards. Those people still in jobs will then be obliged to pay a higher proportion of their income in taxes so that the government can transfer some of their spending power to the unemployed. An increase in unemployment may also lead to a position where the government's total tax revenues do not allow it to maintain the scope and quality of the social and welfare services it seeks to provide.

Central and **local government authorities** must also be prepared to engage in fixed capital formation in order both to protect and to raise the welfare of the community. This requires capital expenditure on health, education and roads, for example. New and better-equipped schools, colleges, hospitals and clinics and a more efficient road and rail system not only enhance the welfare of individuals but also benefit organisations – because improvements in the general level of health and education will raise the quality of the workforce. A more efficient transport network will be of direct benefit to private individuals as well as enabling firms to extend their catchment area for labour, since potential employees will be able to commute longer distances. Organisations also benefit from the more efficient transport of their inputs, such as raw materials and components, as well as the distribution of their finished products.

Working capital

A proportion of capital funds will have to be used to meet the needs of an organisation for working capital. This is because expenditure will be incurred in producing an output before income is derived from its sale. The organisation's production will be planned on a continuous basis, and all the activities, from the receipt of raw materials and components to the distribution of the end product, will need to be financed from one source or another. Some capital will therefore be tied up in the financing of its stocks of raw materials and components and also to pay for the cost of its work-in-progress. At any one time there will be partly completed goods, and this work-in-progress will involve expenditure on labour and other inputs such as energy. Capital will also be absorbed in holding stocks of finished goods.

Table 5.1: Gross domestic fixed capital formation
(a) Analysis by sector and by type of asset

(£ million)

	Total	Private sector	General govern- ment	Public corpora- tions	Vehicles, ships and aircraft	Plant and machinery	Dwellings		Other new buildings and works
							Private	Public	
Revalued at 1980 prices									
1980	41,609	29,361	5596	6652	4571	15,097	5872	2519	13,550
1981	37,928	27,677	4134	6117	3614	14,078	5537	1665	13,034
1982	40,468	30,207	4065	6196	3714	14,404	6047	1990	14,313
1983	42,013	30,466	4836	6711	3925	14,805	6626	2046	14,611
1984	45,259	33,285	5722	6252	4544	15,715	6689	2318	15,993

(b) Analysis by industry group

(£ million)

	Total	Extraction of mineral oil and natural gas	All other energy and water supply	Manufac- turing (revised definition)	Distribution, hotels and catering; repairs	Transport and communi- cation	Financial and business services etc.	Other industries and services	Dwellings	Transfer cost of land and buildings
Revalued at 1980 prices										
1980	41,609	2399	3250	6471	3223	3870	5753	6578	8391	1674
1981	37,928	2669	3290	4853	2947	3067	6080	6035	7202	1785
1982	40,468	2812	3244	4684	3124	2831	6720	6976	8037	2040
1983	42,013	2482	3414	4619	3438	3194	6726	7261	8672	2207
1984	45,259	2876	2931	5265	3844	3592	7547	7846	9007	2351

Source: *Monthly Digest of Statistics*, May 1985.

Table 5.2: Fixed capital expenditure in manufacturing industry

(£ million)

	Total	Metals	Mineral products	Chemicals, etc.	Mech- anical engin- eering	Electrical engin- eering	Vehicles	Food	Drink and tobacco	Textiles, leather and clothing	Paper, printing and publishing	Other manu- facturing industries
Revalued at 1980 prices												
1980	6471	388	447	1038	947	565	863	619	338	234	539	493
1981	4852	273	309	769	689	505	606	546	269	164	402	319
1982	4685	229	318	701	619	508	570	592	254	203	362	329
1983	4619	200	292	756	569	567	548	550	274	181	358	323
1984	5327	265	348	844	663	681	635	647	264	222	413	347

Source: *Monthly Digest of Statistics*, May 1985.

An organisation's stocks and work-in-progress can be financed from the following sources:

1. Obtaining **trade credit** from suppliers.
2. A **bank overdraft** or **loan.**
3. Using **hire–purchase** and **finance companies.**
4. **Ploughing back** part of the profits.
5. In the case of a sole proprietorship or partnership the owner(s) may put in more of their **personal funds.**
6. Large companies that are well established can raise short-term finance by issuing **bills of exchange.** Depending upon the current rate of interest that can be earned by holding such securities, the bill will mature for an amount greater than the price at which it was purchased. If a company raises £97 from each bill that it issues and each bill promises to pay the holder £100 in ninety days, then the company is paying a rate of interest equivalent to an annual rate of approximately 12·4 per cent, i.e. $(3 \div 97) \times (100 \div 1) \times 4$. If, however, it manages to obtain £98 for each bill that it issues then it is borrowing at an annual rate of interest of 8·2 per cent.
7. **Factoring**, whereby a firm will take over the responsibility for collecting a company's debts or the money due on invoices. The firm will buy up these debts and invoices by paying a price lower than the total amount outstanding and will then collect the full amounts itself. The company is in the position of having met its need for finance, but a price is involved. It has sold its debts and invoices for an amount less than what it would have received if it had waited for them to be settled in the normal way.

Internal sources of capital

In 1984 all sources of capital funds provided industrial and commercial companies in the UK with nearly £42 billion. Just under £32 billion of this came from internally generated funds in the form of **undistributed profits.** Retained profits therefore accounted for approximately three-quarters of the capital funds available to these organisations. This demonstrates the essential role that profits play in financing future investment programmes both at home and overseas. They also provide the means by which an organisation can acquire an interest, through share ownership, in another organisation. The link between the level of retained profits and the level of investment in fixed assets is shown in Fig. 5.2.

The extent to which internal capital is available will depend upon (1) current and past levels of profits, (2) the level of corporation tax, (3) tax

Fig. 5.2: Company savings and capital expenditure (as a percentage of GDP)

Source: Based on *Economic Progress Report*, August 1983

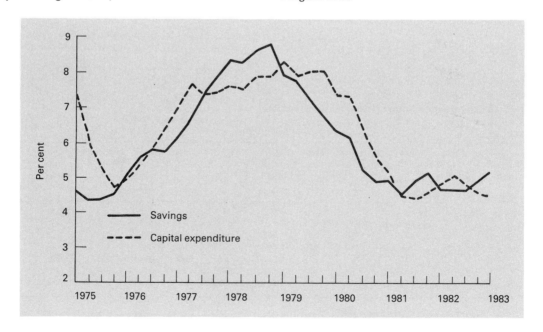

allowances and (4) the policy of the organisation with respect to how much of the resulting net profit should be paid out to its owners, the amount that should be set aside to support its liquid reserves, the need for extra working capital to finance any increase in its output and its planned capital expenditure projects.

In the case of a joint stock company the funds available from undistributed profits are the result of a decision taken by the board of directors to 'save' on behalf of its shareholders. They will be made aware of the organisation's need to pay for capital projects that will help to strengthen its competitive position in the markets where it operates. Greater efficiency and new and improved products or services will help to increase future profits by increasing sales revenue and minimising unit costs. Thus the sacrifice of some profits by shareholders will not only ensure their future dividend payments but should also lead to an increase in total profits. This may allow the organisation to pay out higher dividends in the future while still being able to retain sufficient profits to finance additional capital projects.

The organisation will be aware of what is likely to be an acceptable balance between distributed and undistributed profits. This decision will have been taken after having considered such factors as the current and future business environment, the strategies being pursued by its competitors and how its performance compares with that of other organisations in markets facing the same degree of risk or enjoying the same level of security.

The shares in any particular organisation are just one of a very wide range of alternative outlets for individual investors' funds. Shareholders will compare their previous and anticipated return with the degree of risk involved in a particular shareholding. If they believe that other shares or types of financial asset offer a better return in the light of the risk involved, then they are likely to switch to such alternative outlets for their money.

The return on the funds parted with by an investor must represent at least a 'normal' return. This is what investors in general regard as the minimum return that must be received in order to compensate for the risks involved. What is regarded as a 'normal' return will differ according to the type of financial asset involved. If, for example, a shareholder in a relatively high-risk venture received an average return of only 11 per cent over a period of time, this might fall a long way short of what is regarded as a 'normal' return.

The risk is further heightened by the possibility that the price of such a share may fluctuate a great deal. Shareholders will always bear in mind the prospect of having to sell at a price lower than what they originally paid. A share involving a much lower risk may be offering a similar return and also be less susceptible to sudden fluctuations in its price, while a short-term deposit in a bank may even be offering perhaps 8 per cent, and in this case there is no risk at all of losing any money.

If, therefore, an organisation fails consistently to distribute a sufficient amount of its profits to satisfy its shareholders then its shares will become increasingly less attractive. This will create problems if the organisation then needs some time in the future to raise funds by issuing new shares, because potential investors will not be impressed by its previous record on dividend payments. Moreover the resulting fall in its share prices as investors switch to other shares may eventually undervalue that organisation's assets and make it a particularly attractive target for a take-over bid. An organisation may therefore decide to maintain an acceptable dividend payment to provide at least a 'normal' return to its investors and meet any shortfall in capital funds by making use of external sources of capital.

External sources of capital

In 1984 external sources provided industrial and commercial companies in the UK with capital funds amounting to £9·4 billion. Approximately £7·1 billion of this was in the form of **borrowing from the banks.** The ability of an organisation to borrow from such sources will depend upon (1) its record over recent years with respect to its profits, (2) the lender's opinion of its future prospects and (3) its ability to offer the lender some form of collateral security such as land or property or some other form of asset that the lender can convert into cash if the borrower defaults on the loan.

The rates of interest charged on loans and overdrafts change from time to time. Banks must remain competitive in attracting deposits, and an increase in the rate they pay to their savers will involve a corresponding increase in the rates they charge to borrowers. The banks have what is known as **base lending rates**, and the actual rate charged will be above this level according to the risk associated with the activity the bank is financing and the creditworthiness of the borrower.

Banks usually restrict their lending to the provision of short-term and medium-term finance, as they prefer not to tie up a large part of their funds in long-term loans. They are particularly suitable therefore as a source of working capital. During the course of 1984 the organisations that increased their total borrowing by the largest amounts in terms of loans and advances from banks were those in wholesaling (£2310 m.), oil and extraction of natural gas (£831 m.), electrical and electronic engineering (£820 m.), construction (£662 m.), food, drink and tobacco (£629 m.), retailing (£562 m.), hotels and catering (£545 m.), the chemical industry (£414 m.), transport and communications (£391 m.), metal manufacturing (£316 m.), mechanical engineering (£286 m.) and textiles, leather, footwear and clothing (£273 m.).

Debentures

Part of an organisation's loan capital may be raised by the issue of debentures (also known as **loan stock**). In this case the borrower is committed to paying a fixed rate of interest to the holders of such stock irrespective of the profits made. The interest payments due on an organisation's debentures are therefore regarded as a cost and represent the price it pays to borrow capital. If the organisation goes into liquidation then the debenture holders, as its creditors, will be among those who have a first claim upon the funds realised from the sale of the organisation's assets. In some cases the debentures issued may be secured against a specific part of the organisation's assets; these are known as **mortgage debentures**.

A debenture will carry a maturity date. This means that after a specified period of time the holder will be repaid the full amount that was originally lent to the organisation. If the borrower fails to meet the interest charges on its debentures or is unable to redeem them, the holders – along with other creditors such as a bank and those who have provided trade credit – can force the borrower into liquidation.

From the point of view of the debenture holders, they provide an organisation with funds on a basis that involves them in a much lower element of risk when compared with the shareholders. Even if the company makes very little profit they still receive their fixed rate of interest. In the event of the company going into liquidation, then, depending upon how serious the situation is, they will get back all or at least a proportion of the money owed to them.

Because the element of risk is much lower, the potential holders of debentures may be tempted to part with their money in return for a relatively low rate of interest when compared to the payments that must be paid to satisfy the different types of shareholder facing varying degrees of risk. In other words, the debenture holders will settle for a lower 'normal' return depending upon the risk associated with the type of market in which the organisation is operating.

The issue of debentures, although a relatively cheap way of raising funds, is not a satisfactory method for organisations whose profits tend to be inconsistent and fluctuate considerably from year to year. An organisation that can generally anticipate a fairly stable profit can be confident of meeting its obligations to its debenture holders; but one that periodically experiences a significant fall in its profits may in a particular year find that it cannot meet its fixed interest charges or redeem any maturing stocks. The end result may be the liquidation of the organisation if it fails to convince its creditors that the future is likely to be more buoyant.

The ability to raise loans via debentures and the interest that must be offered will also depend upon the organisation being able to offer suitable security. This security needs to be in the form of assets that can be expected at least to maintain their real value; so those organisations possessing property and land will be in a stronger position to borrow capital and at lower rates of interest compared with those that can offer security in the form only of assets that generally depreciate in value, such as plant and machinery.

Ordinary shares

In contrast to debentures, the raising of capital via the issue of shares does not amount to obtaining a loan. It involves instead inviting investors to buy a 'share' in the organisation, which then entitles them to a 'share' in its profits (Fig. 5.3). There is no guarantee that the ordinary shareholders will receive a minimum return (**dividend**), as the amount paid out to them depends upon the profits made by the company, how much they wish to retain to finance the organisation's future operations and how much of the distributed profit remains after meeting the prior claims of the preference shareholders (see below).

Ordinary shareholders therefore run the risk that in a poor year the dividend payment may represent a very small return on their investment, and they would have been better off holding other shares or financial assets. In an exceptionally bad year there is always the possibility that they do not receive any dividend at all. If a situation is reached where the company is forced into liquidation then they are the last group to be satisfied among those who have a claim upon the funds realised from the sale of the organisation's assets; they may recover only a fraction of the price they paid to acquire the shares. The element of risk is further aggravated by the fact that share prices move in line with the current and predicted performance of the company, and the shareholder may incur a loss if obliged to sell for cash at an inopportune time.

Nevertheless investors do buy ordinary shares. In 1984 the buying and selling of ordinary shares on the Stock Exchange involved dealings worth approximately £73·1 billion. This is because investors regard the risks they are taking as being compensated by an income that represents at least a

Fig. 5.3: Banks now operate schemes whereby the small investor can contribute to a fund, which is used to buy stocks and shares. Their return will depend upon the skills of those who manage and invest the funds

'normal' return and possibly a return that more than outweighs the risks involved in holding the ordinary shares of various organisations. When a company is in a position to distribute a large amount of profit, it is the ordinary shareholders who benefit most, because other providers of capital will still receive a fixed payment irrespective of the high profits made by the company. As described earlier, if a company fails to take the opportunity to reward the providers of 'risk' capital, then the general dissatisfaction among the major shareholders could lead to problems for the company in the future. The risk element is also compensated by the possibility of a significant rise in the price at which the shares can be sold if the company consistently turns in a good performance.

The actual return on ordinary shares will depend upon the price the current holder paid for them. If, for example, a company originally raised extra capital by issuing ordinary shares in units of £1 and in the following year declared a dividend on these shares of 18p, this would provide the holders with a return of 18 per cent – only if they did in fact pay £1 per share to obtain them. If potential investors regarded the company as a particularly attractive outlet for their funds, competition may have pushed the issue price up to £1·30. In this case those of the original buyers who are still holding the shares will earn a dividend of about 13·8 per cent, i.e. $(18 \div 130) \times 100$.

The chances are, however, that after a period of time some of the original shares may have been bought and sold several times; and at any one time the current price that must be paid to obtain such shares will be determined by the market. This price will reflect the general assessment of the company's current and anticipated performance in relation to the risks involved.

If, for example, a current holder bought the shares when the market was still impressed by the company's performance and future prospects, then that holder might have been obliged to pay £1·40 per share. In the case of this particular holder the 18p dividend on each share represents a return of about 12·8 per cent. This lower return reflects the fact that the holder took less of a risk by waiting to see how the company performed in the period just after the new issue.

If the 18p dividend is expressed in relation to their current market price of, say £1·55, then the share is said to provide a **dividend yield** of about 11·6 per cent. Moreover, if the company continues to pay a dividend of about 18p on the shares, then it will establish itself a reputation as being a relatively secure investment with a much lower risk element. This will then be reflected in a further rise in the price of its shares until they reach a level that provides a lower dividend yield; but this will still make them an attractive proposition for those investors willing to settle for a relatively low return in exchange for greater security.

Suppose another company issues the same type of share in units of £1 and its performance on profits does not prove so consistent because it operates in a market with a much higher risk element. Potential investors will be unsure of the company's future profit levels and will be aware that any dividend payments that are made could fluctuate a great deal; they will also face the prospect of a fall in the price of the share and being obliged to sell their holdings when the company is going through a particularly bad period. This general view of the risk being taken may then produce an issue price of only 80p per share. The market's interpretation of the risk involved may then be confirmed by the fact that dividend payments are only 6p and 5p in the next two years.

Those still holding the shares that they bought at 80p each will have received returns of 7·5 and 6·25 per cent. During this period the share prices will also have fallen, indicating the general opinion of investors that the company is becoming an even higher risk. The market price of the share may have fallen to 70p, so the second year payment would mean a dividend yield of 7·1 per cent.

It is possible that the increasing risk could eventually materialise in the company struggling to survive and the shareholders being left with shares whose market price continues to fall. Assume, however, that the company's fortunes suddenly improve and it enjoys a period of success. Rather than facing the possibility of the company going into liquidation, the shareholders receive a dividend payment of 14p, followed by one of 22p. The original buyers who held on to their shares despite the low returns and the fall in their price have now earned returns of 17·5 and 27·5 per cent. Anyone who risked buying them when their price was much lower will receive an even higher return on their investment.

The market will then review its opinion of the risk attached to the shares. The general view of the company's future prospects may be that it has now established itself more firmly in its own particular market. This will be reflected in a rise in the price of the shares until the anticipated dividends are likely to produce at least a 'normal' return in the light of the reappraisal of the risk involved. In this case the very high risks taken by those who purchased the shares when the company was struggling for survival have been well rewarded – not only because of the returns they have received already, but also because future dividend payments, even though they may not be quite as large, will still represent a healthy return on what is now a less risky share. These same holders will also have enjoyed the effects of a rise in the market price of the share upon the value of their shareholding; if they wish they can now sell at a substantial profit.

Voting rights
The other important feature of ordinary shares is that since the holders are 'sharing' in the risks associated with the company's activities they also have a say in running the business. The influence exerted by a shareholder will depend upon the number of shares held, as each share will carry a vote that can be used at the company's annual general meeting.

In most cases, however, shareholders are not sufficiently well organised or knowledgeable about the company's affairs to exert any real influence over the way it is run or over the appointment of its board of directors. As long as they are reasonably satisfied with the return on their shares the investors tend to leave the company in the hands of its directors. In the case of small and medium sized companies, the directors themselves tend to be the major shareholders and are therefore able to command a majority of the votes. A firm may also only issue 'A' shares, which do not carry voting rights. This may be the case with a company that wishes to retain control in the hands of the original owners.

Despite the generally passive role of shareholders there is always the threat of a 'revolt' by those who become dissatisfied with the way the company is conducting its affairs. Any such concerted action is likely to be better informed and more organised and effective if large blocks of shares are held by just a few individuals or by major financial institutions such as life assurance companies and pension funds. Thus a company that issues shares as a means of securing external capital funds cannot afford to abdicate its responsibilities to its shareholders. A failure to reward them with an acceptable dividend when the opportunity arises may eventually threaten the independent survival of the company if they yield to a tempting offer from another company seeking to make a take-over bid.

Preference shares

These are a means of attracting external funds from those investors who are willing to hold assets that involve a lower risk element. Holders of preference shares are paid a fixed dividend regardless of how high the profits are, and they are also given priority over the ordinary shareholders. In some years the distributed profits will enable the company to pay the fixed dividend to its preference shareholders while also allowing it to pay a much higher dividend to its ordinary shareholders. In a year of low profits, however, the company may be able to meet its obligations to its preference shareholders, but the remainder of its distributed profits may represent a much smaller return to its ordinary shareholders.

In the case of **cumulative preference shares** income is made more secure by the fact that if in any particular year the company is not even able to make a fixed payment to such investors, then the outstanding amounts will be paid in addition to the usual dividend when the profit situation improves. The attraction of this type of share to those seeking a less risky asset is not only the more secure return it earns but also the priority they are given over the ordinary shareholders if the company is forced into liquidation. A company may also make its preference shares more attractive by offering a 'participating' version. This allows the holders to receive an extra dividend once the payments to the ordinary shareholders go above a certain level.

Preference shares do not usually carry voting rights, but such rights may be given to holders in connection with matters that are of great importance to them, such as a decision to wind up the company or change the fixed interest payment.

Gearing and external sources of capital

If a company is going to raise capital from external sources, it will need to decide upon the total to be raised by debentures and preference shares and the total raised by ordinary shares. The eventual decision will depend upon how the company views its current 'gearing'. This is the ratio between the existing amount of preference shares and debentures and the amount of the ordinary shares.

When the proportion of prior claimants (holders of preference shares and debentures) to equity capital (holders of ordinary shares) is high, the capital structure of the company is said to be high-geared. When this proportion is low, then the capital is low-geared.

The capital gearing of the company is important from the point of view of the company itself and the potential investor. Table 5.3 shows two companies: company H is high-geared and company L is low-geared. This table can be used to show the implications for the more speculative investor holding ordinary shares.

Table 5.3

Company H

Distributed profits	Payments on debentures £100,000–6%	Payments on preference shares £80,000–8%	Return on ordinary shares £40,000 (%)
£14,000	£6000	£6400	4
£16,000	£6000	£6400	9
£18,000	£6000	£6400	14

Company L

Distributed profits	Payments on debentures £40,000–6%	Payments on preference shares £30,000–8%	Return on ordinary shares £150,000 (%)
£14,000	£2400	£2400	6·1
£16,000	£2400	£2400	7·4
£18,000	£2400	£2400	8·8

Company H

As the level of distributed profits increases, ordinary shareholders will experience a substantial increase in their return because of the fixed nature of the payments made to holders of debentures and preference shares. The increased profits that remain after the prior claimants have been paid is distributed among a relatively small quantity of ordinary shares. The nature of the risk involved, however, is that at one period their dividend was as low as 4 per cent but they received 14 per cent when distributed profits increased.

Such a high-geared company will be an attractive investment during a period of rapid growth and general prosperity, but less so if there is a recession in business activity.

Company H will find it easier to raise additional funds from the issue of ordinary shares with this dividend record and avoid issues with fixed payments. In doing this, however, it will have to take account of the effect upon its original high gearing, which initially gave rise to the high dividends as profits increased. But in a period of very low profits it may find its fixed payments a heavy burden. This may create financial difficulties as well as making it less attractive to potential holders of ordinary shares.

Company L
From the point of view of investors, this company does not offer substantial increases in dividends to ordinary shareholders when profits are growing. But this is compensated for by the greater security provided when there is a downturn in profits. Dividends fluctuate from approximately 6·1 to 8·8 per cent. This record during a period of expansion may make it a less attractive proposition if it is competing for capital with high-geared companies. As profitability falls, however, it will find fixed payments less of a problem compared with company H, as well as making it a more secure investment for ordinary shareholders.

The different capital gearings will also influence the scope that exists for retaining profits for self-financing additional fixed capital assets, as dividend payments that prove acceptable to investors may act as a constraint. What constitutes an acceptable gearing to a company will vary according to such matters as its current and expected financial position.

The acquisition of capital by the public sector

Public corporations
In 1984 the public corporations spent £7·6 billion on capital projects. This compares with £6·8 billion by the whole of the UK's manufacturing sector. In recent years about 78 per cent of the capital funds acquired by the public corporations have come from their profits, and this reflects the policy adopted towards the running of such industries from about 1980 onwards. They have been increasingly expected to earn sufficient revenue to cover their operating costs and to achieve a surplus in order to finance their capital expenditure programmes without having to borrow from the government.

The government was also in favour of a policy whereby such industries would eventually be obliged to raise any additional funds from the capital market by issuing their own bonds. The public corporations would therefore have to compete for capital funds with the private sector. Their ability to do so would depend upon the return they could offer to prospective investors. An attractive interest or dividend payment would depend upon their profits, and the government viewed such a move as a means of promoting greater efficiency and a more commercial approach within the public corporations.

Central government borrowing
In 1984 the capital expenditure undertaken by central government and local authorities amounted to over £6·6 billion. Of the £2·7 billion spent directly by central government on capital projects, about 70 per cent was accounted for by roads and capital projects in the national health service. Apart from this direct involvement in the creation of fixed assets central government also provided a further £2·3 billion in grants to organisations in the private sector to assist and encourage them to undertake certain types of capital project such as those in the Assisted Areas and the building programmes carried out by the Housing Associations. The public corporations received capital grants of £340 million, while a similar amount was paid to local authorities as a contribution towards their various capital expenditure programmes.

Central government therefore raises capital funds not only to finance the capital projects in which it has a direct involvement but also to provide funds for capital spending by local authorities and by organisations in the private sector. The scope and level of such financial assistance by central government is influenced by its political, social and economic objectives.

During the course of a year the government will be obliged to raise short-term finance to help pay for its current expenditure on goods and services, because some of its income from taxes and other sources tends to be peaked at certain times of the year. To obtain this short-term finance the government issues what are known as **Treasury Bills**, which have a maturity period of ninety days. These are purchased by **Discount Houses** – financial institutions seeking a short-term outlet for the funds deposited with them. The implications of this form of borrowing, the rates of interest paid on Treasury Bills and the role of the discount houses are dealt with in detail in Book 2 of *Business Organisations and Environments*, where these matters are examined from the point of view of how the government can influence the amount of credit available in the economy and the general level of interest rates paid on borrowed money.

In the financial year 1983–4 the total level of central government expenditure, including both current and capital spending, exceeded its revenues from taxes and other sources by £12·3 billion. This represents what is known as the **central government borrowing requirement**. Approximately 80 per cent of the borrowing requirement was accounted for by the need to raise capital funds to finance those projects for which it was either wholly or partly responsible in both the public and private sectors. In the course of the year the government also required funds to repay some of its previous loans, which had reached their maturity dates. The main part of its borrowing involved the issue of government stock, which raised £11·6 billion; the various national savings schemes brought in a further £3·2 billion.

The National Debt
The cumulative effect of this borrowing, particularly over the last ten years, has been a large increase in what is known as the **National Debt**. This is the total amount of money that the government still owes to people and institutions both in the UK and overseas. The National Debt now stands at over £130 billion, and in 1983–4 the interest charges amounted to about £15 billion.

Thus in any single year the government borrows not only to help finance the creation of fixed assets in both the public and private sectors, but also to repay the holders of various types of government stock and national savings certificates that are currently maturing or being cashed in. The National Debt has grown because governments have become increasingly involved in capital projects designed to improve the scope and quality of essential services such as health, education and housing, as well as those projects aimed at strengthening the economic infrastructure of the economy on both a national and regional basis. At the same time these capital projects require larger sums of money not only because of inflation but also because of their more complex nature and the advances in science and technology embodied in them.

If governments had attempted to finance all their capital spending in a particular year from their current revenues, they would have needed to raise taxes to very high levels. The entire burden of such spending would have fallen entirely on existing taxpayers. By borrowing long-term, however, via the issue of various types of government stock and national savings schemes, the costs of government's capital projects are borne by a much larger number of people. This is because the cost of the National Debt in terms of interest charges and any repayments of capital will also be shared by future taxpayers, who are also the beneficiaries of the various capital projects completed in an earlier period.

Future generations will benefit, for example, from any recent capital expenditure programmes that involve motorways and hospitals, while support for private sector investment will help to improve the employment prospects for future generations of workers. The taxes paid by such people will contribute to the costs associated with the original creation of the fixed assets from which they benefit. In fact future generations of taxpayers will find it progressively easier to bear their part of the costs. This is because as the economy grows and average incomes rise the government will be provided with higher tax revenues while still leaving people with more spending power when compared with earlier generations.

Government stock
As indicated earlier, the government raises capital funds by issuing stock that pays a fixed rate of interest to the holder. These stocks have maturity dates ranging from one to more than fifteen years; the longer the term of the loan, the higher the return a potential investor would expect to earn from holding such stock. In 1984, for example, one of the new issues was '3% Treasury Stock 1987' in units with a nominal value of £100. This means that the government will pay the holder £3 a year until the stock matures in 1987, when it will also make a payment of £100. In order to sell this stock, however, the government was obliged to sell for only £84 each because it had to compete with other types of existing financial assets where potential investors could obtain a satisfactory return by parting with funds for a similar period of time.

The price of £84 indicates that the general opinion of the market was that investors would be prepared to hold them if they produced a yield of approximately 9·9 per cent a year. If the investors paid a price of £84 per unit then after three years the stock would mature at its nominal value of £100; this would provide a capital gain of £16 on each stock held. In addition to this, each stock will pay the holder a fixed-interest payment that amounts to

£3 a year (3 per cent of its nominal value), and this produces an income of £9 over the three years. Thus an investor will have lent the government £84 for each stock purchased and received a total income at the end of this period of £25. This represents an annual yield of 9·9 per cent, i.e.

$$\frac{25}{84} \times \frac{100}{1} \div 3$$

In the same year another issue involved the sales of stocks described as '8·75% Treasury Loan 1997'. As one would expect, investors would require a return representing a higher yield than the one they were prepared to accept on the stock with a shorter maturity date. This was confirmed by the fact that they were willing to pay a price of £172 for units that in this case had a nominal value of £200 each. Each unit would provide the holder with an annual interest payment of £17·50, i.e. 8·75 per cent of the nominal value of £200 plus a capital gain of £28 when it matured in 1997. The total income earned on each unit is therefore £255·50 and this represents an annual yield of approximately 11·4 per cent.

Government stocks are secure financial assets from the point of view of potential investors. For this reason the government can generally attract funds by offering a return somewhat lower than the rates paid by organisations in the private sector seeking to raise medium- and long-term loans, which involve the investors in varying degrees of risk/security. The government will always be in a position to meet the redemption value of its stocks, while organisations in the private sector have to survive in a much more uncertain environment.

The only element of risk associated with government stock arises from the possibility that a holder may be obliged to sell some of them before the maturity date in order to meet an unexpected need for cash. In the case of the '8·75% Treasury Loan 1997', for example, a holder may be forced to sell after just four years. This may be at a time when there has been a general increase in the level of interest rates in the economy because the total level of borrowing has led to a shortage of funds and the increase in the competitive pressures in the capital market will allow investors to obtain a higher return on their funds. Thus, because of the increased competition from assets offering a higher return with about the same maturity period, the seller may be obliged to sell at the current market price of only £165 per unit. The total income derived from the stock over the four-year period is therefore £70, i.e. 4 × £17·50 minus the capital loss

of £7 per unit when they were sold. This represents an annual yield over the four-year period of approximately 9·1 per cent. The holder has still earned a return, but this may be lower than the return that could have been earned by putting the original funds into some other type of asset that had a maturity period of four years or perhaps even less. Also, having funds tied up in such stock may mean that attractive alternative outlets have to be sacrificed, unless the investor is willing to sell and accept the much reduced return that this involves as a price worth paying in order to acquire new assets with a higher return.

The risk attached to government stock is therefore that its sale before the maturity date may produce a much lower yield than was anticipated, and so the funds could have been used more profitably. The longer the period before maturity, the higher the yield that potential investors will require. This is because they must be compensated for the fact that over a longer period of time there is a greater possibility that the market price for their particular stock may be at a level which, if they were obliged to sell at that time, would have earned them a much lower yield than originally anticipated. Added to this is the fact that a longer period of time will give rise to a greater number of alternative outlets for funds. Holders of long-term assets will not be in a position to exploit such opportunities to the same extent as those investors whose assets can readily be converted into another form without the risk of a capital loss.

In contrast to these less favourable developments, there is the prospect of a surplus of funds in the economy because the total level of borrowing has not grown at the same rate as the supply of 'loanable' funds, and organisations can therefore obtain loans at lower rates of interest. The lack of an acceptable return on alternative assets may therefore make certain types of government stock an attractive proposition for some investors, particularly those who would normally have lent for similar periods to organisations in the private sector. This may then lead to an increase in the demand for the '8·75% Treasury Loan 1997', and in 1990 for example it might command a market price of £189. Some holders may take this opportunity to sell some of their holdings. Over the six-year period, therefore, they would have earned total interest payments of £105 plus the capital gain of £17; this would represent annual yield over that period of approximately 11·8 per cent. This may be very satisfactory in the light of the lower return that would have been earned if the funds had originally been invested in an asset with only a six-year maturity period.

Because of the long-term nature of much of the stock issued by the government, it is generally purchased as assets by financial institutions that are unlikely to be in a position where they need to sell them in order to obtain extra cash. This is the case, for example, with life assurance companies and pension funds, which attract savings from households on a long-term basis; this in turn allows the institutions themselves to lend long-term (Fig. 5.4).

These financial institutions plan their investments in such a way that they maintain some financial assets in a 'liquid' form, in that they are very short-term and can readily be converted into cash when the need arises with no risk of a capital loss. Other funds are used to buy government stock of various periods of maturity. Life assurance companies and pension funds are confident that they will not experience sudden and unforeseen

Fig. 5.4: The role of financial intermediaries in channelling savings into the financing of investment programmes

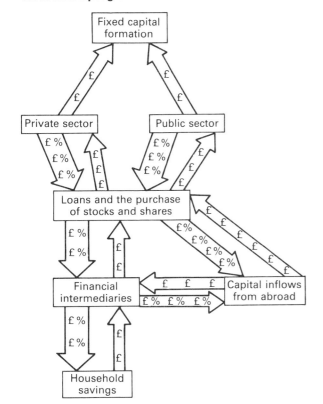

large withdrawals of the savings deposited with them. This allows them to invest their funds in more profitable long-term assets, knowing that they will be able to hold them until their maturity dates. Moreover, since government stock is issued in blocks of perhaps £50,000 or £100,000 then they are most suitable for institutions that have the funds to purchase them in such large minimum quantities.

These financial institutions along with unit trusts and investment trusts also use their funds to buy shares. Because of the amount of money at their disposal they are able to spread their total holdings over a wide range of assets. They can therefore balance the higher-risk shares against those that carry a lower risk, while also enjoying the secure income associated with their holdings of government stock.

Although the banks do not invest their funds in shares, they do hold a small proportion of their total assets in the form of government stock. Because the banking system is more susceptible to a sudden withdrawal of the money deposited with it by its customers, banks are obliged to hold a large proportion of their funds in the form of very liquid short-term assets that can readily be converted back into cash. The banks need these short-term assets as a potential source of cash because of that part of their business which involves them in holding illiquid assets in the form of loans and overdrafts to households and to organisations in both the private and public sectors.

National savings schemes
The role played by financial institutions as intermediaries, whereby household savings are eventually channelled into organisations seeking to raise finance from external sources, means that many people indirectly help to supply the funds needed by organisations for working capital or for the purchase of fixed assets. Very few people have the financial resources to become directly involved in the provision of finance to organisations. This is because a large amount of money would be needed in order to spread such funds over a range of assets providing an acceptable balance of risk, as well as being able to hold some assets that can readily be converted into cash without the risk of a capital loss.

So apart from their longer-term savings in the form of contributions and premiums to pension funds and life assurance companies, the majority of households prefer to hold short-term and risk-free assets. Such outlets for household savings are provided by banks and building societies. In the case of the government, however, it does borrow directly from households by offering them a variety of savings schemes such as National Savings Certificates, Savings Bonds, Premium Savings Bonds, Save-As-You-Earn (SAYE) schemes and deposits with the National Savings Bank (Fig. 5.5).

When issuing stock, the government has to compete with other organisations seeking to raise finance, and its ability to do so depends in particular upon offering a sufficiently high return to attract purchases from the large financial institutions. But in the case of attracting funds directly from households, the government must compete with the returns offered by the savings schemes provided by the banks and building societies. The government must take account not only of the interest rates that these institutions offer on savings deposited for certain periods, but also of the ease with which the depositors can withdraw their money. The government must also be prepared to change its own national savings schemes if they become too uncompetitive, while also ensuring on other occasions that they are not paying unnecessarily high rates of interest to attract funds.

In 1984 the amount of household savings flowing into the national savings schemes and into the banks was about the same. But even this total amount was only about half of the sum attracted into the building societies.

Fig. 5.5: The National Savings Stock Register offers an alternative to buying government stock through a stockbroker

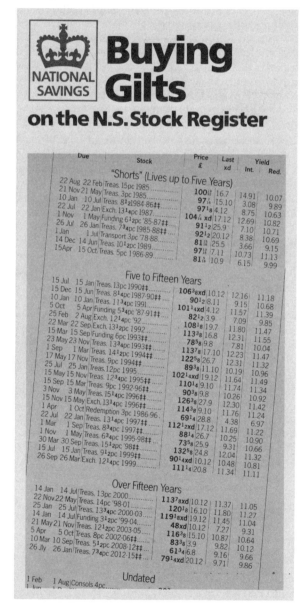

Local government finance

In 1984 local authorities spent £3·9 billion on the capital projects in which they were directly involved. Approximately 50 per cent of this spending was accounted for by education, housing, roads and public lighting. In addition to their own capital expenditure, the local authorities also provided capital grants to households that covered such areas as house purchase and home improvements as well as capital grants to the nationalised transport undertakings. These grants amounted to £1·3 billion in 1984. Approximately £2 billion of local authorities' total capital expenditure of £5·2 billion was financed from the surplus that remained after they had met the current expenditure incurred in providing their various social and welfare services. They received £340 million in the form of capital grants from central government, and the remainder of their capital requirements was met by borrowing.

If the local authorities were obliged to finance all of their capital expenditure from their current sources of income then they would be obliged to introduce much higher rates and perhaps support this move by increasing the rents they charge for local authority housing. Thus the local authorities borrow from the central government in order to help finance their capital projects, and this in turn contributes to the amount of capital that central government has to borrow by issuing stock.

The Stock Exchange

Individuals and the financial institutions are willing to purchase the wide variety of stocks and shares offered by organisations in both the private and public sectors in the knowledge that their holdings of such assets can readily be turned into cash. They can also always change the type of stocks and shares they hold in order to take advantage of favourable developments that they anticipate in connection with prospective movements in their prices and the returns the various assets offer.

If the provision of funds to organisations involved a complete loss of liquidity, because shares could not be resold or cash was required before a debenture or government stock matured, then few people would be willing to part with their money unless they were offered exceptionally high returns. The Stock Exchange therefore fulfils a valuable role in that it increases the **liquidity** of claims on the government and private sector organisations by providing a market in which existing financial assets can be sold.

In 1984 there were just over six billion transactions in securities listed on the Stock Exchange. About 64 per cent of these transactions involved ordinary shares. Total transactions involved a turnover of £364·6 billion, and approximately £268·6 billion of this was in central government securities. Only a relatively small part of the business on the Stock Exchange does in fact involve the issue of new shares and debentures. In 1984 total issues amounted to only £3·5 billion, and £1·2 billion of this was concerned with **'rights' issues**, whereby a company makes direct contact with its existing shareholders who are given the right to take up new shares. Shares will be offered in proportion to their existing holdings, and this option may be made on particularly favourable terms. Shareholders may then sell their allotted quota if they wish. In 1984 only £1·1 billion was raised by industrial and commercial companies through the issue of ordinary shares, while issues of debentures and preference shares raised £250 million.

The Stock Exchange is therefore essentially a market for 'second-hand' securities. But without this role organisations would find it more difficult to raise funds from external sources by the issue of shares and loan stock.

6. The Organisation and its Costs

Costs and profitability

The description of the organisation and its objectives in Chapter 1 emphasised the importance, for organisations in the private sector in particular, of the **maximisation of profits** and how this objective dominates their long-run business strategy. Profit maximisation depends ultimately upon the ability of an organisation to obtain the best possible price for its good or service while at the same time achieving the desired level of output at the lowest possible unit cost. It is possible that the organisation may be willing to some extent to sacrifice an element of profitability in the short run in order to help achieve objectives associated with its future market share and security. In this case the level of sales and output that allows the organisation to maximise its profits at any one time will not necessarily coincide with the sales and output that help it to secure a balance of objectives designed to both protect and raise profits in the long run. Nevertheless, the organisation will still be concerned about achieving such a sales and output level at the lowest possible unit cost, because this will minimise the effect upon current profitability of achieving long-run objectives.

As far as the nationalised industries are concerned, the extent to which they are directed to give priority to such matters as increasing their profits by minimising unit costs will depend to some extent upon the government's approach. One government may believe that the national interest is best served by employing methods of production that are dictated mainly by considerations of efficiency, as this may be seen as ensuring that such industries make sufficient profits to finance their future investment programmes and reduce their financial assistance from the government.

A different government, however, may believe that the introduction of new methods of production and the application of new technology may have to be tempered in order to help the government achieve certain social, political and overall economic objectives. Such a government may hold the view that the maximisation of the profits earned by the nationalised industries will conflict with the attainment of these other objectives. In this case the government may be willing to provide financial support to the nationalised industries which incur costs that would otherwise have been avoided, had they been concerned solely with the maximisation of profits. If, however, the nationalised industries are given a clear indication of what areas of their operations must take account of certain non-commercial objectives, then they will also be aware of the remaining areas where scope exists for the minimisation of costs.

There are also different views concerning the advantages and disadvantages of placing a greater emphasis upon the introduction of cost-cutting programmes in the public sector organisations concerned with the provision of social and welfare services. The essential difference between the two views is the extent to which a greater emphasis upon costs will lead to a reduction in the scope and quality of the services provided.

Unit costs

The very survival of an organisation, particularly those facing stiff competition in both home and overseas markets, depends on constant attention being paid to ways of reducing or controlling unit costs. Attempts must be made to minimise the impact upon unit costs of unavoidable increases in the prices paid to obtain the inputs required to achieve output targets.

In the mid-1970s, for example, there was a massive rise in the world price of oil and essential raw materials. At the same time, organisations faced a substantial rise in their total labour costs because of the pay increases negotiated during that period. The organisations that were most successful in surviving this very difficult period were those that raised their prices by a smaller amount than their competitors. They were able to do this by absorbing a larger proportion of the increase in their costs through the introduction of techniques that made a more efficient use of energy and raw materials, and by adopting methods of production and working practices that raised the productivity of their workforce.

The competitive position of the organisations that responded in this way was protected by an ability to moderate the rise in their unit costs. The result was that they increased their prices by a smaller amount than their less efficient competitors. The impact upon their profits of the higher prices for their inputs was therefore cushioned by improved efficiency that helped to moderate the rise in their total costs and by their ability to offer prices that helped to sustain the demand for their output.

Effects of recession

In more recent years the major problem facing organisations has been the depressed state of the home market, which has been aggravated by the world-wide recession. In many markets the demand has been either stagnant or in decline; redundancies and closures are the penalties for organisations that have failed to introduce cost-saving programmes and improve their performance with respect to productivity. The sales, profitability and survival of organisations have depended upon paying strict attention to costs, as buyers have increasingly shopped around to obtain the best value for money. This has been the case with households purchasing consumer goods and services, and with organisations themselves buying materials, components, machinery and equipment.

Effects of costs on profits

The costs of production influence an organisation's profits in two ways. In the first place they have a direct effect upon profits. Given the total revenue earned from sales, the lower the total costs incurred in achieving the necessary output the larger will be the level of profit. Secondly, there is an indirect effect. The lower the total costs associated with a particular level of output then the lower will be the **costs per unit of output**. This will allow the producer to lower the price of the good or service offered to potential customers without having to accept a cut in the profit margin on each good or service supplied. This more competitive price will lead to an increase in the level of sales and thus an increase in **total profits**.

Assume, for example, that a producer incurs a cost of £4 per unit, and a price of £5 is charged in order to provide an acceptable profit margin of £1 per unit. Output and sales of 100,000 per period of time will therefore produce a total profit of £100,000. If changes are then introduced which

lower production costs to £3.50 per unit, this means that a price of £4.50 can be charged. This more competitive price may then lead to sales of 140,000 units per period of time, and this produces profits of £140,000. As will be seen in subsequent sections of this chapter, the higher output of 140,000 is likely to be produced at a lower unit cost than the output of 100,000, and the profit will therefore be even higher than £140,000.

This profit can also be used to help pay for the installation of more efficient machinery and equipment, which will contribute to a further reduction in the unit costs of production. This will give the producer an even stronger competitive advantage in the market where the output is sold. As illustrated in Fig. 6.1, the advantages of lower unit costs are likely to prove circular and self-reinforcing.

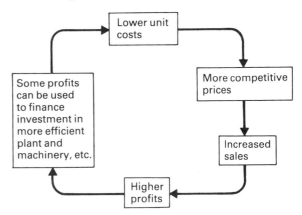

Fig. 6.1: Advantages of lower-cost units

The influence of the law of diminishing returns upon output

The reaction of a firm to more favourable market conditions that leads to the decision to increase output will be influenced by the time period considered. In the short run it is possible to identify certain restraints under which the firm operates in its efforts to increase output.

The short run

This is defined as a period of time during which the input of some factors of production is regarded as fixed. Output can be raised only by increasing the employment of those factors that the firm regards as being variable. This involves the firm in an increase in output, which is achieved by using the existing capacity, as dictated by the fixed factors, more intensively through the addition of more units of variable factors.

Because of this inability to vary the input of all factors in the short run, the firm will be susceptible to the **law of diminishing returns**. This law predicts that if increasing quantities of variable factors are added to a fixed quantity of other factors, then eventually the resulting increases in output will get progressively smaller.

If, for example, some important items of the plant, machinery and equipment are fixed, and the firm increases output by employing more units of labour, the marginal product of labour will eventually start to diminish. The marginal product of labour is the addition to total product (output) resulting from the employment of an additional unit of labour. The implications that this law holds for the firm in the short run are shown in Table 6.1. This firm cannot increase its inputs of capital and employs additional units of labour to raise output in the short run.

Table 6.1

Units of labour	Total product	Marginal product	Average product
1	20	20	20
2	120	100	60
3	290	170	96·7
4	520	230	130·0
5	800	280	160·0
6	1120	320	186·7
7	1450	330	207·1
8	1770	320	221·2
9	2060	290	228·9
10	2300	240	230·0
11	2480	180	225·4
12	2560	80	213·3
13	2560	0	196·9
14	2460	−100	175·7

When one unit of labour is employed, total product is 20 units, and the employment of a second unit of labour raises total output to 120 units. The marginal product (MP) of the second unit of labour is thus 100 units, as this is the increase in total product that results from the employment of this second unit of labour. Similarly, total product increases from 120 to 290 units when the third unit of labour is employed and thus the MP of this unit of labour is 170. The initial employment of labour results in an increase in its MP. This implies

that there are some economies of scale associated with increases in output, such as being able to take advantage of the division of labour. The MP of the fifth unit is 280 units, but this is not to say therefore that this fifth unit personally contributes 280 units to the total product. There is a direct contribution from this additional unit of labour but its presence also allows certain economies that make other units more productive. The MP of labour increases at first but eventually the point of diminishing marginal returns is reached when 7 units of labour are employed, as beyond this point the MP of labour declines.

The data in Table 6.1 is transferred to Fig. 6.2, where the point of diminishing marginal returns is indicated at the peak of the curve showing the MP of labour. The employment of the thirteenth unit of labour leaves total product unchanged and thus the MP of this worker is zero. The employment of the fourteenth actually leads to a decline in total product and so the MP of this unit of labour is actually negative.

The average product (AP) per unit of labour is shown in Table 6.1, and this has also been transferred to Fig. 6.2. An interesting feature is that the *MP* and *AP* curves intersect at the latter's highest point. It is useful to understand this relationship as it contributes to the understanding of cost curves dealt with in subsequent sections of

Fig. 6.2

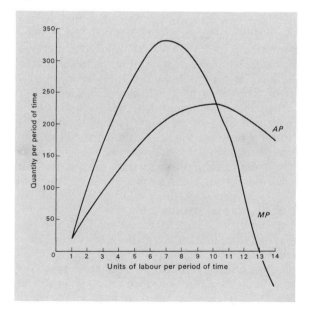

this chapter. Both the data and the curves show that after the employment of the seventh unit of labour the AP of labour continues to rise, despite the fact that the MP of labour is falling. This occurs because although the MP of labour (the addition to output) is declining, it is still greater than the existing AP of labour and thus the latter must be pulled up.

For example, the MP of the ninth unit of labour is 290 units, and this is greater than the AP of 221·2 units relating to the previous 8 units of labour. Thus the AP of 9 units of labour must be higher than the AP of 8 units of labour. In fact, as long as the MP of labour is greater than the existing AP of labour, the latter will continue to rise. Once, however, the MP of labour falls below the existing AP of labour, then the AP of labour will also start to fall. Thus it is no coincidence that the *AP* curve falls once it is cut by the *MP* curve, and this point of intersection is the point of diminishing average returns.

The long run
Firms will eventually experience diminishing returns during their efforts to increase output in the short run to meet a change in market demand. In the long run, however, the firm is freed from the restraints imposed by some factors of production being fixed. This long run is defined as a period of time that enables the firm to vary the input of all factors of production and adjust more fully to a larger level of output. There will be scope to introduce more units of capital, train more labour and generally have an opportunity to exploit greater economies of scale.

The duration of the short run will vary between industries according to the nature of their products and the technical conditions surrounding their production. If, for example, there is an increase in the demand for ceramic floor tiles, firms may at first expand production by using their existing capital items, such as kilns, more intensively through employing more labour. It may, however, be only a question of weeks or months before producers can obtain and install more or larger kilns and train the necessary operatives. Similarly, the oil-refining industry may be able to expand output in the short run by increasing the employment of variable factors such as labour. It may be a question of years, however, before a long-term adjustment can be made as oil refineries are large complex plants and this will be reflected in the time taken to construct them.

The decision to expand the scale of operations to accommodate a larger demand will be taken only if the firm believes that the more favourable conditions are of a fairly permanent nature and so make investment expenditure worth while. Business expectations are therefore an important factor in determining the extent of the long-term adjustment.

The influence of the law of diminishing returns upon the costs of production

The identification of time periods is important since it highlights the expected relationships between inputs and outputs. These relationships will have repercussions upon a firm's costs of production according to the time period considered. Changes in costs will affect profits, so it is important to distinguish between the main categories of costs and how they are likely to vary with output.

Fixed costs
These are costs that do not vary no matter what changes occur in output. In many cases they can expect to include such items as the interest that must be paid on borrowed capital and the repayments on such loans, the depreciation on items of capital equipment, rent and rates levied by local authorities. Fixed costs are also known as overhead or indirect costs, and the latter description implies that, since fixed costs are incurred regardless of the level of output, they cannot be directly related to any particular unit of output. Fixed costs must also be paid even if the firm ceases production.

Variable costs
These costs vary directly with the level of output and are incurred only when output takes place. If output increases, so will the variable costs associated with such inputs as labour, raw materials and energy. These costs can be more readily attributed to certain units of production and therefore are also known as direct costs.

This division into fixed and variable costs does become a little blurred on occasions, as the category into which some costs are placed depends upon the time period considered. Some costs may remain constant over a particular range of output but then suddenly jump once output reaches a certain level.

For example, plant and machinery are to varying degrees indivisible and their capacity cannot be increased by marginal amounts to cope precisely with an increase in output. In the long run this involves the installation of more items of capital and these costs can be of a variable nature when the firm expands output. These costs become fixed over the next range of output before further capacity is installed.

It also becomes possible to reduce some fixed costs in the long run if the firm believes that it should reduce the scale of operations because of business expectations of a more permanent fall in the market demand for its output. In these circumstances, the firm will not replace machines as they wear out; it will reduce the size of its plant and also produce an administrative structure more in keeping with its reduced output.

Some variable costs may, in turn, display a certain degree of indivisibility. For example, a firm may require more man–hours to increase output, but the nature of the conditions surrounding the employment of labour may oblige the firm to hire an additional worker on a full-time basis, although this additional labour may not be fully utilised by the desired increase in output. Similarly, raw materials may be available only in standard amounts that may be surplus to immediate requirements, while services such as heating and lighting cannot always be controlled in line with changes in output. Within a firm it will be the task of the cost accountant to identify the firm's total costs and provide management with the unit costs of their finished products for purposes of establishing the relative profitability of its activities.

This greater variability of all costs in the long run does not prevent a useful division of costs into our two categories, as the firm will decide in its own interest whether they should be regarded as fixed or variable. Subsequent sections will thus concentrate upon using the two broad headings under which costs are generally placed by a firm.

Marginal costs (MC)

This is the addition to total costs as a result of producing and selling one more unit of output. As output is expanded the increase in costs will be those attributable to an increase in variable costs which rise with output, since by definition fixed costs remain unchanged. Marginal costs are therefore comprised entirely of marginal variable costs.

Table 6.2 can be used to show the likely characteristics of a firm's marginal costs as output

changes. The MC of the first unit is £280 as this is the addition to total costs as output is raised from zero. The MC of the second unit is £100 as total costs increase from £480 to £580 as a result of this extra unit of output. Column 5 shows that this firm's MC falls rapidly at first, but then the fall becomes less pronounced, and eventually reaches a minimum level when the eighth unit is produced. Beyond this point MC rise at an increasing rate. This is reflected in the *MC* curve in Fig. 6.3, which relates to the data contained in column 5 of Table 6.2.

The shape and direction of this *MC* curve will be influenced by the marginal product of the variable factors associated with its marginal costs. Since labour is generally a variable factor then Table 6.1 can be used to illustrate the impact of the marginal product of labour upon marginal costs. This table shows that in the initial stages a proportionate or percentage increase in the employment of labour brings about a larger proportionate or percentage

Fig. 6.3

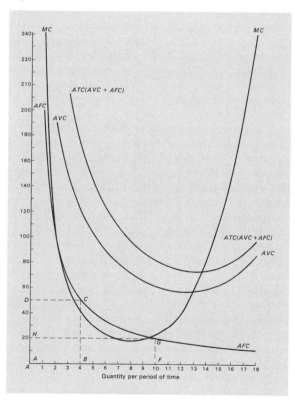

Table 6.2: Costs (in £)

1 Units of output	2 Fixed costs	3 Total variable costs	4 Total costs	5 Marginal costs	6 Average fixed costs	7 Average variable costs	8 Average total cost (6 + 7)
0	200	0	200	0	0	0	0
1	200	280	480	280	200·0	280·0	480
2	200	380	580	100	100·0	190·0	290
3	200	440	640	60	66·6	146·7	213·3
4	200	480	680	40	50·0	120·0	170·0
5	200	510	710	30	40·0	102·0	142·0
6	200	534	734	24	33·3	89·0	122·3
7	200	554	754	20	28·5	79·1	107·6
8	200	572	772	18	25·0	71·5	96·5
9	200	592	792	20	22·2	65·8	88·0
10	200	614	814	22	20·0	61·4	81·4
11	200	644	844	30	18·2	58·5	76·7
12	200	682	882	38	16·7	56·8	73·5
13	200	742	942	60	15·4	57·1	72·5
14	200	822	1022	80	14·3	58·7	73·0
15	200	932	1132	110	13·3	62·1	75·4
16	200	1082	1282	150	12·5	67·6	80·1
17	200	1282	1482	200	11·8	75·4	87·2
18	200	1542	1742	260	11·1	85·7	96·8

increase in output. For example, an increase in the employment of labour from 4 to 5 units resulted in an increase in output from 520 to 800 units. This amounts to changes of 25 per cent and 53·8 per cent respectively. Thus initial increases in output would require a much smaller proportionate increase in the employment of labour, and total variable costs would therefore increase by a smaller proportion than the desired increase in output.

This prospect of certain economies as output is expanded is also reflected in Table 6.2, where the increase in output from 3 to 4 units causes total variable costs to increase from £440 to £480. These are changes of 33·3 per cent and 9·1 per cent respectively. Thus, because the firm's marginal product associated with variable factors, such as labour, can be expected to increase quite sharply at first, then the marginal costs will fall.

This influence of the marginal product can be identified at other stages of the cost data since, as the marginal product slows down, so also will the decline in marginal costs. Eventually the point of diminishing marginal returns will be reached, and this will exert an upward pressure on marginal costs at higher levels of output. For example, the increase in the level of employment from 10 to 11 units in Table 6.1 raises output from 2300 to 2480

units, and these are changes of 10 per cent and 7·8 per cent. Thus a proportionate increase in the employment of a variable factor is now met by a much smaller proportionate increase in output. This relationship can again be seen in Table 6.2, where the increase in output from 14 to 15 units causes total variable costs to rise from £822 to £932. An increase in output of 7·1 per cent has required an increase in variable costs of 13·4 per cent and marginal costs are now increasing.

This upward pressure on the firm's marginal cost can also be added to by what may soon become another important factor. Not only is the firm being forced to employ proportionately more units of variable factors to achieve the desired increase in output, but at the same time may eventually be obliged to pay a higher price to obtain them. Increased demand for labour may involve firms in paying a higher wage or salary for labour in order to secure its services. Thus marginal costs may start to rise even before the point of diminishing marginal returns is reached.

Average variable costs (AVC)
These are the total variable costs of producing any given level of output divided by that level of output. The data in column 7 of Table 6.2 shows

that the average variable cost per unit produced falls as output is at first expanded. Again this is partly explained by the expected increase in the average product associated with the employment of additional units of variable factors. In the case of the firm in Table 6.1 the average product per unit of labour increases at first as total output rises at a faster rate than the employment of labour. The firm in Table 6.2 is experiencing a similar rise in the average product of its variable factors as it employs more of them. When, for example, output is increased from 5 to 6 units, the total variable costs (which reflect the employment of variable factors) increase from £510 to £534. Thus output has increased by 20 per cent with an increase in total variable costs of only 4·7 per cent, and so the average variable cost associated with each unit of output must fall, and column 7 of Table 6.2 shows this to be the case.

Eventually, however, the firm will experience a fall in the average product of its variable factors, as total output will increase at a slower rate than the employment of variable factors. For example, the increase in output from 17 to 18 units requires an increase in total variable costs from £1282 to £1542 and these are changes of 5·8 per cent and 20·2 per cent respectively. The average variable costs associated with each unit of output must therefore increase, as is shown by column 7 of Table 6.2. Not only will the fall in average product be exerting an upward pressure on the average variable costs, but they will also be pushed up by the increased price that the firm may be forced to pay in order to obtain additional units of variable factors. The average variable costs may therefore start to rise even before the point of diminishing average returns is reached and the general shape and direction of such a curve is illustrated in Fig. 6.3.

Average fixed costs (AFC)
These costs will fall continuously as output is expanded, as a fixed amount is being divided by a progressively larger level of output. Average fixed costs fall quite steeply at first but the fall becomes less significant as higher levels of output are reached, as shown by column 6 of Table 6.2. The average fixed cost curve is depicted in Fig. 6.3 and its shape is that of a rectangular hyperbola. The feature of such a curve is that if a level of output is selected and then multiplied by the average fixed costs associated with that output, the result must always be the same, i.e. total fixed costs. The curve in Fig. 6.3 shows average fixed costs are £50 when

output is 4 units and this produces the total fixed costs of £200. The same result is achieved when 10 units is multiplied by their average fixed costs of £20. These amounts are represented by the areas *ABCD* and *AFGH*. They must be the same and equal to any other areas shown by a combination of output and corresponding average fixed costs. A rectangular hyperbola will have this particular property.

Average total costs (ATC)
These are determined by adding together the total fixed cost and total variable costs and dividing them by the level of output in question. The same result would be achieved by adding together the average fixed costs and average variable costs associated with a particular level of output. Column 8 of Table 6.2 shows that average total costs fall at first and then eventually rise. The initial fall is due to the fact that both the average variable costs and the average fixed costs fall as output is expanded. Eventually, however, the average variable costs start to rise, and although the average fixed costs fall continuously, the progressively larger increases in average variable costs will more than outweigh the progressively smaller fall in average fixed costs. The average total cost therefore starts to rise, as shown by the curve in Fig. 6.3. Note that the gap between the average variable cost curve and the average total cost curve in the diagram is equivalent to the average fixed costs at a particular level of output. The average total cost curve is after all the result of adding the average fixed cost curve to the average variable cost curve.

It may have been noticed in columns 5 and 7 of Table 6.2 and in Fig. 6.3 that in a range of output beyond 8 units the marginal costs are rising, while the average variable costs are still falling. The explanation is that as long as the addition to total costs (i.e. marginal costs) is still less than the existing average variable costs, then production of one more unit will still cause the average variable costs to fall. Once, however, the marginal costs exceed the existing average variable costs, the latter must start to rise. This occurs between the production of the twelfth and thirteenth units, and therefore it is no coincidence that the marginal cost curve cuts the average variable cost at the latter's lowest point. Similarly, the average total cost curve is cut by the marginal cost curve at its lowest point.

If cost curves are to be used to illustrate a particular point, it is important that they are drawn

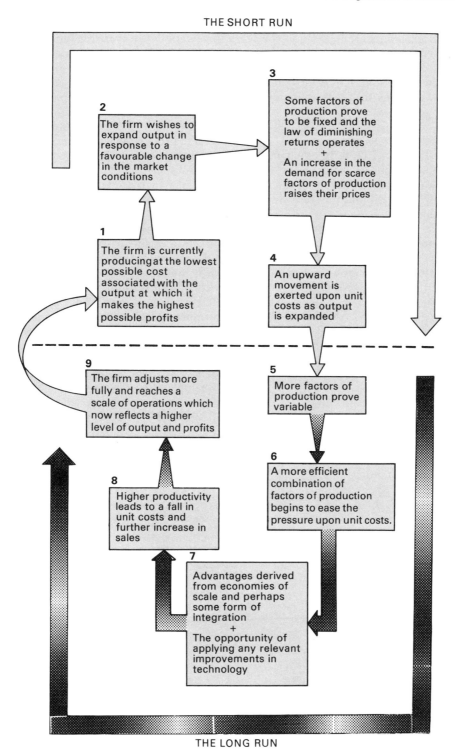

THE SHORT RUN

2 The firm wishes to expand output in response to a favourable change in the market conditions

3 Some factors of production prove to be fixed and the law of diminishing returns operates
+
An increase in the demand for scarce factors of production raises their prices

1 The firm is currently producing at the lowest possible cost associated with the output at which it makes the highest possible profits

4 An upward movement is exerted upon unit costs as output is expanded

9 The firm adjusts more fully and reaches a scale of operations which now reflects a higher level of output and profits

5 More factors of production prove variable

6 A more efficient combination of factors of production begins to ease the pressure upon unit costs.

8 Higher productivity leads to a fall in unit costs and further increase in sales

7 Advantages derived from economies of scale and perhaps some form of integration
+
The opportunity of applying any relevant improvements in technology

THE LONG RUN

Fig. 6.4

in a manner which does demonstrate their basic shape and direction. Points of intersection should occur at the correct places rather than being drawn in a haphazard fashion. Cost curves can prove useful aids when discussing and illustrating the output decisions of firms that seek to maximise their profits.

Long-run costs

The analysis of the firm's costs has so far been conducted from the point of view of the likely impact on costs of increases in output in the short run (see Fig. 6.4). When diminishing returns were an important influence on these costs, the firm had to make the best of the situation by employing more units of those factors of production which were more immediately variable, and was not able to expand the scale of its operations by varying the inputs of all factors of production and combine them in the most productive way. The firm has fixed factors, such as plant and equipment, geared to its current level of output and these will not be the most economic means of producing a higher level of output.

In the long run, however, all factors of production are variable and the firm can be expected to adjust the quantity and combination of its inputs of any factors of production in order to achieve the higher output at the lowest possible unit cost. The firm will be able to take advantage of potential economies of scale, with the result that a proportionate change in output will be met by a smaller proportionate increase in costs. Some likely opportunities for economies of scale are outlined on pages 98–100. The long-run cost curves show the cost associated with producing a higher level of output when a period of time has elapsed which allows all factors of production to be varied, and Fig. 6.5 can be used to illustrate the likely shape and direction of such curves.

It is assumed that the firm is currently producing OQ_1 units of output and this output is produced with a combination of inputs specifically geared to this level of output. This position represents a production technique that is the result of a previous long-run and planned adjustment to this level of output OQ_1, and this is produced at an average total cost of OC_1. If market conditions now change and

Fig. 6.5

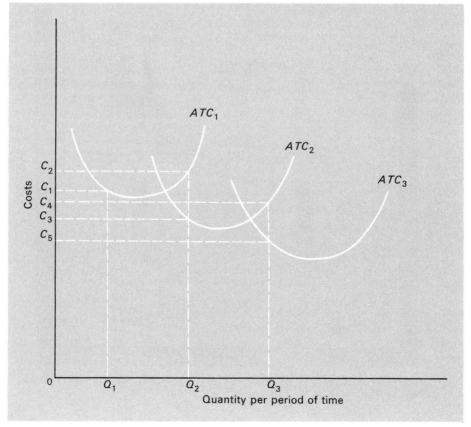

this firm wishes to increase output, then in the short run it will have to operate with some factors such as plant and equipment being fixed. The average total costs associated with the higher level of output OQ_2 is shown by a movement along the curve ATC_1 and produces OC_2.

In the long run the method of production can be adjusted more fully to cope with the increase in output by, for example, expanding the capacity of plant and equipment. Because of the economies of scale associated with such a move, it then becomes possible to produce OQ_2 units at an average total cost of OC_3. The curve ATC_2 now represents the likely experience of the firm as far as unit costs are concerned if it again varied output in the short run with its new set-up of plant and equipment being regarded as fixed. Thus a further increase in output, in response to market changes, to OQ_3 will see an expansion along ATC_2 to produce an average total cost of OC_4. A long-run adjustment will permit output OQ_3 to be produced at an average total cost of OC_5, as ATC_3 is the new relevant cost curve.

This exercise can be repeated and gives rise to costs that reflect a complete adjustment to increases in output and traces the shape and direction of the long-run average total cost curve ($LRATC$). Such a curve is illustrated in Fig. 6.6 and shows that at any one moment a firm can only produce on a single short-run average total cost curve ($SRATC$) because some factors are fixed. In the long run it will select the most suitable combination of input and this will have its own $SRATC$ curve at any given level of output.

The decline in the $LRATC$ curve shows that the firm benefits from economies of scale, and in our example in Fig. 6.6 the eventual rise in the $LRATC$ curve indicates that this particular firm does experience diseconomies once output is increased beyond a certain level.

The $LRATC$ curve envelopes the $SRATC$ curve, and is always at a tangent to a point on a $SRATC$ curve. No point of a $SRATC$ curve could lie below the long-run curve as this would imply that a certain level of output could be produced at a lower unit cost in the short run than in the long run. It is very unlikely that opportunities for reducing unit costs would be taken advantage of in the short run and then neglected in the long run. The flatter nature of the $LRATC$ curve suggests less dramatic changes in costs as output is expanded when compared with the short-run situation. This situation is thus reflected in a long-run marginal cost curve ($LRMC$), which is also flatter and indicates that additions to costs are less significant when compared with the experience in the short run.

The previous analysis has shown that unit costs will be lower in the long run than in the short run when output is expanded. This will also be the case, however, when the firm is obliged to contract output because of unfavourable developments in its market. The firm in Fig. 6.7 is currently producing OQ_1 at the lowest possible unit cost of OC_1. If the firm is forced to reduce output to OQ_2, the new unit costs are shown by a movement along the relevant curve ATC_1 and produce an average

Fig. 6.6

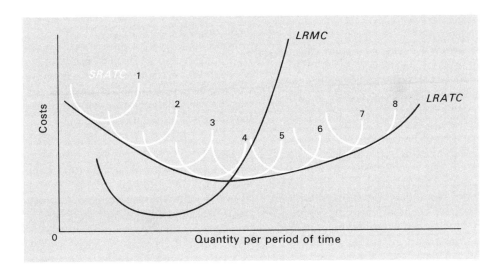

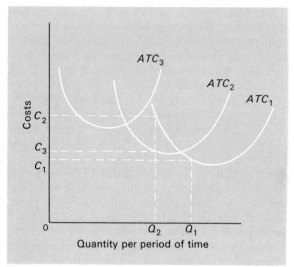

Fig. 6.7

total cost of OC_2. The capacity set by the fixed plant and equipment is now too large for the lower level of output for which it was not specifically designed. In the long run the firm will adopt a combination of factors of production more closely geared to the lower level of output. Plant and equipment may be fixed in the short run, but in the long run they can be reduced by not replacing items as they wear out and installing units that provide a capacity that is more suitable to the lower level of output. The long-run adjustment results in OQ_2 being finally produced at a unit cost of OC_3 on ATC_2, which is also a point on the $LRATC$ curve. This $LRATC$ curve is thus relevant for both increases and reductions in output that the firm believes are to be sufficiently permanent to warrant an alteration of its scale of operations.

For most of the analysis of costs it has been assumed that the fixed factors were items of real capital such as plant and equipment. However, there may be circumstances where the skills of labour are such that additional employees are not readily available and certain types of equipment may prove more variable. In this case, a short-run situation would involve the addition of extra units of capital in order to use the existing labour force more intensively. Again the concept of diminishing returns would apply and influence short-run costs as the marginal and average returns from additional units of capital would eventually decline. A long-run adjustment may then involve the firm in concentrating upon training extra labour to meet its specific requirements.

Economies of large-scale production

In the long-run adjustment to a higher level of output, an organisation will be able not only to use a combination of factor inputs that seeks to minimise its unit costs, but also to benefit from other economies associated with the increase in the scale of its operations. An organisation reaps economies of scale if for a given proportionate increase in its output it incurs a less than proportionate increase in its total costs, with the result that there is a fall in the unit costs of production. It is possible that economies of scale will be derived in the following areas:

1. *The larger a firm becomes, the greater the opportunities for taking advantage of the increased specialisation or division of labour.* As the volume of output expands, an employer can be kept fully occupied on a narrow range of tasks and consequently become more skilled. The breaking down of a complicated job into a series of what may become routine operations allows the employment of relatively unskilled labour and allows more specialised skills to be used in aspects of production that use these skills more fully. Training periods can be shorter and therefore the worker becomes more productive at an earlier stage, and an easily acquired skill will reduce wastage during the learning period.

The splitting up of a complex task into easily identified operations is likely to hasten the introduction of increased mechanisation. A single worker will need only the equipment relevant to his/her own specialist task. Time is saved in that he/she does not have to move around between operations to use different items of plant and equipment.

Some aspects of the increased specialisation of labour can to some extent be implemented in the short run. It is their combined contribution to the productivity of labour that accounts for the initial rise in the average product per unit of labour depicted in Fig. 6.2 (page 90).

2. *There will also be economies associated with purchasing and marketing.* Raw materials, components and other inputs can be obtained at a lower unit cost if bought in bulk. The supplier will offer a discount because he/she in turn will benefit from the economies of scale associated with a long production run and bulk distribution. Purchasing staff will not have to be increased in the same proportion, particularly if the expansion of output

produces increased orders placed with existing suppliers, and the staff may also be organised to deal with specialist areas of purchasing. When sales increase, the costs incurred in marketing will not rise in the same proportion, especially if increased sales are mainly to existing customers, where again distribution economies may arise.

3. *Small firms suffer from the existence of the indivisibility of plant and machinery and other items of fixed capital in that they are generally available only in a limited range of working capacities.* A small firm will be forced to operate such items below full capacity, but the maximum utilisation of capacity will be necessary to keep unit costs to a minimum and develop a strong competitive advantage. Only an increase in output may make this possible.

The fuller utilisation of the existing items of fixed capital make such a significant contribution to the reduction in unit costs of production as organisations respond in the short run to an increase in the demand for their output. This is reflected in the effect that the fall in the *AFC* curve has upon the *ATC* curve in Fig. 6.3 (page 92). In the long run, however, the organisation may be sufficiently confident that the more favourable market conditions are likely to persist and is willing therefore to increase its productive capacity. This will involve the installation of items of fixed capital with larger capacities, and this aspect of the increased scale of output will also yield certain economies.

For example, an organisation may replace an item of machinery with one capable of handling a 50 per cent increase in the work-load for a particular operation. When compared with the smaller machine it is replacing, the new machine is likely to involve a less than 50 per cent increase in the purchase price and also in its running and maintenance costs. The smaller machine may be priced at £200,000, whereas the machine with a 50 per cent larger capacity may cost £250,000. The energy costs associated with running the machine rise from £3000 to £4000 per annum, while the labour input for its operation remains at £8000 per annum, and the maintenance costs rise from £2000 to £2500. Thus a 50 per cent increase in the output from this particular area of the organisation's activities will give rise to only a 24 per cent increase in the costs associated with such an operation.

4. *Financial economies will be open to a large, well-established firm that can raise funds on more favourable terms than a small firm.* The former can offer greater security and has a proven record of success, while the latter will be regarded as a more risky venture and accordingly be obliged to pay a higher rate of interest. The costs of floating a large public issue of shares does not increase in the same proportion as the size of the issue.

5. *The position of a large firm will be further strengthened by the availability of funds for research and development and the employment of specialist staff in this department.* New products and techniques can then be put to profitable use and make it progressively more difficult for the small firm to close the competitive gap that exists between it and the large concerns.

6. *As the organisation expands, the improvement in its financial position brought about by the economies of scale will put it in a stronger position when seeking to recruit experienced people with the skills, abilities and attitudes that will make an important contribution to its future productivity and efficient management.* The organisation will be in a position to offer more attractive salaries and rates of pay, while the increased scale of its operations will allow it to offer good career and promotion prospects to people with ambition and drive.

The increase in the size of its workforce and labour requirements will also make it viable to set up its own specialist personnel department. Experienced and trained personnel staff will improve selection procedures and help to reduce labour turnover. The training and management development programmes they operate will not only improve the skills of existing employees but also make the organisation an attractive employer from the point of view of people who recognise the importance of training as a means of enhancing their career and promotion prospects. As the organisation expands it will therefore be able to attract and retain employees of a higher calibre.

Diseconomies of scale

The fall in the long-run average total cost curve (*LRATC*) in Fig. 6.6 (page 97) illustrates the potential benefits of economies of scale. But the same curve also shows the possibility that an organisation may eventually experience developments that exert an upward pressure upon its unit costs. It is difficult to imagine a situation where the cause of such pressures can be linked directly to the use of additional items of fixed capital, as the description in point 3 above indicated that they are a very important source of potential economies of scale. This is because their productive capacity increases more rapidly than the capital expenditure involved in acquiring them and the costs incurred in operating and maintaining them. This is the case even though the long run is seen as a period of time during which the additional items of machinery and equipment do not yet embody any significant advances in science and technology.

A simple example of this is the fact that a commercial vehicle capable of carrying a four-ton load will not cost twice as much to purchase and operate as a vehicle capable of carrying a two-ton load. In fact the transport industry continues to use larger lorries, aircraft and oil tankers; retail organisations build ever-larger supermarkets; and the production of motor vehicles, steel and chemicals is increasingly concentrated in factories, works and plants that use items of fixed capital with very large operating capacities. Even if the technology embodied in computers remained static for a period of time, all types of organisations would endeavour to match their expansion by using computers with a capacity to handle higher work-loads. One must therefore look elsewhere for the factors that will eventually exert an upward pressure upon an organisation's unit costs.

The sources of such diseconomies tend to be human in nature, whether at management or shop-floor level. A large and complex organisation will make demands upon management skills that cannot readily be met, because the supply of such skilled personnel at any one moment will be limited. The firm may grow at a rate that exceeds the improvement in managerial techniques required to guarantee the smooth and successful running of the business and to take advantage of potential economies of scale. The decision-taking procedure may be slowed down, and sections within the organisation may sense a feeling of remoteness from each other. The process of expansion may have involved a greater degree of specialisation among workers, which in turn may produce a deterioration in industrial relations.

A disadvantage of the specialisation of labour is that workers become dissatisfied with the continuous repetition of a single routine operation and a consequent loss of job satisfaction. They may seek a higher monetary reward as compensation, and at the same time the greater bargaining strength that results from increased specialisation will make the threat of industrial action all the more serious for the firm, as the whole productive process may come to a halt if certain workers use strike action.

As an organisation expands the scale of its operations it may be obliged to offer higher wages and salaries in order to recruit certain skills because they are increasingly in short supply. The higher rates of pay will also have to be paid to the existing employees with similar skills. If the expansion of an organisation coincides with a general upturn in the overall level of activity in the economy, then the increased competition in the various sections of the labour market, combined with the greater bargaining power of trade unions, may oblige an organisation to pay substantially higher wages and salaries both to recruit labour and to retain its existing employees. Such developments in the labour market will not only raise the total labour costs of an organisation but also increase the prices that have to be paid for other inputs such as components and equipment. This is because the manufacturers of such inputs will also be experiencing similar pressures upon their labour costs. Depending upon the extent to which they are able to make more efficient use of their labour, they too will be forced to raise the prices of their outputs.

Similar pressures may push up land and property prices in those parts of the country where there is a high concentration of organisations that require additional premises to accommodate their expansion of output.

As has been described (page 91), the period of time that generally elapses before an organisation can complete its long-term adjustment to a higher level of output will differ between industries. In particular those organisations involved in the extraction of raw materials may encounter serious problems in their efforts to expand output from existing sources or to develop new deposits. If the growth of an organisation coincides with a general expansion of its industry both at home and abroad, therefore, it may face a large increase in the prices of its essential raw materials because of the shortages produced by the inability of the suppliers to cope with a sudden large rise in the world demand for their output.

Rises in the prices of inputs create problems for organisations to which they may respond by accelerating the development and introduction of new technologies, materials and skills. These are the changes one would expect in the very long run, as organisations adapt their operations to developments in the markets for their goods and services and in the availability and prices of their inputs.

The very long run

Effects on the organisation

This is defined as a period of time during which organisations may not only vary the input of all factors of production but also take advantage of **developments in science and technology**. Such developments lead to new and improved items of plant, machinery and equipment and more efficient processes and materials, as well as improvements in the design and other important features of both components and end products. This is also a period of time that recognises the progress that can be made in education, training and management development programmes.

All these potential areas of development add a further dimension to the continuing efforts of organisations to introduce production and management techniques that both minimise unit costs and raise the quality of their output. In recent years, for example, organisations involved in processing, manufacturing and assembly work have increasingly turned towards the use of more highly automated plant and equipment while also exploiting the scope that exists for the use of robots. Rapid advances in the computer field have radically changed the administrative and financial systems used by all types of organisations. The application of advances in science and technology has not been restricted to organisations in the manufacturing and industrial sectors; those concerned with the provision of services such as banking, insurance, retailing, transport, communications and hotel and catering have also sought where possible to take advantage of the latest technology in many parts of their operations.

In the very long run, organisations are also able to respond to changes in the **relative price of inputs**. It is possible, for example, that if the price of the labour input rises more slowly than the input of capital, because the prices of capital items and interest charges increase more rapidly than wages and salaries, then organisations may seek to minimise their costs by shifting towards more labour-intensive techniques of production. Similarly, if there is a rise in the price of the labour input relative to the capital input per unit of output then organisations will seek to adjust to this by adopting more capital-intensive methods of production that economise on labour.

The rise in the price of labour due to shortages of certain skills and other developments in the labour market during much of the post-war period has perhaps been the main driving force behind the adoption of more capital-intensive techniques. Such techniques not only allow a reduction in the labour input per unit of output but also provide scope for the substitution of less expensive unskilled and semi-skilled labour for the more costly skilled labour.

Such is the potential impact of recent advances in science and technology upon the output per unit of new capital employed, however, that even a very large fall in the price of labour relative to capital may only slow down rather than reverse the shift towards the use of more capital-intensive techniques of production. Even those organisations that, because of the nature of their business, have traditionally been labour intensive, such as those providing retailing and hotel and catering services, have increasingly expanded the scale of their operations by designing premises and using equipment allowing expansion with a less than proportionate increase in their employment of labour.

Effects on the consumer

In the very long run the continued advance of science and technology and the development of new materials and skills provide organisations with further opportunities to introduce cost-saving innovations and to supply new and improved products and services. Such developments affect not only business competitiveness and profits but also the standard of living of households when measured in material terms. Prices, of course, continue to rise at various rates in different sectors of the economy; but in the long term the rise in the cost of living for the majority of households is more than outweighed by the average increase in the earnings.

Thus because unit costs and hence price increases in the long term have been less than the increase in earnings, the real price of the goods and services supplied by organisations has actually fallen. One way of looking at this is to compare the amount of time that must be worked by someone on average earnings in order to pay the current price for a medium-range washing-machine, for example, and to compare it with the amount of working time that would have been required, say, twenty years ago.

In this particular example, the amount of working time fell from about 160 hours in 1965 to approximately 55 hours in 1985. The average washing-machine is now also more efficient and sophisticated than its predecessor of twenty years ago, because of developments in both materials and technology. A washing-machine does therefore cost more to buy, but its real price has fallen dramatically over the last twenty years.

It is even possible to find some examples of products that in recent years have fallen not only in terms of their real price but also in terms of their actual purchase price. This has been the case with video-recorders, home computers and calculators. A combination of economies of scale and advances in science and technology have more than outweighed increases in the prices of factors of production. In future years these items may start to go up in price, but further long-run improvements in technology and productivity will ensure that their real prices continue to fall.

Thus even though a long-run average total cost curve (Fig. 6.6, page 97) starts to rise and illustrates certain diseconomies that push up unit costs, the good or service is still likely to be offered at a lower real price thanks largely to the effects of employing larger units of capital. Then, in the very long run, unit costs and hence price rises are further moderated by the ability to apply new technology, skills and materials with the result that the real prices continue to fall.

Integration

So far the description of the resource decisions taken by organisations in their efforts to minimise unit costs has concentrated upon how their ability to alter the combination of inputs is largely influenced by the time period under consideration. The time factor is also important with respect to other decisions taken by an organisation in pursuing policies formulated in response to changes in the relative price of factors of production or developments in the markets where they sell their goods or services.

An organisation may believe that its long-term interests are best served if it embarks upon some form of integration with another organisation. When two organisations decide to join forces and pool their resources the resulting amalgamation is usually the result of a **merger** agreed to by both parties. Mergers are in fact far more common than **take-overs**, though it is the latter that tend to capture the headlines in the media. If an organisation finds that another rejects its proposal for a merger, then it may make a take-over bid by

trying to buy up enough shares in the other organisation to give it a majority holding.

This occurred in 1985, when Guinness, the brewers, successfully made a bid for Arthur Bell, the whisky distiller. This particular bid involved Guinness in £356 million to secure control. Because of such vast sums of money that must be raised to finance take-over bids, the integration of organisations usually occurs as a result of a voluntary merger.

Organisations commonly believe that mergers are a means of achieving their objectives. This is confirmed by Table 6.3 and by the fact that the largest 100 organisations in the UK account for about 50 per cent of industrial output. Mergers have also taken place within the financial, retailing and hotel and catering sectors. This rapid concentration of industrial and commercial activities means that the output of many goods and services now lies increasingly under the control of a few large organisations. There is continuing debate as to whether or not the net effect of this trend is in the public interest.

The potential advantages and disadvantages of mergers from the point of view of an organisation's customers are discussed in Chapter 9. The following sections therefore concentrate upon the part that mergers and hence integration can play in assisting the organisations involved to achieve their objectives in the long run. A merger will involve both parties in some form of adjustment, such as the resource decisions concerning the management structure and the production methods, so a relatively long period of time may elapse before the anticipated benefits begin to accrue to the single and larger organisation produced by the merger.

Horizontal integration
This involves a merger between two organisations involved in the same line of business and does not give rise to any significant departure from their range of goods or services. Horizontal integration would therefore take place when, for example, there is a merger between two banks, two retail chains, two motor vehicle manufacturers or food-processing companies. The motives behind this form of integration may be to achieve some of the following objectives:
1. *As independent organisations, neither may have been able to raise their market share to a level that enabled them to reap further economies of scale, while their respective unit costs may also have been adversely affected by levels of output that left each of them operating with a*

Table 6.3: Acquisitions and mergers within the UK

| | Total all acquisitions and mergers [1] | | | Acquisitions of independent companies and mergers | | | | | | | | | | |
| | | | | Total | | | Acquisitions of independent companies | | | Mergers [2] | | | Sales of subsidiaries between company groups | | |
	Number acquiring	Number acquired	Value £m	Number acquiring	Number acquired	Value £m	Number acquiring	Number acquired	Value £m	Number acquiring	Number acquired	Value £m	Number acquiring	Number acquired	Value £m
1972	928	1 210	2 532	716	938	2 346	710	931	2 337	6	7	9	212	272	185
1973	929	1 205	1 304	724	951	1 058	722	949	1 055	2	2	2	205	254	247
1974	427	504	508	307	367	459	306	366	452	1	1	8	120	137	49
1975	276	315	291	180	200	221	177	197	215	3	3	6	96	115	70
1976	315	353	448	218	242	348	217	241	348	1	1	–	97	111	100
1977	427	481	824	333	372	730	331	370	701	2	2	30	94	109	94
1978	484	567	1 140	387	441	977	384	438	926	3	3	50	107	126	163
1979	447	534	1 656	353	417	1 470	352	414	1 437	1	3	33	103	117	186
1980	404	469	1 475	320	368	1 265	320	368	1 265	–	–	–	90	101	210
1981	389	452	1 144	288	327	882	288	327	882	–	–	–	105	125	262
1982	399	463	2 206	264	299	1 402	261	296	1 373	3	3	29	140	164	804
1983	391	447	2 343	272	305	1 907	269	302	1 783	3	3	125	123 [3]	142 [3]	436
1984	508	568	5 474	355	398	4 353	354	396	4 252	1	2	100	153	170	1 121

[1] The number of acquiring companies may be less than the sum of the components because some companies acquire both independent and subsidiary companies.   [2] A merger (which takes place when two companies combine to form a new company) is reckoned as the acquisition of the smaller company by the larger and is valued at the market value of the smaller company's share of the newly formed company.   [3] Includes one merger.
p Provisional.

Source: *British Business*, 16 August 1985.

significant margin of unused capacity. A merger will allow the closure of the most uneconomic of their productive units and provide scope for concentrating output in the remaining units where capacity can be more fully utilised. A single and much larger organisation will also become more competitive through the lower unit costs associated with additional opportunities for economies of scale.

In the case of the motor vehicle industry, for example, two producers may possess several manufacturing and assembly plants between them, and many areas of their activities may be operating well below capacity. A merger will provide scope for the rationalisation of the model range and the concentration of their output into fewer factories. Similarly, a merger between two producers of beer will allow the closure of the less efficient and outdated breweries and the concentration of the various types of beer in those breweries where future investment is to be directed. Such a merger may also provide savings from rationalisation schemes in the areas of management, administration, marketing and distribution.

2. *The striving for higher and more secure profits in the long run rather than their maximisation in the short run would also suggest a merger or take-over that will strengthen an organisation's control over a market.* Amalgamations that reduce the level of competition in a market will help to reduce the risks to an organisation's investment project caused by a rival adopting a competitive strategy that could make serious inroads into its future market before it had completed its new investment programmes, or before it had received an acceptable return on the capital expenditure involved. Such risks may cause an organisation to hesitate over long-term investment, and this is the form of investment likely to make the most significant contribution to efficiency and competitiveness.

Investment projects can involve many millions of pounds. A greater control over the market and a subsequent reduction in the risks may be an important precondition for new projects if they are to yield an acceptable return. A long period often exists between the start of such projects and the time when they come into operation and make a contribution to revenue that more than covers the initial outlay. This is the case in particular with high-technology projects that involve a radical change in the methods of production or in the end product with respect to design or performance.

A reduction in the risk involved in operating in a market will also make it easier to raise funds from external sources.

3. *A merger may be promoted by a mutual interest in pooling resources to withstand the growing strength of an*

overseas producer attempting to make inroads into the domestic market. A new entrant is more likely to gain an initial foothold in a market if it has to contend with only relatively small organisations that are already engaged in fierce competition with each other and do not benefit from potential economies of scale nor possess the financial resources to survive a price-cutting war. A merger may also be the means of creating an organisation that is capable of entering into competition with the foreign rival in its own domestic market.

4. *An organisation may have identified a threat from the current development of a new technology or substitute product by a rival organisation that will greatly strengthen the competitive position of the latter, which has protected its innovation by the acquisition of patent rights.* The organisation threatened by these developments may propose a merger, and the other organisation may recognise that their combined resources will enable yet further development of the innovation and its much wider application throughout a larger organisation.

5. *Even during a recession, mergers are likely to take place.* The problems of falling sales and excess capacity will be particularly acute, and neither organisation may be sure which of them has the greatest potential for riding out a period of exceptionally low demand.

Vertical integration
The objectives of the firm may point to expansion in a vertical direction, whereby the firm involves itself in additional stages of production or distribution. An enterprise may seek to engage in *either* more of the processes undertaken before it receives a product as a raw material or component, *or* those that contribute to the end product before it is purchased by the consumer. A brewery, for example, may expand horizontally via amalgamations with other breweries and then expand vertically towards the market by securing more retail outlets in the form of public houses and off-licences. The same brewery may then decide to expand vertically backwards towards the source of its raw materials by securing its own hop fields and bottle-manufacturing plant.

This type of expansion may also allow a firm to achieve those objectives associated with increasing profits through greater efficiency, as well as increasing its power over the market. Thus the firm will become more secure and ensure its survival.

Vertical expansion is likely to benefit the firm in the following areas:

1. *By securing the sources of its raw materials and other inputs, such as components, the firm will make supplies more secure.* This will prove particularly advantageous when the market demand is rising rapidly, as the firm might otherwise experience shortages and delays when, for example, component manufacturers do not possess the capacity to deal with an increase in both the size and number of orders.

2. *Adjustments in the productive capacities necessary to cope with changes in demand may be more quickly and accurately achieved if more of the processes are under the control of a firm.* Market trends will be more readily transmitted down the line and help reduce the problem of either an excess or a shortage of capacity as independent firms would not co-ordinate their investment plans. This will assist the integrated firm in developing a more effective investment programme.

3. *Some industrial processes are more efficiently undertaken if they are conducted in close proximity to each other.* Several processes may, for example, require that each of them is carried out at very high temperatures. If they were undertaken by separate firms, then the need to reheat the inputs would result in much higher production costs. This would be the case, for example, with the production of metals, oil products and chemicals.

4. *The firm would also have greater control over the quality and design of its inputs and from the very beginning they can be geared to suit the firm's individual requirements.* An independent component manufacturer, for example, may produce a standard product with certain features that are superfluous to a particular firm's need, yet in other ways it may have certain limitations. The supplying firm may not consider it worth introducing improvements that do not coincide with the needs of a sufficiently large number of its customers. A user firm may be particularly interested in developments in the areas of heat resistance, electrical conductivity and a longer life for its components, and such improvements are more likely to occur if the firm can control the manufacture of its own components.

5. *The firm may believe that it has now reached a size where it becomes viable to enter into the field of distribution.* The first move may be to introduce its own transport fleet, which will make it independent of outside hauliers and the public transport system. The size of its business may not only make this commercially viable but will allow greater flexibility in delivery dates and times, as

well as reducing the impact of outside influence, which may restrict deliveries.

6. *Rather than deal with an independent wholesaler, the firm may absorb this role itself if retail outlets or customers place sufficiently large orders.* The manufacturer may therefore deal directly with retail units or users, and the next move may be the opening up of its own retail outlets if it is producing consumer goods. This movement towards the market may be to increase the presence of its goods in the market itself, particularly during a period of recession. Having direct contact with the consumer will also give the firm first-hand knowledge of changes in tastes and preferences and enable it to act accordingly.

The vertical integration of a firm will mean in some cases that the advantages derived from specialising in a narrower range of activities will have to be sacrificed to a certain extent. The firm may believe, however, that the increased security and power that such vertical expansion brings more than compensates for the tendency for some costs to increase.

Lateral integration

Diversification of a firm's activities is also a feature of lateral integration whereby a firm increases the range of its output. A pharmaceutical company, for example, may have recognised in the course of its development that additional products could be produced with very little adjustment. The process involved, the skills and inputs, may readily lend themselves to multi-product growth; it may be possible to utilise a by-product; and the same retail outlets can be used to sell additional products.

Diversification may also be motivated by the desire to reduce the firm's reliance upon a single product for its revenue, and to enable it to spread risks over a wider range of products and markets. This reduction in risks may outweigh any advantage lost by moving away from a specialised output.

International expansion

The firm's expansion plans may go beyond its home market and seek to expand its sales in overseas markets, and this may be the case when the domestic market shows a lack of sustained growth or is experiencing a prolonged recession. A rapid rise in the size of overseas markets may see a firm seeking to enter the export field by establishing a specialist department to promote its product abroad. It may, however, be entering a highly competitive market and its position and sales contacts might be improved by setting up production units in the overseas market itself. This objective could also be secured by take-overs or mergers involving a company already resident in the overseas market. This will also help the firm overcome any restrictions in the form of tariffs or quotas that have been placed upon goods entering the particular overseas market concerned.

For example, a motor vehicle manufacturer may face a heavy import duty on its exported vehicles and so decide to set up an assembly plant in the overseas market itself. This pattern of expansion has led to the growth of **multinational companies** such as Ford, Philips, IBM and ICI, which have production units in several countries. They have been motivated by several factors, such as possessing the ability to switch production from plant to plant when external events in a particular economy are mitigating against efficiency.

This type of expansion also allows them to move into those areas where they can take advantage of relatively abundant and cheap supplies of labour. They may select a location where they can minimise their tax burden and they have the power to decide where, within their organisation, their profits should accrue. As far as possible, they will ensure that profits are allocated to the subsidiary resident in a country where the tax laws are most favourable to them. This quest for overseas operations, whether in selling or actual production, can also perhaps be interpreted as a desire to extend the power and influence of the firm beyond the boundaries of the country of origin.

7. The Role of Employment Law

It may be argued that people are an organisation's most important resource. In order to produce goods and services, the organisation needs efficient and effective manpower. This chapter will consider 'people' in the employment situation and the laws and constraints which affect that situation.

'Rules' of employment

Like all aspects of life in a civilised society, employment is governed by 'rules'. Rules ensure that individuals are treated fairly and equally. If one person breaks a rule, he or she is treated in exactly the same way as another person who breaks the same rule in the same organisation. In employment, 'rules' are made by three groups of people: employers, employees, government – see Fig. 7.1.

Each group directly affects the other. Therefore, by using the model in Fig. 7.1 we can firstly define the role of each of the parties involved in the rule-making procedure and then discuss the way each affects the others.

Employer

The definition is 'one who employs others for wages' (*Penguin English Dictionary*). Employers may belong to an employers' association – an

Fig. 7.1: Parties involved in rule-making in employment

Employers
• Employers' associations

Employees
• Trade unions
• Trade Union Congress (TUC)

organisation that represents employers in given industries and will negotiate national industry-wide agreements with trade unions for the particular industry. The association also provides other services for employers, such as guidance with personnel, training and employment legislation matters.

Employee
'One who is employed by another and paid wages' (*Penguin English Dictionary*). Employees may belong to a trade union – an independent organisation of workers 'whose principal purposes include the regulation of relations between workers and employers'. Every worker has the right under law to join an independent trade union, but there is nothing under the law that compels an employer to 'recognise' the presence of that union or to deal with it.

There are three types of trade union: craft, industrial and general.

Craft unions. The oldest form of trade union – they derived from early groupings of skilled craftsmen who combined during the eighteenth and nineteenth centuries to negotiate with their employers for improvement in wages and conditions of employment. Early recorded examples include the Woollen Weavers (1721) and the Society of Compositors (1792). In modern times, some craft-workers still belong to specific craft unions. However, these are now either small unions, as is the case with the Bakers' Union, or have amalgamated with other unions in order to increase membership, for example the electricians and the engineers.

Industrial unions. These were the second type of trade union to be formed, whereby the work-force of an industry may choose to join one union (supervisors and management, however, may join another union). Examples of industrial unions include the National Union of Mineworkers (NUM) and the National Union of Railwaymen (NUR).

General unions. These large unions were originally for unskilled workers who were not eligible to join either of the other two categories. Now two of the largest trade unions in Britain are general unions: the Transport and General Workers' Union (TGWU) and the General, Municipal and Boilermakers' Union (GMBU).

A fourth category is sometimes added to the list: '*White-collar unions*'. These are the largest-growing type of trade union in Britain. Although some white-collar workers such as foremen may belong to the industrial or general unions, there are many examples of trade union that are specifically for white-collar workers – for example, bankers, civil servants, teachers and local government officers. The largest of the white-collar unions is the Association of Scientific, Technical and Managerial Staffs (ASTMS).

Trades Union Congress (TUC)
Most trade unions belong to the TUC, an organisation formed in 1868 as a permanent association of trade unions. The TUC holds an annual conference at which delegates from all affiliated trade unions have the opportunity to meet and to discuss trade union matters.

The role of government: employment legislation

Historical aspects
Governments have been involved in the regulation of wages and conditions of employment since the Middle Ages. Justices of the Peace had power to fix wages under the Statute of Labourers 1351 and the Statute of Apprentices 1563. At this time it was prohibited for workers to join forces 'against their employers' in order to negotiate for higher wages. In 1799 and 1800 the Combination Acts made any combinations of workers illegal. Thus for many years trade unions themselves were illegal.

Another example of government involvement in the employment situation was the Truck Acts of 1831. These Acts made it illegal for employers to pay employees in anything other than 'coin of the realm'. Prior to this intervention by government an employer could pay wages 'in kind'; i.e. a miner could receive a bag of coal in payment for a week's work, etc.

Recent employment legislation
During the past sixteen years a large quantity of employment legislation has been passed. Governments have had increased involvement in the rule-aspects of employment. A check-list of recent legislation is shown in Fig. 7.2.

It is useful to consider some of the current employment legislation and to discuss its practical implications in rule-making within employment.

The contract of employment
A contract does not have to be in written form.

Fig. 7.2: Recent employment legislation

Under English law a contract between two or more parties can be a verbal agreement. Thus the employee does not have to receive a written contract on the commencement of employment. The contractual agreement between employer and employee will state the agreed rate at which the employer will pay the employee for his or her labour – the employee sells his or her labour to the employer. Also included in the agreement will be other terms and conditions, such as hours of work, holiday entitlement, overtime rates and sick-pay arrangements.

Under the Contracts of Employment Act 1972, which was incorporated into the Employment Protection (Consolidation) Act 1978, an employee has the right to receive written terms and conditions of employment within thirteen weeks of employment. This statement is not the contract itself but the terms and conditions agreed in the contract. The statement must include the following information:

1. Names of the parties involved.
2. The date of issue of the statement.
3. The date of commencement of employment.
4. The job title.

5. The rate of remuneration and pay intervals.
6. The number of hours normally worked under the contract.
7. The employee's holiday entitlement including public holidays.
8. Sick-pay arrangements.
9. Arrangements for pensions and pension schemes.
10. The employee's notice entitlement.
11. Disciplinary rules that apply to the employee.
12. Grievance procedures.
13. Appeals procedures in matters of discipline and grievance.

Dismissal of employees
The Industrial Relations Act 1971 was repealed in 1974 by the Trade Union and Labour Relations Act 1974, but some of the provisions of the 1971 Act were retained, in particular the provision relating to the dismissal of employees. Under the Act employees have the right 'not to be unfairly dismissed'. Thus an employer cannot dismiss an employee without reason or a proper 'fair' procedure. An employee who considers that he or

she has been unfairly dismissed has the right to take the employer to an industrial tribunal, provided that the employee

- has been employed for a period of two years and works for at least sixteen hours a week, *or*
- works for fifteen hours a week or less but has been employed over a period of five years.

What constitutes 'fair' dismissal?

It is automatically unfair to dismiss an employee because he or she is a member of a trade union or because they refuse to join a staff association that is funded by the company or organisation. In order to stipulate that unfair dismissal of employees could lead to an industrial tribunal case against the employer, the legislation must also indicate the type of reason for dismissal that might be considered 'fair' provided that the employer has followed the correct disciplinary procedure.

The reasons for a dismissal to be considered 'fair' are:

- *Capability* – the employee cannot do the job for which he or she has been employed.
- *Misconduct* – the employee's conduct is such that he or she could not remain in employment.
- *Redundancy* – the job for which the person was employed no longer exists.
- *Contravention of statutory requirements* – the employer would break the law by employing the employee in a given capacity: e.g. in the case of a driver losing his or her driving licence, the employer could not continue to employ that person in that capacity.
- *Other substantial reason* – the legislation allows some leeway in that an employee may be deemed to have been fairly dismissed for a reason other than those stated.

Constructive dismissal

This term is used to describe a situation whereby an employee leaves an organisation (terminates his or her own contract) because the employer's behaviour is such that the employee considers he or she has no alternative but to leave the organisation. It can therefore be considered an act of unfair dismissal on the part of the employer if an employee is given no alternative other than to leave the organisation.

Industrial tribunals

An employee who meets the necessary requirements (as stated above) may if he or she considers that his or her dismissal is unfair take a case against the employer to an industrial tribunal. Tribunals were established in 1964. Besides cases of unfair dismissal they also deal with claims of sex and race discrimination (in matters of employment) and claims for equal pay, redundancy payments, etc. Tribunals are located in towns around the country, and approximately sixty tribunals sit each day.

Industrial tribunals are informal courts in that the employee, who is called the 'applicant' in the case, does not need legal representation and may choose to put his or her own case to the tribunal. However, in cases where the applicant is a member of a trade union, that trade union may represent its member at the tribunal. The employer (the 'respondent') must demonstrate that he or she has acted fairly in the dismissal of the employee.

Who sits on an industrial tribunal? Each tribunal has three members: the chairperson (a legally qualified member), an employer representative (elected by the Confederation of British Industry) and an employee representative (elected by the Trades Union Congress) – see Fig. 7.3.

Employees who win their case at an industrial tribunal for unfair dismissal can be awarded cash compensation. If they wish to return to their former job they may ask the tribunal for reinstatement. The employer must then decide whether or not he or she wishes to reinstate or re-employ the employee in question. If he or she does not wish to do so, he or she may choose to pay an additional compensatory award.

Health and safety

The Health and Safety at Work Act 1974 is legislation concerned with the health, safety and welfare of people in the work situation, and with the general public who come into contact with that work situation. The Act creates a framework for a healthy and safe working environment. It puts responsibility on both the employer and the employee to ensure that health and safety at work are both created and maintained.

Under the Act the employer has 'a general duty' to ensure, as far as is reasonably practicable, the health, safety and welfare at work of all his or her employees. The employee has a 'general duty' to take reasonable care for the health and safety of himself or herself and of other people who may be affected by his or her acts or omissions at work. The employee's duty is also to co-operate with the employer as far as is necessary to meet or comply

Employer representative   Chairperson   Employee representative

Fig. 7.3: Industrial tribunal

with any duty requirement concerning health and safety. Employees must not interfere with or misuse anything provided in the interests of health, safety or welfare.

Main functions of the Act
- It completely overhauled and modernised the existing law dealing with safety, health and welfare at work.
- It put new general duties on employers, ranging from providing and maintaining a safe place to work to consulting with their work-force.
- It created the Health and Safety Commission to oversee the legislation.
- It reorganised and unified the various government inspectorates into a body called the Health and Safety Executive.

Health and safety policy
Under the Health and Safety at Work Act employers with five or more staff must provide a written statement of their health and safety policy. An employer can face prosecution for failure to provide a policy statement.

Health and safety representative
In unionised work-forces (work situations where one or more trade unions are 'recognised' by the employer for collective bargaining purposes – see 'trade union recognition', page 115) employees may, if they wish, elect 'safety representatives' to represent them to the employer in matters of health and safety. Safety representatives must be employees who are employed in the work-place where they carry out their function. They must also have at least two years' employment with their present employer. Exceptions may be made in cases of high labour turnover or in newly established work-forces.

Functions of the safety representative include:

- Inspection of the work area at least every twelve weeks.
- Inspection of accidents or dangerous occurrences that take place.
- Inspection of any documents that are relevant to health and safety.
- Recording each inspection in a register provided by the employer for this purpose.

Safety committees
Employers are required to establish a safety committee in organisations where there are safety representatives and where at least two safety

representatives make such a request in writing. The purpose of the safety committee is to review the health and safety situation within the organisation frequently, to ensure that the work-place is safe.

Discrimination in employment

There are three pieces of legislation that deal with the question of discrimination in employment: the Equal Pay Act 1970, the Sex Discrimination Act 1975 and the Race Relations Act 1976.

Equal pay act 1970
This legislation is now incorporated into the Sex Discrimination Act. The aim of this Act was to create a situation whereby employers could not discriminate between male and female in terms of the payment made for work. Prior to the legislation it was possible to pay females a lower rate than that paid to a male for the same work. The Act states that a woman who is doing the same *or broadly similar* work for the same or for an associated employer should receive the same rate of pay.

Under the legislation a person of either sex can bring a case to an industrial tribunal if they wish to have their job compared with that of someone else doing the same or broadly similar work who is receiving a higher rate of pay.

Sex Discrimination Act 1975
This Act makes it illegal to discriminate between males and females in matters of employment, training and education, unless there is a 'genuine occupational qualification' (Fig. 7.4). The Act established the Equal Opportunities Commission to 'help enforce the legislation and to promote equality of opportunity generally' (*A Guide to the Sex Discrimination Act*, 1975).

Under the Act any individual – whether male or female – has the right to take an employer to an industrial tribunal if they consider that they have been discriminated against in matters of employment on the basis of their sex. An individual may take a case without actually commencing employment if they consider that the employer did not offer them the job because of their sex.

Fig. 7.4: Sex Discrimination Act helping to change roles within the working environment

Naturally in cases of this kind it is up to the applicant to prove to the tribunal that discrimination did in fact take place.

The Act applies to all employment situations where five or more people are employed, provided that the employment situation is not a private house.

'Discrimination' is defined under Section 1 of the Act in the following way. A person discriminates against a woman if he or she treats her less favourably on the grounds of her sex than he or she would treat a man, *or* if he or she applies to her a requirement or condition that he or she applies or would apply equally to a man *but*

- which is such that the proportion of women who can comply with it is considerably smaller than the proportion of men who can comply with it; *and*
- which he or she cannot justify irrespective of sex; *and*
- which is to her detriment because she cannot comply with it.

It is therefore illegal for an employer to advertise a job stating the sex of the applicant unless there is a 'genuine occupational qualification'.

Genuine occupational qualifications
It is lawful to discriminate between one sex and the other provided that there is an accepted reason for doing so. The Act indicates the criteria for discrimination under the heading 'general occupational qualification', of which there are eight.

1. *Physiology*. A job may specifically require a male or female, not for reasons of physical strength, but for the physiology of the person, as is the case with models, actors and 'bunny-girls'.
2. *Decency or privacy*. People employed as public toilet attendants or in changing rooms may be expected to be of the same sex as the people using the facility for reasons of decency and privacy.
3. *The nature of the establishment*. If it is necessary for employees to live in and share accommodation, it may, depending on the accommodation, be appropriate to have employees of the same sex.
4. *Single-sex establishment*. Within single-sex establishments such as some hospitals and prisons it may be considered appropriate for some of the posts to be held by a person of the same sex. In some cases, for example, women prefer to attend single-sex hospitals to be treated by women doctors.
5. *Education or welfare* – where the services provided by the job-holder promote the education or welfare of the individual, as could be the case with welfare workers and marriage guidance counsellors.
6. *Other legislation*. Women are restricted by the Factories Act from working in certain places at certain hours, e.g. in factories throughout the night. Thus it might be necessary to employ a man.
7. *Other countries' legislation*. The legislation of another country may restrict women from employment that could involve women employed in Britain working abroad. An example would be a driving job that involved travelling to a country where it is illegal for women to drive.
8. *Married couples*. Some jobs require a couple comprising of a male and female, an example being the landlord and landlady of a public house.

Race Relations Act 1976
This Act makes it illegal to discriminate on grounds of race in matters of employment, training and education, unless, again, there is a genuine occupational qualification. The Act established the Commission for Racial Equality to 'help enforce the legislation and to promote equality of opportunity and good relations between people of different racial groups generally' (*A Guide to the Race Relations Act*, 1976). Under the Act discrimination on racial grounds is unlawful in terms of colour, race, nationality and ethnic or national origins.

The Act states that 'direct racial discrimination arises where a person treats another person less favourably on racial grounds than he treats, or would treat, someone else.'

'In considering whether a particular kind of treatment of a person constitutes direct racial discrimination it is necessary to inquire: (1) whether it was less favourable than the treatment which was (or could have been) accorded to another person and, if so (2) whether the less favourable treatment was on racial grounds, i.e. whether the reason for the treatment was the colour, race, nationality or ethnic or national origins either of the victim or of someone else' (*A Guide to the Race Relations Act*, 1976).

Genuine occupational qualifications

The Race Relations Act recognises only one 'general occupational qualification'. This is on grounds of 'authenticity'. Thus an employer can state that he or she wishes to employ a Chinese waiter in a Chinese restaurant for reasons of authenticity.

Wages councils

Some countries have a national minimum wage, which is a statutory weekly wage for an agreed number of hours worked. This minimum wage is set by the government of the country. Employers in all industries must not pay below that rate; to do so would mean prosecution. In Britain there is no national minimum wage. But government does get involved in wage determination in industries that are not able to negotiate terms and conditions of employment because of weak trade union representation of employees within that industry and thus limited bargaining power. The government becomes involved in such industries by means of wages councils (Fig. 7.5).

Wages councils establish minimum rates of pay and conditions such as holiday entitlement and overtime rates for approximately 3 million people employed in industries such as hotels and catering, retail, hairdressing and clothing. Each such industry has at least one wages council. This produces an order each year setting out the minimum rates of pay and conditions for that particular industry or sector of an industry.

History of wages councils

In 1909 Trade Boards were established within industries where pay was low and conditions were very poor. The industries involved were known as 'sweated trades', and the aim of the boards was to improve the conditions in which people were employed and to establish improvements in rates of pay.

In 1945 the government of the day passed the Wages Council Act establishing for the first time governmental responsibility in wage determination. The Act converted the Trade Boards into wages councils with statutory rights to set minimum rates of pay within given industries

Fig. 7.5: The structure of a wages council

Employee representatives   Independent members   Employer representatives

that were unable to establish free collective bargaining because of low union representation. The Act also enabled wages councils to agree certain minimum conditions of employment such as holiday pay.

In 1975 the Employment Protection Act increased the scope of wages councils, giving them greater involvement in establishing terms and conditions of employment. The 1975 Act also enabled wages councils to be abolished if it could be shown that they were no longer required in a particular industry or sector of an industry, because that industry was able to establish its own terms and conditions by means of collective bargaining. Thus the industry would have to provide evidence that trade union membership had increased to a level sufficient to be considered representative of staff interests within it, *and* that employers' and employees' representatives were able to sit down together and negotiate.

In 1985 the government considered disbanding wages councils in favour of employers paying the rates that they could afford. The government argued that because the councils set rates of pay, some employers found the rates too high and were thus discouraged from employing people. However, a compromise was reached. Wages councils will continue to exist, but the rates that they set will apply to employees of 21 years of age onwards, thus excluding all young people from 16 to 20 years of age; and there will be some reduction in the scope of the councils.

Structure of wages councils
Wages councils are made up of equal numbers of employer and employee representatives and up to three independent members (usually academics). The members do not actually negotiate, since there are three parties involved; but with the help of the independent members a compromise is reached and an annual wages council order is produced. This relates only to the employees within a given industry.

Enforcement of wages council orders
Wages orders are legally binding on employers within the particular industry. Employers may choose to pay above the minimum rate, but they cannot pay below that rate. An inspectorate is employed to ensure that wages council orders are adhered to. Inspectors may visit an organisation, and if an employer is found not to be complying with the appropriate wages council order he or she

will face prosecution. If found guilty, he or she can expect to be fined and to be ordered to pay compensation to his or her employees.

The employer must also ensure that the wages council order is accessible to all his or her staff, displayed on a notice-board in a staff area such as a rest room. Failure to do this can also lead to prosecution.

Discipline and grievance procedures

Employers are expected to establish with their staff procedures to deal with matters of discipline and grievance. The Employment Protection Consolidation Act 1978 requires that written statements of terms and conditions of employment should include disciplinary rules applicable to the employee, or should refer to a document that is reasonably accessible to the employee and specifies such rules. Also under the Act, all employees must be made aware of the organisation's grievance procedure.

Disciplinary procedures

Employer
↓
Employee

Grievance procedures

Employer
↑
Employee

A procedure can be seen as an established way of carrying something out, the course to follow to reach a particular goal. In matters of employment it is important to ensure that employees are treated fairly and uniformly. It is therefore necessary to both employers and employees that there are agreed procedures within the organisation to deal with matters of staff discipline and grievance.

Disciplinary procedures
ACAS has produced a code of practice entitled *Disciplinary Practice and Procedures in Employment.* This gives guidance to employers as to how to draw up a disciplinary procedure. A code of practice is not legally binding, but it does have similar status to that of the Highway Code: employers will be expected to follow the code

when disciplining and dismissing staff. An industrial tribunal will take into consideration the procedure that was followed by the employer prior to dismissal if a case for unfair dismissal is brought before it.

The ACAS code states that the purpose of a disciplinary procedure is to promote fairness and order in the treatment of individuals and in the conduct of industrial relations. Such procedures also assist an organisation to operate effectively. Rules set standards of conduct at work, and procedures help to ensure that these standards are adhered to and also provide a fair method of dealing with alleged failures to observe them.

A disciplinary procedure is not intended to be simply a means of dismissing staff. Instead it is a means of providing employees who may have broken work-place rules with the opportunity to improve. If this does not happen, then ultimately dismissal may be the only sanction left to the employer.

The guidelines given by the ACAS code of practice to employers drawing up a disciplinary procedure include the following:

- The procedure must be in writing.
- It must specify to whom it applies.
- It must specify levels of management that have the authority to take the various forms of disciplinary action.
- The procedure must allow for individuals to be informed of the complaint against them and to state their case prior to action being taken.
- Individuals must be given the right to be accompanied by a trade union representative or a friend of their choice.
- Except for reasons of gross misconduct, no employee should be dismissed for a first breach of discipline.
- Disciplinary action should not be taken until the case has been carefully investigated.
- Individuals should be given an explanation for any penalty imposed.
- A right of appeal is provided.

A disciplinary procedure will usually include the following stages:

Stage 1. Verbal warning.
Stage 2. First written warning.
Stage 3. Second written warning.
Stage 4. Dismissal notice.

The procedure may vary slightly in different organisations. But in all cases the employee must be informed of the next stage of the procedure should the need arise for it to be used. An example could be: 'As this is your second written warning in this matter, Mr Jones, if you continue to be fifteen minutes late for work each day, we shall have no alternative but to terminate your employment with this organisation.'

Gross misconduct
Disciplinary procedures will state the actions that are considered to be 'gross misconduct' in the eyes of the particular organisation, and therefore are reasons for instant dismissal. Examples of gross misconduct could include – theft, arson and assault (Fig. 7.6).

Grievance procedures
Employees have the right to seek redress for grievances relating to their employment. Employers should establish with employees' representatives or trade union a procedure through which an employee can take up a grievance and expect to get it settled both fairly and promptly. Thus a formal procedure should exist.

The aim of a grievance procedure is to settle grievances fairly and as near as possible to the point where the grievance began. Procedures should again be in written form. A usual format would be as follows:

- Discussion of grievance with immediate supervisor.
- If the grievance cannot be resolved at this stage it goes to management, where the employee should be given the right to be accompanied by either a friend or a trade union representative.
- If the employee is not happy with the outcome of his or her meeting with management he or she should have a right of appeal against the decision reached.

Trade union recognition and collective bargaining

Trade union recognition is the name given to the process through which an employer agrees to deal with a trade union representing the interests of some or all of the employees, for the purpose of collective bargaining. The definition of the process in the Employment Protection Act 1975 is as follows: 'Recognition of the union by the employer, to any extent, for the purposes of collective bargaining'.

In Britain there is no legislation that directly

Fig. 7.6: Gross misconduct

enforces trade union recognition. Even if such legislation did exist, it could be argued that it would be extremely difficult to enforce. Good working relationships between an employer and his or her work-force, and with the representatives of that work-force, can be developed only on a basis of goodwill and not through the law of the land.

Thus trade union recognition is, in Britain, a voluntary process. An employer agrees to negotiate with an independent trade union representing all or some of his or her employees, provided that a sufficient number of employees wish to be represented by that particular trade union. (There is no set number of employees held to be a viable number for recognition purposes. The decision is the employer's.)

The recognition agreement

Management and representatives of the trade union (usually full-time paid officers, as opposed to elected shop stewards) meet and draw up the formal recognition agreement, which is usually in writing. This will state both who is covered by the agreement and the scope of the agreement – that is, what the agreement entitles both parties to

negotiate, when, where and how it will be enacted.

The agreement will state who the group of employees are. It could be that the whole of the work-force, including management, chooses to belong to the same trade union; thus only one agreement will exist. However, many organisations deal with more than one trade union, because management may choose to join a white-collar union, the craft-workers a craft union, and the remainder of the staff a general union. It is probably easier for employers to deal with fewer unions; and the trend at present seems to be for employers to try to draw up an agreement with one union that will represent the interests of all of the work-force.

Having decided who is to be covered by the agreement, the next stage is for the parties to decide exactly what the agreement is going to cover. A trade union will wish to represent its membership in various ways. These include negotiating terms and conditions of employment (collective bargaining) and involvement in procedures such as discipline, grievance and redundancy, whereby the union assists in drawing up the procedures and is involved through the representation of its membership.

Employment law: the rights of recognised trade unions

Once a trade union has gained recognition from an employer it acquires certain legal rights within the organisation as a representative of some or all of the work-force. These rights include the following:

- Health and Safety at Work Act – employees have the right to elect safety representatives.
- Employment Protection Act. Under this Act trade unions have several rights:
  1. Disclosure of information – employees' representatives have the right to ask for specific information about the company, e.g. its profits and plans, that will assist the union to bargain with employers.
  2. Redundancies – in the case of an organisation intending to make members of its work-force redundant, the union has the right to be consulted on the matter.
  3. Time off – trade union officers (shop stewards) and members have the right to take time off, in agreement with management, for trade union matters.

Under the Employment Act 1980 trade union members have the right to be provided with facilities for secret ballots, as long as at least twenty people are employed by the particular organisation.

Collective bargaining

This is the process whereby management and unions agree to sit down together and bargain or negotiate the terms and conditions of employment of the work-force. The bargaining process may take place *locally*, in that in a small organisation an employer may negotiate with the shop stewards who represent the work-force. They may meet on an annual basis or more frequently, negotiating wage increases, overtime rates, staff holiday entitlement, etc.

In the case of a large organisation, which may have outlets around the country, it will be necessary to hold negotiations either nationally or at least 'company-wide' in order to achieve uniformity in wages and conditions. Examples of national negotiating bodies in the public sector include the Whitley Councils. These are negotiating bodies which represent civil service and health service employees and on which representatives from the various (recognised) trade unions sit down with representatives of the employers and agree national terms and conditions of employment. Teachers and college and university lecturers also have their terms and conditions of employment negotiated on a national basis.

In conclusion it can be seen from this chapter that government plays an important role in the rule-making process within employment, giving both employers and employees recognised rights, and imposing sanctions.

8. The Organisation and Market Forces

Markets

A market is formed by the existence of the forces of demand and supply. It is the means by which buyers and sellers are brought into contact with each other.

Geographical size of markets
The geographical size of the market within which an organisation operates will depend mainly upon the nature of the good or service it produces.

Markets for goods
An organisation involved in the extraction and refining of oil from the North Sea may conduct its operations in the context of the world market for oil. Its output will be part of the world's supply of oil, and it will hope to capture a share of the world's demand for oil. Such an organisation will therefore pay attention to those factors likely to affect the total demand for oil in the world, and how the action taken by oil producers in other parts of the world is likely to influence its own sales of oil in the world's markets.

A UK motor vehicle manufacturer producing a certain range of cars may believe that the potential market for each of its models includes most of the major countries of Western Europe. It may, for example, have developed a model aimed at satisfying the demand for small-engined hatchbacks and another model specifically aimed at the luxury car market. The manufacturer must therefore be prepared to respond to developments that may influence the total size of these potential markets and its market shares. It must also monitor and respond to the policies pursued by its competitors operating in the same markets, which contribute to the supply side of the markets.

Other organisations may operate in much smaller markets. A packaging company, for example, may concentrate upon marketing its products solely in the UK. It may have neither the resources nor the particular type of product that would allow it to compete in overseas markets. As far as a brewery or bakery is concerned, the output may be aimed at more local markets, while a small organisation involved in the repair and installation of central heating systems may regard its potential market as being confined to an even smaller geographical area.

Markets for services
Apart from the markets for visible, tangible items such as consumer goods, capital goods, components and raw materials, there are also markets for services. These too will vary a great deal in size.

An airline or a firm of architects may operate in several overseas markets. A road haulier, by contrast, may believe that its current interests are best served by concentrating upon the demand for road transport within a specific area of the UK. It will therefore be most concerned with developments affecting the demand for its services within that particular area.

In the case of personal services, the potential markets tend to be limited to a much smaller geographical area. The customer or client has to be in attendance to 'consume' the service. Manufactured goods can be transported over relatively large distances; this is because in many cases the transport costs incurred are such a small part of the unit costs that their prices are still sufficiently competitive to make them attractive to potential buyers in markets some distance from the factory where they were made. Some services, such as banking and insurance, do embrace national and international markets; these are served by maintaining branches and representatives at more local levels in order to reach as many potential customers as possible.

With the more personal services, however, such as leisure and recreation, catering and retailing, then the suppliers will be concerned mainly with local markets. They will not be particularly affected by changes in the supply of and demand for similar services in other parts of the country. In the case of a personal service such as hairdressing, the owner may regard the market as being limited to the immediate neighbourhood where the salon is situated.

An important determinant of the size of a market for personal services is the extent to which a customer or client is willing to travel to avail themselves of the service provided by one particular supplier. Thus the more an organisation involved in the provision of a personal service can convince people that it offers good value for money, then as households become more mobile the larger will be the size of their potential market.

The provision of a personal service in a certain area may also involve suppliers that are part of very large organisations operating on a nation-wide basis. Examples include retail and fast-food chains. Although such an organisation may operate in the national market, it will be very concerned about developments in the local markets where its outlets are located. In the case of a shoe shop that is part of a large chain organisation, its sales will be influenced by developments in the local demand for footwear and by the strategy adopted by other shoe retailers in the same area.

Because of the regional differences in the distribution of income and social groups, and the different degrees of competition existing in various parts of the country, it is possible that the UK is regarded essentially as being made up of many small markets rather than one large homogeneous market.

Market information

An organisation needs as much information as possible about the market(s) in which it is operating – in terms of both its potential size and the factors likely to influence total sales and market share. It must also monitor the activities of other organisations that compete with its own products or services. This is the type of information that an organisation obtains when analysing the results of its **market research**. A detailed description of market research and related activities can be found in Book 2 of *Business Organisations and Environments*.

Factors that influence demand

The following sections identify important economic factors that, if they were to change, can be expected to influence the demand for goods and services. Whenever one of these factors is being analysed it will be assumed that all the remaining factors remain unchanged in order that one can attribute subsequent changes in demand to this single factor.

1. Demand for a product in relation to its price

In the vast majority of cases the demand for a product is inversely related to its price. As the price of a product increases, it becomes more expensive relative to possible substitutes and the demand for it can be expected to fall. The relationship between the demand and the price of shirts, for example, can be shown by the use of a demand curve as in Fig. 8.1.

Fig. 8.1

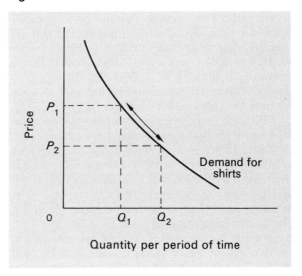

This curve is concerned with the total market demand for shirts in general rather than the demand for the particular shirts of any single producer. The price axis therefore refers to the average price of shirts as an item of clothing. An analysis of how the demand for the particular output of a single producer is likely to respond to a change in the price charged by that producer is given in the latter sections of this chapter, where account is taken of the degree of competition that a producer is faced with in the market where the output is sold.

The demand curve in Fig. 8.1 therefore shows the quantity of shirts that the total market is prepared to purchase at different price levels. If, for example, the price of shirts was OP_1 then the market would be prepared to purchase the quantity of shirts as shown by OQ_1. However, at a lower price of OP_2 consumers would be prepared to purchase a quantity of shirts totalling OQ_2. In order to register the quantity demanded at various price levels, it is necessary to describe demand in the context of a particular period of time – per month or per year. Demand is a flow, and the absence of a time period over which this flow is measured would not allow an estimation of the strength of demand.

Perhaps the rationale behind this relationship between the price of a product and the demand for it can usefully be explained. Consumers always seek to maximise the level of satisfaction or well-being which they can derive from using their income in various ways. The consumer is said to be in equilibrium when buying less of some products in order to release income for other uses is not considered to be worth while. The reaction of a consumer to a fall in price can be analysed in the light of the **law of diminishing marginal utility** (satisfaction or well-being). The amount of extra utility that a consumer derives from additional purchases of a product falls and thus total utility does increase, but by progressively smaller amounts.

Whenever consumers contemplate a change in their patterns of expenditure between existing products or to include new products, they ask themselves, 'Is it worth it?' The eventual decision is then taken on the basis of how much a move will affect their own level of satisfaction. The aggregation of these individual decisions regarding changes in relative prices leads to their combined expression, via the market demand for a product in relation to its price. Thus a fall in price will encourage a greater demand because the lower price will compensate for the diminishing marginal utility associated with increased consumption of the product.

This inverse relationship between prices and the quantity demanded exists with the majority of products but there are some areas where a perverse relationship may exist. This arises with products associated with the 'demonstration effect' whereby some consumers derive increased satisfaction from a product because it actually increases in price. Consumers are expected to behave rationally and reduce by various amounts their purchases of products whose relative price has increased. If some consumers, however, are observed to increase their demand for a product when it increases in price, they are not acting irrationally.

This is because one assumes that consumers always seek to maximise their satisfaction. Producers have discovered that in certain cases if a product is relaunched at a higher price, supported by advertising and promotional activities that seek to raise its image, sales increase. This does, however, raise the question of whether one is still dealing with the same product. If the producer succeeds in up-marketing the product, this increase in sales may be largely due to the campaign that seeks to influence tastes and preferences in favour of the product. Thus another factor likely to influence demand – tastes and preferences – has not remained unchanged. This influence on demand is described in section 5 (pages 125–6).

This 'demonstration effect' does exist, but the conclusion should not necessarily be drawn that a fall in price will lower the demand. Any reduced purchases by those who feel the product no longer has sufficient exclusiveness or prestige may be more than outweighed by those who would be keen to buy for the first time now that the price is reduced to within their reach and the product still possesses a favourable image.

There are some markets where the reason for a perverse relationship is more readily identified. In markets such as those for securities, foreign exchange and commodities, there is always the element of speculative trading present. An increase in market prices may provoke speculative buying in anticipation of further price rises which may produce a capital gain when sold at a higher price. Similarly, if prices in such markets start to fall, then speculative pressures may lead to a fall in demand. The holding of cash may be seen as preferable, thus avoiding any capital loss if an unforeseen need for cash forces the holder of such assets to sell when market prices are even further depressed.

2. Demand for a product and the price of substitutes

Although there are a large number of items competing for the consumer's income, there are some markets where this competition is particularly strong – where the consumer's need can be satisfied from a range of products which can be substituted for each other. In this case the demand for a product will vary directly with the price of a substitute, and this will be particularly apparent when products are very close substitutes.

For example, the demand for various types of meat is shown in Table 8.1. The changes in the pattern of consumption would have been due largely to changes in their relative prices as the different types of meat are substitutes for each other.

Table 8.1: Meat consumption in ozs per person per week, 1979–83

	Ozs per person per week				
	1979	1980	1981	1982	1983
Beef	8·27	8·13	6·96	7·06	6·57
Lamb	4·28	4·51	4·25	3·59	3·87
Pork	3·63	4·13	3·82	4·02	3·53
Beefburgers etc.	4·57	4·70	4·81	5·19	5·18
Poultry	6·82	6·67	7·30	6·85	6·99

Similarly, if there were a change in the price of timber, the demand for products such as plastics would be influenced. This is because scope exists to employ either of them in some aspects of building and furniture-making, for example.

Fig. 8.2 shows this expected relationship between the demand for a product and the price of a substitute. This diagram refers to paint and wallpaper, which compete for the income of those consumers who regard them as possible substitutes. When the price of wallpaper is at OP the demand for paint is OQ_1, but when the price of wallpaper rises to OP_2 the demand for paint increases to OQ_2.

Since the satisfaction of a need provides a consumer with welfare, then all goods and services are possible substitutes for each because they are all a potential source of welfare. On this basis it might be possible to find a relationship between seemingly unrelated areas of expenditure.

If, for example, there is a rise in the price of foreign holidays then some households may decide that a holiday at a resort in the UK now offers better value for money when comparing the money that must be parted with for the two types of holiday and the level of welfare each of them provides.

Some households, however, may decide that even a holiday in the UK does not match the welfare that could be derived from using the money that would be needed to pay for a holiday to buy a video-recorder, refurnish part of the house or build a greenhouse. Thus an increase in the price of foreign holidays will increase the demand for holidays in the UK, while the effect of this price rise may also be seen in an increase in the demand for a wide range of consumer goods and services.

3. Demand for a product and the price of complementary products

The description 'complementary products' is given to those products that must be used in conjunction with each other so that a particular need can be satisfied. For example, cameras and film are complementary products, as are cars and petrol.

Fig. 8.3 shows such a relationship by suggesting how the demand for oil-fired central heating systems is influenced by a change in the price of oil. When the price of oil is OP_1 the demand for this type of heating system is OQ_1, but it falls to OQ_2 when the price of oil rises to OP_2. In 1984 in the UK

Fig. 8.2

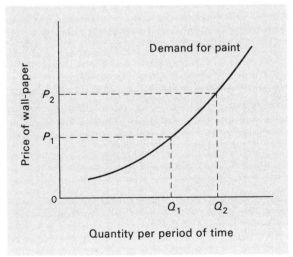

Fig. 8.3

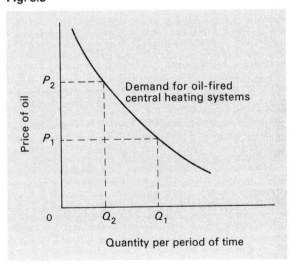

less than 60 per cent of households had central heating, which suggests that a significant rise in the price of oil would reduce sales, both to the first-time buyer and to those replacing an obsolete or inefficient system, by firms engaged in manufacturing oil-fired central heating systems.

One would then anticipate an increase in the demand for gas as a central heating fuel and thus a rise in the demand for gas-fired boilers. This is because oil and gas are substitute central heating fuels, while gas and gas-fired boilers are complementary products.

4. Demand for a product and the average level of real disposable household income

In 1983 in the UK total personal income was £258,382 m. After taxes and national insurance contributions, total personal disposable income was £204,652 m. £22,232 m. of this latter amount was 'disposed' of in the form of personal savings. Various forms of savings also compete for household income, since savings are a source of welfare in that they satisfy the need to feel that future living standards can be protected.

Because of the **effect of inflation** upon the purchasing power of households, this must be taken into account when discussing how the demand for various goods and services is likely to respond to a change in income. Thus the data on real disposable income in Table 8.2 gives the change in purchasing power because an allowance has been made for the fact that some of the increase in income would immediately have been absorbed by the need to pay higher prices for the various goods and services.

Between 1979 and 1980, for example, total personal disposable income rose from £136,648 m. to £161,328 m. But once account is taken of the general increase in prices over the year the level of real disposable income rose by approximately only 1·2 per cent. It is important therefore that money and disposable income are adjusted to produce real disposable income.

Another important assumption when tracing the effect of possible changes in real disposable income upon the demand for various goods and services is that the existing distribution of income between different groups of the community remains unchanged. This is because changes in the level of real disposable income accompanied by a **redistribution** of real disposable income will change the anticipated pattern of consumer expenditure.

Suppose, for example, that there is a change in the distribution of income in favour of the lower income groups as total income rises. The rise in average real disposable incomes may then produce an increase in the demand for certain goods and services larger than one would have anticipated when simply looking at the rise in average real disposable incomes as a possible reason for the increase in demand. There may, for example, be an increase in the demand for food products and the more essential household items larger than would have been the case if the previous distribution of income had been maintained.

Similarly, a rise in income that coincides with a redistribution in favour of the higher income groups may produce a larger than anticipated increase in the demand for the goods and services upon which such groups tend to spend their disposable income. Moreover the total increase in spending may not be as large as expected because the higher income groups also tend to save a larger proportion of an increase in their disposable incomes.

Certain income groups for example may succeed in obtaining a wage or salary increase significantly in excess of the rate of inflation, while others experience an increase in their income well below the rate of inflation; but throughout the economy in general the average increase in income is approximately the same as the rate of inflation, and thus total real disposable income shows no significant change. Nevertheless there will be a change in the pattern of consumer expenditure. One group has experienced a rise in its real disposable income while the other group has suffered a fall in its real disposable income.

Fig. 8.4 contains the demand curve X, which shows that the demand for this particular product varies directly with the average level of real disposable income. As they become better off, households have the opportunity of increasing their purchase of items that will add to their total satisfaction with the obvious advantage of not having to cut the purchase of other products. The consumer will distribute an increase in real disposable income in such a way that, having regard to relative prices and the satisfaction derived from various products, a new equilibrium will be reached and satisfaction again maximised within the budget imposed by this higher real disposable income.

Demand curve Y in Fig. 8.4 shows the case where demand increases at first, and then actually

Fig. 8.4

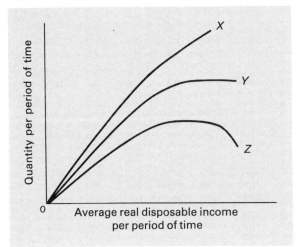

Fig. 8.5

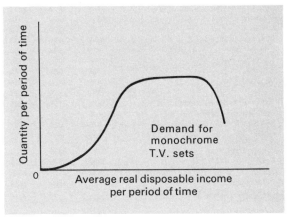

remains constant at a certain quantity per period of time despite further increases in income. Table 8.1 shows this to be virtually the case with items of food, suggesting that once incomes have reached a certain level these needs are completely satisfied. The consumer may, however, alter the composition of food consumption in favour of those items which could not be purchased on a lower income.

There is also the possibility, as shown by demand curve Z in Fig. 8.4, that the demand for some products may eventually fall once incomes reach a certain level. This will be the case when the higher income allows the consumer to replace some existing purchases with what are regarded as superior substitutes. Table 8.2 shows, for example, that coal and coke have experienced a decline in domestic demand as households have been able to afford superior means of heating.

In the long run, virtually all products are replaced by superior substitutes, and this is the driving force that helps to maintain the momentum of industrial and commercial organisations. Research and development produce new materials and technologies that are incorporated into new or improved products. Producers will then inform the market of the superior nature of these products through advertising as higher incomes widen the market for them.

Fig. 8.5 shows the life cycle of monochrome television sets. On the assumption that income is not evenly distributed, there will be some televisions demanded at a low average income as the better off will be able to purchase them. As average household income increases, a larger number of households will have reached a level of income which allows them to purchase a television set, while perhaps some of the higher-income households will purchase a second set. Eventually a position will be reached when the demand is completely satisfied.

In order to maintain sales, producers may restyle the sets to make them more attractive and to induce households to replace their existing models. Any additional increase in sales may then require the development of a set that is a very superior product, which higher incomes allow households to purchase as a substitute for their existing models. This has been the case with colour television sets. In 1976 nearly 96 per cent of households in the UK possessed a television set, and the market had been virtually saturated for many years. The development of colour sets, however, gave fresh impetus to sales as there was a substantial increase in the replacement demand. In 1969 colour sets accounted for 15.5 per cent of total sales, whereas by 1974 they had already reached 74·4 per cent of sales.

The life cycle of many products can be identified, although in some cases the fall may eventually be arrested and even off at a lower level. For example, as real disposable incomes increase, the demand for bread may fall; but some bread will still be consumed because of the advantages bread may possess in terms of food value, convenience and versatility in its uses.

Table 8.2: Consumers' expenditure at 1980 prices

£ million

	1973	1974	1975	1976	1977	1978	1979	1980	1981	1982	1983
Food (household expenditure): total	22,442	22,122	22,001	22,159	21,883	22,501	22,893	22,873	22,676	22,587	22,858
Bread and cereals	3121	3053	3017	3044	3034	3034	3055	3056	3086	3105	3117
Meat and bacon	5761	5809	5976	5971	6116	6272	6475	6471	6275	6228	6093
Fish	703	625	688	690	635	648	668	731	750	752	778
Milk, cheese and eggs	3657	3606	3613	3617	3480	3520	3480	3423	3341	3303	3329
Oils and fats	939	939	952	937	927	950	931	920	894	861	849
Fruit	1208	1173	1133	1203	1105	1148	1193	1273	1248	1185	1255
Potatoes	786	786	730	644	675	750	779	789	823	843	898
Vegetables	1476	1432	1456	1449	1452	1540	1563	1621	1659	1618	1669
Sugar	391	375	325	353	348	345	332	322	320	298	284
Preserves and confectionery	2237	2158	1949	2013	2026	2098	2054	1959	2032	2141	2181
Coffee, tea and cocoa	740	787	760	770	665	694	733	746	734	732	819
Soft drinks	618	637	701	763	735	776	874	856	815	843	873
Other manufactured food	855	800	772	791	719	726	756	706	699	678	713
Alcoholic drink: total	9211	9435	9350	9448	9487	9930	10,382	9954	9612	9383	9730
Beer	5394	5396	5567	5623	5467	5548	5588	5320	5000	4838	4914
Spirits	2334	2495	2378	2325	2428	2616	2890	2720	2561	2428	2494
Wine, cider and perry	1522	1564	1459	1554	1618	1766	1904	1914	2051	2117	2322
Tobacco	5309	5247	4995	4821	4602	4982	4960	4822	4470	4128	4082
Clothing and footwear: total	8346	8244	8354	8406	8529	9333	9996	9863	10,170	10,734	11,683
Clothing other than footwear	6860	6750	6828	6838	6961	7596	8149	8103	8334	8676	9405
Footwear	1476	1487	1522	1569	1565	1737	1847	1760	1836	2058	2278
Housing: total	16,961	17,152	17,191	17,346	17,626	17,979	18,483	18,827	19,041	19,388	19,814
Rents, rates and water charges	14,121	14,387	14,655	14,941	15,232	15,516	15,790	16,044	16,279	16,530	16,764
Maintenance, etc. by occupiers	2835	2761	2534	2406	2394	2463	2693	2783	2762	2858	3050
Fuel and power: total	6145	6253	6107	6050	6202	6314	6622	6353	6335	6211	6220
Electricity	3399	3407	3308	3239	3275	3303	3425	3370	3314	3237	3245
Gas	1143	1244	1343	1425	1496	1627	1816	1851	1942	1946	1986
Coal and coke	1085	1138	959	851	865	790	797	677	667	654	626
Other	672	592	571	582	603	594	584	455	412	374	363
Household goods and services: total	10,286	9816	9512	9615	9117	9787	10,354	9937	9791	10,001	10,629
Furniture and floor coverings	3403	3151	3278	3417	3155	3322	3696	3429	3354	3424	3724
Major appliances	1869	1807	1625	1685	1597	1784	2018	1997	1950	2056	2225
Other household goods	3288	3218	3086	3100	3061	3355	3291	3123	3126	3164	3330
Household and domestic services	1760	1673	1551	1422	1313	1326	1349	1388	1361	1357	1350
Transport and communication: total	20,470	18,948	19,062	19,598	19,374	21,022	22,499	22,462	22,628	22,923	24,861
Cars, motorcycles and other vehicles	6365	4855	5152	5325	4725	5804	6668	6307	6366	6510	7909
Petrol and oil	4256	4125	4044	4294	4333	4445	4492	4604	4657	4827	4909
Vehicle excise duty	622	619	631	637	638	670	682	726	701	755	811
Other running costs of vehicles	3223	3274	3276	3399	3541	3719	3768	3768	3820	3892	4009
Rail travel	1075	1072	1034	961	1023	1073	1102	1088	1041	919	1035
Buses and coaches	2012	1988	1921	1823	1756	1655	1633	1498	1407	1344	1407
Air travel	982	894	956	971	980	1121	1332	1510	1639	1700	1670
Other travel	670	650	608	598	604	621	671	715	719	688	723
Communications	1488	1542	1534	1633	1733	1914	2151	2246	2278	2288	2388
Recreation, entertainment and education: total	10,468	10,825	10,733	11,075	11,333	11,989	12,478	12,621	12,772	13,132	13,615
Radio, television and other durable goods	1037	1078	1076	1203	1243	1374	1581	1587	1816	2203	2601
TV and video rental, licence fees, etc.	1019	1163	1252	1386	1419	1482	1547	1578	1626	1706	1828
Recreational goods not elsewhere specified	2820	3076	3080	3055	3016	3189	3401	3538	3575	3640	3799
Recreational and entertainment services	2994	2930	2814	2825	2902	3032	3015	2970	2805	2722	2711
Books, newspapers and magazines	2044	1999	1892	1831	1822	1840	1856	1856	1805	1744	1671
Education	761	740	736	810	964	1072	1078	1092	1145	1117	1005
Other goods and services: total	16,455	16,549	16,545	16,500	16,872	17,234	17,709	17,248	16,867	17,184	18,078
Pharmaceutical products and medical goods	556	560	531	528	506	536	559	575	564	562	574
NHS payments and other medical expenses	619	611	542	559	588	594	632	684	754	839	921
Toilet articles; perfumery	1469	1484	1389	1341	1302	1359	1419	1337	1398	1439	1493
Hairdressing and beauty care	873	852	815	792	797	799	804	783	757	763	773
Jewellery, etc. and other goods	2335	2485	2433	2528	2686	2893	2802	2349	2368	2431	2325
Catering (meals and accommodation)	7773	7569	7643	7649	7778	7736	7964	7853	7269	7146	7644
Life assurance, etc. costs and other services	2814	2962	3149	3085	3211	3317	3529	3667	3757	4004	4348
Real disposable income at 1980 prices	144,064	142,831	143,296	142,499	140,921	150,696	159,080	161,185	157,263	157,564	161,319

Source: *Annual Abstract of Statistics* (HMSO, 1985).

Table 8.2 shows how the demand for various categories of goods and services may have been influenced by changes in real disposable incomes. Just as money disposable income needs to be converted into real disposable income in order to make valid comparisons between different years, it is also necessary to change money expenditure into real expenditure.

In 1973, for example, the total amount of money spent on air travel was in fact £567 m. But when this amount is reflated and expressed in terms of the general level of air fares that existed in 1980 it represents spending of £982 m. Similarly, the amount spent on air travel in 1983 was £2142 m. But when this is deflated to the fares of 1980 it amounts to £1670 m. This means that between 1973 and 1983 the total money expenditure on air travel rose by 277 per cent, but real expenditure rose by only 70 per cent. Thus because Table 8.1 has expressed expenditure at 1980 prices it is possible to identify and compare changes in the *quantities* of goods and services purchased in different years.

In analysing the data in Table 8.2, bear in mind that some of the changes in the patterns of demand could have been caused by consumers switching between certain items that they regard as substitutes because of changes in relative prices. In the case of gas and electricity, for example, the increase in the demand for gas could have been produced by a combination of higher real disposable incomes and gas prices rising less rapidly than electricity prices over much of the period covered. We also need to take account of possible changes in tastes and preferences that could have influenced demand.

Nevertheless the magnitude of some of the changes in demand that can be identified in Table 8.2 does suggest that increases in average real disposable incomes were a major influence on the pattern of expenditure emerging over the period covered. It is also possible to see the effect of the economic recession and higher unemployment in the years after 1979.

A useful exercise for the reader at this stage is to plot the total expenditure between 1973 and 1983 on some of the goods and services in Table 8.2 against the level of real disposable income. This will prove a useful guide to how demand for various goods and services responds to changes in the level of real disposable income.

Since increases in real disposable incomes are the result of disposable incomes rising faster than the general level of prices, it is important to review the factors that help to produce this increase in purchasing power. In Chapter 6 it was described how a combination of economies of scale and advances in science and technology allowed organisations to offset to varying degrees the impact of higher input prices upon their unit costs of production. In the long run, therefore, they are able to moderate their price increases, and this is particularly important for those organisations operating in a highly competitive market. In particular organisations have to cope with wage and salary increases, which increase the price of labour.

Organisations generally respond to a rise in the cost of labour by ensuring that other costs are kept to a minimum and by raising the productivity of labour. If the output per employee can be increased, then this will help to moderate the increase in the labour costs per unit of output; along with other cost-saving programmes it will lead to a price increase that is a smaller percentage increase than the rise in the price of labour.

If this happens throughout the economy as a whole, then prices in general will rise less than the price of labour, i.e. the wages and salaries received by households. The end result, assuming that other factors such as tax rates remain unchanged, is a rise in real disposable incomes – or, looked at from another point of view, a fall in the general level of real prices.

There is, therefore, a very important link between productivity and real disposable incomes. If, for example, pay and salaries rise by an average of 10 per cent while productivity in the economy as a whole rises by only 2 per cent, then prices are likely to rise on average by about 8 per cent. Income tax and national insurance contributions will be deducted from the extra income received by households, and the final rise in average real disposable income will, therefore, be less than 2 per cent. If productivity had risen by 4 per cent, then the general increases in prices would have been smaller and this would have meant a larger increase in the average level of real disposable income.

Similarly, if pay and salaries rise by an average of only 6 per cent, but productivity as a whole rises by 4 per cent, then the rise in average real disposable income is higher than is the case of a 10 per cent rise in incomes and a productivity rise of 2 per cent.

5. Demand and changes in tastes and preferences
Tastes and preferences are an area upon which producers seek to operate by the use of persuasive

advertising suggesting that greater satisfaction can be achieved by purchasing a particular product rather than its alternatives. There may be certain features of the product that make it superior and attractive as incomes rise, but it is assumed here that tastes and preferences may stem directly from consumers and be expressed in a change in the pattern of expenditure.

For example, there are many ways of filling leisure time. Increased preference for sporting activities would be reflected in the increased demand for sports equipment and sportswear. The growth of DIY and garden centres, and the increasing range of what they offer to their customers, is to some extent a reflection of the trend towards these particular uses of leisure time. Eating habits may also change, as has occurred in the UK with the increased popularity of foreign dishes. The consumption of food may also be influenced by factors that cause consumers to be more discriminating between alternatives on the basis of calories or cholesterol content, and ingredients of a health food or nutritional nature.

This influence on demand can also be seen in the market for consumer durables as, for example, the popularity of hatchback cars and cassette-players. Male toiletries have also been a rapid growth area in recent years, as men have shown a greater interest in various lotions and talcs, which previously were in minority use. Fashion is an important element in some purchases, and this may give rise to an increase in the demand for denim, cheesecloth and leather at the expense of other materials from which clothing is made. An important feature of tastes and preferences is that although some may seem to have led to permanent changes in demand, trends may eventually develop that reverse the process and traditional products can regain their popularity.

Other important factors that influence the level and pattern of demand arise out of long-run **demographic changes.** As was described in Chapter 2, changes in the population with respect to its size, age and social structure, its geographical distribution and its occupational structure will have repercussions upon organisations supplying goods and services in both the private and public sectors.

The elasticity of demand

As one factor that influences demand alters,

producers will be concerned about the repercussions of this change upon the demand for their products. The producer may be aware of the direction of this change in demand but will be equally concerned about its expected magnitude. The elasticity of demand is used to determine the size of this change as it measures the extent to which the quantity demanded responds to a change in one of the factors that influence demand. If a value can be attached to these elasticities, the producer may be able to estimate the total effect upon demand of one or more of these factors changing at the same time.

1. The price elasticity of demand

This is a means of measuring the extent to which the demand for a product responds to a change in the price of that product. Figs. 8.6 and 8.7 show demand curves relating to two different products, X and Y. When the prices of the two goods are raised from OX_1 to OX_2 and OY_1 to OY_2 respectively, the demand for good X is much less sensitive to this price change than is the demand for good Y. The percentage increase in price is the same in both cases, but the percentage fall in the demand for good X is much smaller than the percentage fall in the demand for good Y. Similarly, if one starts at the prices OX_2 and OY_2 and then lowers them to OX_1 and OY_1 respectively, the percentage increase in the demand

Fig. 8.6

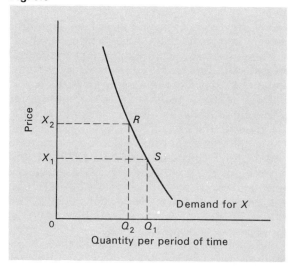

Fig. 8.7

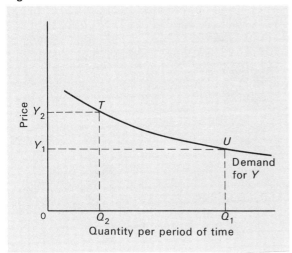

for good X is much smaller than the percentage increase in the demand for good Y.

As far as the price change in Fig. 8.6 is concerned, the demand for X does not prove to be very sensitive and is said to be inelastic in that the percentage change in price is met by a smaller percentage change in the quantity demanded.

In Fig. 8.7 however, the demand for Y shows itself to be much more sensitive and is said to be elastic as the percentage change in price is met by a larger percentage change in the quantity demanded. A numerical value can be given to this **price elasticity of demand** (E^d) by the following formula:

$$\text{Price } E^d = \frac{\text{percentage change in the quantity demanded}}{\text{percentage change in price}}$$

An example will help to illustrate this means of determining the E^d. When the price of petrol is raised from £2 to £2·25 a gallon, the demand falls from 10 million gallons to 9·5 million gallons per period of time. The rise in price amounts to an increase of $12\frac{1}{2}$ per cent whereas the percentage fall in the demand for petrol is 5 per cent. Using the above formula, this produces a price E^d for petrol in this price range of 0·4. For every 1 per cent increase in the price of petrol there is a 0·4 per cent change in the demand, and as long as the formula produces a value of less than one, then demand is said to be inelastic within this price range.

Another example can be used to illustrate the case where demand proves to be elastic with respect

to a change in prices. When the price of lager is increased from 90p to £1 a pint, the demand for lager falls from 5 million pints to 4 million pints per period of time. The rise in price amounts to an 11·1 per cent change, while the fall in the quantity demanded is a 20 per cent change. The formula for the price E^d produces a value of 1·8 per cent for lager within this price range, and for every 1 per cent change in price there is a 1·8 per cent change in demand. As long as a value greater than one is achieved, then demand is said to be elastic.

Producers will be concerned not only about the extent to which the demand will respond to a rise in the market price, but also with how sensitive demand is to a fall in the market price. This is because the total expenditure on a product and hence the total revenue earned from sales by producers will depend upon the direction of the price change and the demand for the product. The following analysis will concentrate upon a general price increase or decrease brought about by all the producers in a particular market raising or lowering their prices by approximately the same percentage in response to increases or decreases in the prices they pay for certain inputs, such as raw materials and components.

If demand is inelastic, then an increase in price will raise total revenue, while a reduction in price will reduce total revenue. This can be seen in Fig. 8.6. If the price is OX_1 then the total revenue earned from sales is the price OX_1 multiplied by the quantity which consumers are prepared to purchase, which is OQ_1. This can be represented by the area OX_1SQ_1. If the price is raised to OX_2 then the total revenue is represented by OX_2RQ_2. Since OX_2RQ_2 is greater than OX_1SQ_1 then producers have succeeded in raising total revenue because, although sales have fallen, this is more than outweighed by the higher price obtained from each of the units still being sold. If one starts at OX_2 then total revenue falls from OX_2RQ_2 to OX_1SQ_1, since although sales have increased this is more than outweighed by the lower price which was necessary to induce a greater demand.

Similarly, if demand is elastic, as in Fig. 8.7, then a fall in price will raise total revenue from OY_2TQ_2 to OY_1UQ_1 as the reduction in price does not have to be substantial to attract greater sales which are large enough to outweigh the lower price received per unit sold. Similarly, if the price is raised in Fig. 8.7, then total revenue falls from OY_1UQ_1 to OY_2TQ_2, as the rise in price is more than outweighed by the fall in demand.

As far as producers are concerned when contemplating a price change, they are primarily interested in whether or not demand is likely to prove elastic or inelastic. There are certain areas of elasticity of interest to the student of economic theory, but the descriptions elastic or inelastic will suffice to deal with the majority of cases when dealing with the response of demand to a change in price.

The value of the price E^d will vary according to the current position of price and demand in relation to the market demand curve and possible changes in the slope of this demand curve. In Fig. 8.8 the initial price is £9, as a result of which consumers are willing to purchase 12 units. Although this part of the demand curve is very steep, this does not necessarily imply that demand is inelastic, as a fall in price to £8 is a relatively small percentage change when compared with the percentage increase in demand which this price reduction produces. Thus a price of £9 produces a total revenue of £108 while a price of £8 produces an increase in total to £120, as shown in the table attached to Fig. 8.8. If, however, the price is lowered further from £8 to £7, this is met by a smaller percentage increase in demand as total revenue falls from £120 to £112. As one moves downwards along this steep part of the demand curve, the percentage fall in price is increasing while the percentage increase in demand is falling. Thus the demand is becoming increasingly inelastic, as shown by the fall in total revenue produced by a reduction in price from £7 to £6.

Fig. 8.8

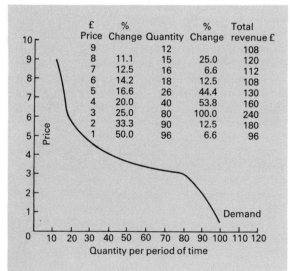

£ Price	% Change	Quantity	% Change	Total revenue £
9		12		108
8	11.1	15	25.0	120
7	12.5	16	6.6	112
6	14.2	18	12.5	108
5	16.6	26	44.4	130
4	20.0	40	53.8	160
3	25.0	80	100.0	240
2	33.3	90	12.5	180
1	50.0	96	6.6	96

Eventually, however, the demand for this particular product becomes much more sensitive to price reductions and it must have entered a range that makes it more attractive to a larger number of consumers working within the constraints imposed by their income and other prices, and engaging in spending which maximises their respective level of satisfaction. For example, a price reduction from £6 to £5 produces a larger percentage change in demand as total revenue increases from £108 to £130. Demand is now entering a price range where it proves elastic, and as long as this is the case, the firm will be adding to its total revenue as it lowers its price. Below a price of £3, demand becomes inelastic again as additional price reductions promote significantly smaller percentage increases in demand. In fact a price reduction from £3 to £2 is a change of 33·3 per cent yet the percentage increase in demand is only 12·5 per cent.

If consumers are to be persuaded to buy more, then as far as this product is concerned a large price reduction is necessary. The diminishing marginal utility that they derive from extra units must be met by a large reduction in price to make such extra purchases worth while when compared with the satisfaction which must be given up elsewhere in order to finance such purchases. This reduced sensitivity of demand to further price reductions is shown by the steep nature of the final section of the demand curve.

The fortunes of an industry as a whole are, therefore, closely connected with the extent to which its customers will respond to a price change. An increase in the price of petrol, for example, caused by a rise in the price of crude oil will not lead to a significant reduction in petrol sales, because the demand for petrol tends to be very inelastic. Companies in the petroleum industry can be reasonably confident, therefore, that there will be only a slight reduction in the demand for their output and they can earn the extra revenue to cover their higher costs. They will also be aware, however, that a general fall in petrol prices will not increase the total market by an amount to make such a price reduction worth while.

Similarly, a rise in the price of meat and meat products brought about by a rise in the price of animal feed or processing costs will not produce a marked reduction in the demand for such products. At the same time, a substantial price reduction may be necessary to encourage consumers to purchase even a slightly larger quantity of such products.

In the case of video-recorders, a general increase in their price of, say, 10 per cent may produce a larger percentage reduction in the industry's annual sales, because many people who were potential buyers and considered them value for money at the previous price may now be deterred from purchasing them. If the producers could find a way of reducing their prices by 10 per cent, this may be a sufficiently large price reduction to expand the industry's sales by more than 10 per cent; this is because the price cut will enable the industry to capture those households that previously regarded video-recorders as not giving sufficient value for money at their original prices.

The demand for fruit juices may also prove to be elastic with response to a price change. Many of the existing consumers may regard them as coming somewhere near the bottom of their list of priorities, and a price rise may cause many people not to buy them at all, and others to buy them less frequently or in smaller cartons. On the other hand, there may be a large number of consumers who believe that at their current price fruit juices do not represent sufficient value for money, and that they would be better off buying other food products or beverages. These consumers, however, have been only marginally lost to the producers and may be persuaded to buy if faced with slightly lower prices. A price reduction may also encourage existing customers to increase the amount of fruit juice they are buying at the moment.

The value of the price E is also of major importance to the government when seeking to raise money from indirect taxes in the form of excise duties and VAT. In the financial year 1983–4 the government raised £35·5 billion from various indirect taxes: taxes of petrol contributed £6·2 bn., tobacco £4·1 bn., beer £1·8 bn., spirits £1·2 bn., wine £600 m., car tax (not to be confused with the road-fund licence) £740 m. and VAT contributed £18·5 bn. Excise duties have been heavily concentrated therefore upon those products that are in inelastic demand, so that the government can be confident that when these taxes are raised it will collect more revenue. If demand was not inelastic then the tax increase would produce a reduction in the quantity purchased more than outweighing the increased amount of tax per unit sold, and the result would be a fall in tax revenues.

A tax that had a significant impact upon the demand for a product would obviously affect the future prospects of that industry. The firms involved would have to make even greater efforts to minimise their costs in order to avoid additional price increases that would depress the market demand even further.

VAT is more widely spread throughout the economy and is not levied on essential items such as certain food products and children's clothing. Nevertheless there is the possibility that VAT could be extended to cover goods and services not taxed at the moment, and this could have an effect upon their total sales. In recent years VAT has been extended to include home improvements and take-away foods.

In the 1970s the government experimented with a two-tier rate of VAT: a standard rate of $12\frac{1}{2}$ per cent and a rate of 25 per cent on 'luxury' goods such as domestic appliances. The latter had such an adverse effect upon certain parts of the consumer durables industry that the higher rate soon had to be abandoned.

Table 8.2 on page 124 suggests that higher excise duties could be one of the factors that has either slowed down or reduced the demand for tobacco products, beer and spirits.

Factors that influence the price E^d

The price E^d for a product will depend upon several factors:

(a) *If the product has very close substitutes, a price change can be expected to create relatively large changes in demand over a wide range of prices.* At this point it is important to distinguish between the demand for a product in general and the demand for a particular type or variety of a product. The market demand for petrol as the product of the petroleum industry is inelastic, but the demand for the petrol produced by any single company that helps to make up the industry may prove to be very sensitive to a price change. This is because the average motorist regards the different brands of petrol as being more or less perfect substitutes for each other. In this case even a small price change by one petrol company is likely to have a significant impact upon its sales, and this would be reflected in a very elastic demand curve for that particular company's petrol, although the market demand curve for petrol as a whole is very inelastic.

Similarly the market demand for paint may be relatively inelastic, but the demand for any particular brand of paint could prove to be relatively elastic, as many consumers may regard the various paints as close substitutes for each other. The greater the degree of brand loyalty displayed by its customers then the smaller the number of consumers lost to competing brands if the company has to raise its price. At the same time, however, a price reduction will not necessarily produce a significant increase in sales, as other companies will also have their loyal consumers who are not easily attracted by a fall in the price of a competing product.

Depending upon the nature of the product, producers seek to strengthen the loyalty of their customers by concentration upon such features as quality, design, style, performance, ingredients, material, packaging and after-sales service. They also ensure that any such relevant features and other characteristics of the product are brought to the attention of consumers through advertising.

Thus the price E^d for a product can be viewed from the point of view of the total market demand for a product or service in general or the demand for a particular product or service produced by a company that operates in that market.

(b) *There is often a temptation to conclude that the demand for necessities is inelastic while the demand for luxuries is elastic.* Definitions of 'luxuries' and 'necessities' depend upon the type of consumer one is dealing with. Some people may regard dishwashers or microwave ovens as a very necessary part of the way they run their homes; whereas others may regard them as luxuries when compared with other demands upon their income. At one time, freezers, music centres and colour TV sets were seen as distinct luxuries, but many people now treat such consumer durables as essential items when first setting up home. Nevertheless necessities can be identified as products that consumers continue to purchase in significant quantities despite a substantial price rise; e.g. petrol, heating and lighting, and essential food products.

(c) *The price E^d for a product or service will also depend upon the proportion of disposable income accounted for by the expenditure on that product or service over a certain period of time.* Demand may prove inelastic if expenditure is a small part of disposable income. A rise in the price of ballpoint pens or shoe polish will not seriously affect the demand for such items. This is because, even a very large percentage increase in their prices may not cause consumers to economise on their use, as the savings might not be considered worth while.

(d) *The purchase of some products and services is dictated by personal habits, which leads the consumer to regard them in some sense as necessities.* This would include tobacco, tea, coffee and alcoholic drinks.

(e) *With some products the demand may be more inelastic in the short run than in the long run.* This is because a reaction to a price change may involve consumers in a complementary expenditure. A fall in the price of gas relative to electricity will not cause an immediate rise in the demand for gas, because such decisions will be taken when existing heating and cooking systems need replacing.

The longer the time period considered, the greater the number of households that have to make such a choice. Moreover, as time passes new homes will be set up, and this will influence the choice of first-time buyers. The relative fall in the price of gas may, however, cause some increase in the short run, since those about to install heating systems for the first time may be persuaded to change their plans and opt for gas as a fuel rather than for electricity.

2. The income elasticity of demand

This refers to the responsiveness of demand to a change in real disposable income and is measured as follows:

$$\text{Income } E^d = \frac{\text{percentage change in the quantity demanded}}{\text{percentage change in real disposable income}}$$

If, for example, average real disposable income rises from £80 to £120 per week and the quantity of long-playing records demanded rises from 30 million to 40 million per period of time, these amount to changes of 50 per cent and 33·3 per cent respectively. Using the above formula, this produces an income E^d of 0·6 per cent, which means that for every 1 per cent rise in real disposable income the demand for records increases by 0·6 per cent. As far as this range of real disposable income is concerned, demand is said to be inelastic as it has a value less than one.

If, however, a percentage change in the level of real disposable income is met by a larger percentage change in the demand for a product, demand is said to be elastic. The value of the income E^d will depend upon the product in question and the existing level of real disposable income. As real disposable incomes rise from very low levels, households will increase their purchases of those products which play an important part in satisfying their most urgent needs. The income E^d for food, heating, basic items of clothing, and essential furnishings, for example, will be positive and possibly increase as real disposable incomes first rise. Once, however, a certain level of real disposable income is reached the income E^d for them will start to fall, and when the demand remains constant the income E^d will be zero. Further increases in real disposable income may then lead to an increase in the demand for consumer durables, and those goods and services associated with entertainment and recreational activities, while some of the existing purchases may be replaced with superior substitutes. The availability of superior products means that as real disposable incomes rise the income E^d for those actually replaced will become negative.

Fig. 8.5 (page 123), dealing with the demand for monochrome television sets, can be used to illustrate areas of income E^d. The initial part of this demand curve shows that percentage increases in real disposable income cause smaller percentage increases in the demand for such television sets. As the gradient of the curve increases, this indicates that demand is becoming more sensitive to changes in real disposable income, and eventually the income E^d becomes greater than one. The demand for monochrome television sets then becomes less responsive as sales reach their maximum and the value of the income E^d falls. When the demand curve levels off, the income E^d has reached zero, and then displays an increasingly larger negative value when it starts to fall. If, for example, the income E^d at higher levels of real disposable income is -1.5, a 10 per cent rise in income will produce a 15 per cent fall in the demand for monochrome sets.

The income E^d is important for a producer, as sales will depend not only upon their relative competitive position in a market, but also upon what is happening to the total market in which the producer is selling. Those engaged in products with a low income E^d will need to direct a great deal of effort towards capturing a greater share of a stable market by persuading consumers that their particular product is superior to that of its competitors. Producers of household cleansers and foodstuffs would come into this category and can be expected to monitor tastes and preferences very closely to gain a competitive advantage.

Producers of some consumer durables may also be faced with what is virtually a saturated market, and those involved in vacuum cleaners and refrigerators, for example, will attempt to increase replacement demand by developing superior products. In other cases, there will be producers dealing in products which have a high income E^d, such as domestic appliances, more sophisticated furnishings and household goods and those goods and services associated with recreation and entertainment. Further increases in real disposable income may then also leave these latter producers with a saturated market and a need to develop superior products, or – like many firms – seek to diversify into new and growing areas of demand for which they see trends developing.

If real disposable incomes were to fall, however, producers of products with a high income E^d may experience a recession in their markets, as not only would sales not be maintained but the actual fall in real disposable income may cause consumers to react by reducing their replacement demand.

3. The cross-elasticity of demand

This refers to the extent to which the demand for one product responds to a change in the price of another product. This concept is particularly noticeable with products which are regarded as substitute or complementary products. For example, if the price of coffee rises from £1 to £1·50 per jar and the demand for tea rises from 1 million to 1·25 million packets per period of time, a 50 per cent rise in the price of coffee has caused a 25 per cent increase in the demand for tea. The formula for the cross-E^d would be:

$$\text{Cross-}E^d = \frac{\text{percentage change in the demand for tea}}{\text{percentage change in the price of coffee}}$$

The cross-E^d for tea, with respect to a change in the price of coffee, would thus be 0·5. For every 1 per cent rise in the price of coffee there is a 0·5 per cent rise in the demand for tea.

The more closely that two products are regarded as substitutes the greater will be the value of the cross-elasticity of demand. If the bulk of the reduced demand for one product is transferred to another, the value of the cross-E^d will be correspondingly larger. If, however, there are a range of substitutes available, a rise in the price of one of them will result in a shift in demand which is more widely spread among the remaining products, and the cross-E^d will also be correspondingly smaller for any one of them. The value of the cross-E^d will also be smaller the less the opportunity for substituting one product for another.

The larger the cross-E^d the greater the increase in demand which a producer can expect to experience when there is a rise in the price of a substitute product, but equally important is the fact that he can expect to lose sales if the other product is reduced in price. This will act as an incentive for a producer to keep prices at a competitive level in order that an advantage can be derived from a price rise elsewhere, while hoping to minimise the loss of sales in the event of another product being reduced in price. As long as the cross-E^d is greater than zero, the producer benefiting from a switch of consumer expenditure will increase his total revenue as there will be more demand for this product at its existing price level. One of the objectives of continuing to monitor demand in a test market is to determine the effect upon a particular product of price changes in competing products, and so to be able to adjust and deal with these trends in the market as a whole.

A significant cross-E^d will also exist with products which are complements. If, for example, there was a change in the price of deep-freezes then this would have repercussions upon the demand for frozen foods designed for storage in deep-freezes. This again is a reason for continuing market research as trends in certain markets may open up profitable opportunities for products that are complementary to the product which is in increasing demand. The use of BMX bikes, for example, provided a market for producers of safety equipment. The research may show, however, that a complementary product is increasing in price which may lead to a significant reduction in sales and the need to seek alternative markets.

Profitability as a factor influencing supply

The following analysis of the factors that influence the supply of a product will initially concentrate upon the major influence exerted by the desire of a firm to make profits. When the objectives of organisations were discussed in Chapter 1, it was suggested that firms had several objectives, one of which was a desire to maximise profits. Other objectives, such as maximising sales or achieving a position of security, might involve the sacrifice of some profits so that maximum profits were not necessarily obtained. A conclusion was drawn, however, that when this sacrifice of short-run profits was analysed, there was not necessarily a conflict with other objectives when a longer period of time was considered.

For example, the aim of maximising sales while engaging in vertical and lateral expansion may have meant a level of profits which was not at the maximum. But the increased security derived from a larger market share and a degree of diversification would allow the firm to secure its future with a

view to ensuring profits in a later period. The firm will assess the position in the market for its own output, and also developments in other product markets and those where it purchases its resources. The firm will then adopt policies in pursuit of certain objectives that in its opinion will be in its long-run interest, and then concentrate upon maximising profits while adhering to those other objectives.

The firm will conduct its activities within the business environment, as dictated by developments in both product and resource markets and by the general economic, social and political climate. The possible sacrifice of profits can be likened to a cost which the firm is willing to accept because of the return which accrues in a non-monetary form. For example, the firm may have increasingly involved itself in producing or processing its own components or materials, when strictly speaking the resulting diversification may have resulted in a loss of some of the advantages stemming from increased specialisation. In this case, the firm will have placed a value upon the increased security which control over important inputs may bring. The extra costs and effect on profits that may be incurred as a result of this vertical expansion will produce a return in the form of increased security.

Similarly, accepting a lower profit margin in order to maintain or increase sales may place the firm in a stronger market position against its rivals, and this lower profit margin may be regarded as a price worth paying in order to reduce the strength of existing or potential competition. Also the firm may agree to comply with the government's current policies as they affect the company, as it may be in the interest of their long-term existence to do so.

Thus the pursuit of objectives that would seem to detract from maximum profits provides the constraints within which the firm is then able to seek maximum profits. It can be assumed, therefore, that the firm does seek to maximise profits and is prepared to accept what at first may seem non-profit-maximising activities.

The higher the price a firm can obtain for its product the more it is prepared to supply. Different levels of output will involve the firm in various levels of unit costs, and an increase in output will only be forthcoming if the price of the product in question is such that the extra output adds more to total revenue than it does to total costs, with the result that total profits increase. The supply from a firm will be dictated by the price of the product and the unit costs of producing it, as these two factors will dictate profitability. The determination of the level of output that a firm is prepared to supply in order to maximise profits can be shown with the use of diagrams which involve revenue curves and cost curves.

Revenue curves

It is assumed that a firm is faced with a demand curve as shown in Fig. 8.9. This curve shows that if the firm wishes to raise its prices, it must be prepared to accept a fall in the demand for its product. The important point about the market is that a firm cannot dictate both price and quantity sold. If it sets a price, it must then accept the amount which consumers are prepared to purchase at that price. Similarly, if it decides upon a level of output then the firm must be prepared to accept the price at which the market is willing to absorb that amount. Thus this demand curve provides us with information concerning the total revenue which the firm can expect to receive from various levels of sales.

As with Figs. 8.6 and 8.7 (on pages 126 and 127), any point on these demand curves is a combination of price and quantity and this was used to indicate the total revenue earned by the firm from these particular price and quantity combinations. Total revenue will differ according to which level of

Fig. 8.9

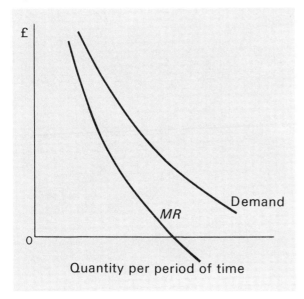

Quantity per period of time

output is selected and it proved useful to discover what happened to total revenue as output was changed. Comparing areas is a tedious and cumbersome process but a marginal revenue curve will provide this information on changes in total revenue.

Marginal revenue (MR) is defined as the addition to total revenue as a result of selling one more unit. If, for example, a firm is selling 8 units a week at £80 each, then the total revenue earned over this period is £640. In order to sell 9 units, however, the firm may be obliged to lower the price to £78 and the total revenue is now £702. In this case, the addition to total revenue as a result of selling the ninth unit is £62 (i.e. £702–£640). The firm gains an extra £78 by selling the extra unit, but it will have to lower the price of the existing 8 units to the same price which means that the extra £78 is partly offset by the reduced revenue from existing sales of £16. The firm is not in a position where it could charge 8 consumers £80 and the remaining consumer £78. If this same firm wished to sell 10 units, the price may have to be lowered to £75, which means that the marginal revenue of the tenth unit is £48 (i.e. £750–£702). An eleventh unit, involving a price of £70, will produce a marginal revenue of £20.

Thus the marginal revenue is always below the price received for each unit sold, and in Fig. 8.8 this is reflected in the fact that the marginal revenue curve lies below the demand curve. The gap between them also widens, as not only must greater price reductions be given to attract more sales, but these price reductions must be given on an increasingly large number of units.

As long as the marginal revenue schedule is above the horizontal axis, additional sales (although at a lower price) must be raising total revenue. This is because the marginal revenue, although falling, is still positive. This section of the demand curve must reflect an elastic market demand curve within the various price ranges, as any percentage fall in price is matched by a larger percentage increase in demand, and this leads to an increase in total revenue. Where the marginal revenue curve cuts the horizontal axis, the marginal revenue is zero and increased sales have left total revenue unchanged. When this is the case, it implies that the percentage fall in price was accompanied by an equal percentage increase in sales so that total revenue remained unchanged. The firm is now maximising its sales revenue but, as will be shown, it is not necessarily at a point where it is maximising its profits. Once marginal revenue becomes negative, however, this means that total revenue is now beginning to fall. For this to happen, the percentage fall in price must have been met by a smaller percentage increase in demand and thus the firm has reached an area where demand for its product is increasingly inelastic.

Another relevant point is that the extent to which the marginal revenue curve lies below the demand curve will be dictated by the general nature of the demand curve. If demand is essentially inelastic as in Fig. 8.10, very large price reductions are necessary to induce even a small increase in sales. Thus the marginal revenue will fall very rapidly soon becoming negative, and this reflects the generally inelastic nature of the demand curve itself. Fig. 8.11, however, shows a demand curve that is essentially elastic and only relatively small price reductions are necessary to stimulate extra demand, with the result that the marginal revenue falls more slowly and the point at which marginal revenue becomes negative is postponed till much later.

This is the basic information that one can derive from demand and marginal revenue curves and it is now possible to proceed with the determination of the output at which a firm will maximise profits. These revenue curves are combined with cost curves in Fig. 8.12 and the basic shape and direction of the cost curves facing this firm demonstrate their characteristics as explained in Chapter 6. The firm

Fig. 8.11

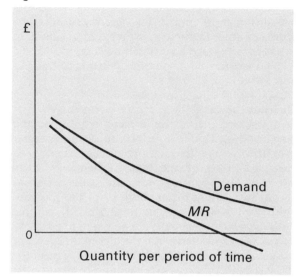

Quantity per period of time

will increase production until the last unit produced adds as much to total revenue as it does to total costs.

Fig. 8.12

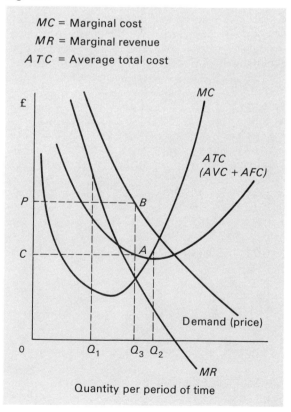

Quantity per period of time

Fig. 8.10

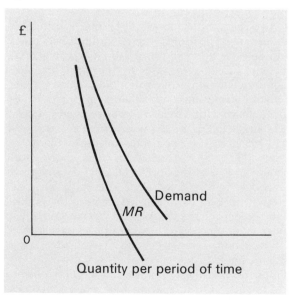

Quantity per period of time

If, for example, this firm was producing OQ_1 units then this would not be a level of output at which the firm would be making maximum profits. This is because additional units of output beyond OQ_1 would add more to total revenue than to total costs, as the marginal revenue associated with extra units of output is greater than the marginal costs of these extra units. Total profits will thus increase. Although the marginal revenue is falling and the marginal cost eventually rises, extra units will still increase total profits, but of course by progressively smaller amounts. Nevertheless the essential point is that it is profitable to expand output as long as marginal revenue is greater than marginal costs. Similarly, output OQ_2 would not represent a position where the firm would be maximising profits, as it has moved into an area of output where additional units of output have added more to total costs than to total revenue. This is because marginal cost is greater than marginal revenue, and the losses made on these higher units of output will start to reduce the total profits made on earlier units of output. The level of output where this firm will be making maximum profits is in fact at OQ_3.

The total cost incurred by this firm at OQ_3 will be that level of output multiplied by the average total costs of those units which make up OQ_3. In Fig. 8.12 this is represented by the area OQ_3AC. The total revenue derived from selling OQ_3 units is the same quantity multiplied by the price received per unit, which is OP. As predicted in Fig. 8.9, the selling price is greater than the marginal revenue resulting from the sale of the last unit. Total revenue is thus OQ_3BP. The total profits made by this firm are therefore $CABP$. This firm is more than covering its costs at OQ_3 and within costs is an element of profit which is regarded as normal profit. This is the minimum return that the firm is prepared to accept, taking account of the risks involved in this particular line of production. This normal profit must be covered for the venture to be worth while, and it can therefore be likened to a cost and is accordingly included in the average total cost curve. Since this firm is more than covering total costs, it is said to be making **super-normal profits**.

The effect of price and cost changes on supply

Profitability has thus dictated the amount of the product that this firm is willing to supply, and since profitability is determined by the revenue and cost curves, any change in these factors will influence profits and hence the supply of the product. A change in the demand for the product will mean that the firm is faced with a different revenue situation. Similarly, a change in the factors that influence total costs will mean that the firm is faced with a different cost situation. The repercussions of changes in these two situations on the firm will now be examined.

1. A change in demand

The demand curve with which the firm is faced shows the relationship between the price of the product and the quantity demanded, on the assumption that all other factors that influence the demand for the product remain unchanged. If the price of the product itself changes, the demand curve tells us what happens to the demand. A rise in the price in Fig. 8.13, for example, from OP_1 to OP_2, results in a *movement along* the existing demand curve indicating that the quantity demanded falls from OQ_1 to OQ_2. If price were lowered from OP_2 to OP_1, then again the increase in the quantity demanded is shown by a movement along the existing demand curve, indicating that the quantity demanded has increased from OQ_2 to OQ_1.

A change in any of the other factors that influence the demand for this product will cause the demand curve to *shift*. If, for example, there is an

Fig. 8.13

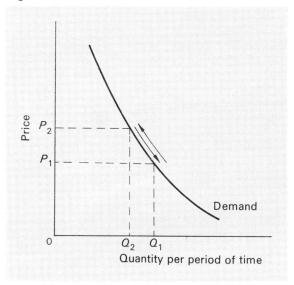

Quantity per period of time

increase in the average level of real disposable income and the income E^d for this product is positive, more of this product will be demanded at each price than previously. The producer can expect a percentage increase in the demand for his product at all the possible price levels. In Fig. 8.14, for example, consumers are now prepared to purchase the quantity OQ_4 at the price OP_1, rather than the quantity OQ_1; and at the price OP_2 they are now willing to buy OQ_3 rather than OQ_2. The demand schedule has shifted to the right from D_1 to D_2.

If the average level of real disposable income falls, however, then the demand for this product will be lower at each price than previously, as shown by the leftward shift of the curve in Fig. 8.15, from D_1 to D_2. At the price OP_1 the quantity demanded has fallen from OQ_1 to OQ_4, whereas at the price OP_2 demand has fallen from OQ_2 to OQ_3. The factors that can cause such a shift can be summarised as follows.

Rightward shift of demand
(a) A rise in average real disposable income.
(b) A rise in the price of a substitute.
(c) A fall in the price of a complement.
(d) A change in tastes and preferences in favour of the product.

Leftward shift of demand
(a) A fall in average real disposable income.
(b) A fall in the price of a substitute.
(c) A rise in the price of a complement.
(d) A change in the tastes and preferences away from the product.

There are other factors that may influence the demand for a product and thus cause a shift of the demand curve, such as a redistribution of income, a change in the size of the population and a change in the structure of the population. As will be shown in *Business Organisations and Environments Book 2*, demand can also be affected by the availability of credit and the level of interest rates.

Fig. 8.16 shows the effect of a rightward shift of the demand curve from D_1 to D_2 upon the amount which the firm is willing to produce. The higher price in fact makes the firm more profitable and it is therefore encouraged to expand output to make even higher profits. The cost situation and demand curve D_1 initially produced a level of output where profits were maximised at OQ_1, as this was the level of output where marginal cost was equal to

Fig. 8.14

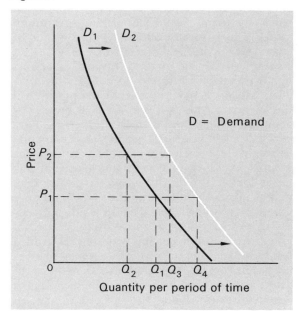

Fig. 8.15

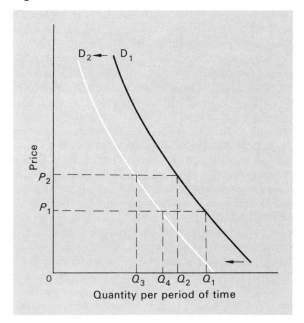

marginal revenue. The shift of the demand curve from D_1 to D_2 now means much higher profits at this level of output, as the price received for each of the units can be shown by continuing the vertical line from OQ_1 until it reaches the demand curve D_2. The difference between total revenue and total

Fig. 8.16

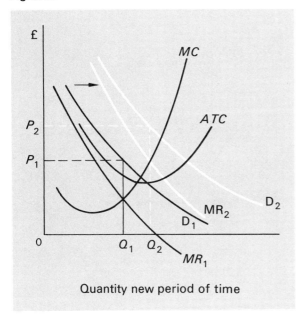

Quantity new period of time

costs at OQ_1 is now much larger. There is now every incentive to expand output as the demand curve D_2 has produced a new and higher marginal revenue curve MR_2. Therefore at output OQ_1 the marginal revenue is now greater than the marginal cost, and additional units of output will mean more is added to total revenue than to total costs. The firm will continue to expand output until once again a level of output is reached where marginal revenue is equal to marginal costs. Profits will be at a maximum at the output OQ_2, and had the firm remained at OQ_1 it would have been denying itself profitable units of output. The difference between total revenue and total costs at OQ_2 will be much larger than that which existed at OQ_1.

By extending the vertical line to D_2 the new and much higher price that existed at OQ_1 has fallen to OP_2. This was the result of the firm expanding output to take advantage of profits from higher output, and this would involve a lowering of price if the extra output was to be absorbed by the market. This is shown by a movement downwards along D_2. The firm was prepared to accept this fall in price as extra units of output still raised total profits.

This analysis can be reversed if one starts with the demand curve D_2 and then shifts it to D_1. The initial output is now one where marginal cost exceeds marginal revenue and output will be

contracted to OQ_1, where once again profits are being maximised, although at a lower level.

The conclusion is that the quantity supplied is influenced by profitability and the higher the price the larger the quantity the firm is prepared to supply, and the lower the price the smaller the quantity the firm is prepared to supply. This relationship between price and supply is thus reflected in the supply curve in Fig. 8.17 in that when the price is raised from OP_1 to OP_2 the quantity supplied is increased from OQ_1 to OQ_2, while a fall in price from OP_2 to OP_1 will lower supply from OQ_2 to OQ_1. This supply curve relates to the reaction of one producer to a change in price, and a market supply curve relating to the same type of product coming from all producers involved in the market would also slope upwards from left to right, showing the relationship between the price and the total quantity which will be supplied to the market. Since firms can expect to have different cost structures because, for example, of their size and productivity, a certain price will produce different levels of output from each firm within the market as a whole.

Fig. 8.17

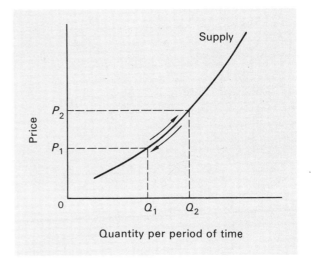

Quantity per period of time

Let us assume that the market for a particular product X is supplied by five different firms, and the quantities which each of them is prepared to supply at various price levels, so that each of them maximises its profits, is as shown in Table 8.3. The total of the individual amounts which each firm is willing to supply at each of the price levels can then be used to produce the market supply curve for the product *X* in Fig. 8.18. The most efficient is firm A because it can afford to supply more at each price than the others, indicating that its marginal costs do not rise as rapidly as the others; so firm A is thus provided with greater scope to increase output as the price increases. This is in contrast to firm E which experiences rapidly increasing marginal costs that soon reach the marginal revenue associated with any extra units it produces.

Table 8.3

Price in £s	Units of product X supplied per period of time					Total supply
	Firm A	Firm B	Firm C	Firm D	Firm E	
1	10	9	7	4	2	32
2	25	21	17	12	10	85
3	45	36	29	22	19	151
4	75	48	39	30	25	217
5	95	56	45	36	28	260
6	105	60	48	38	29	280

Fig. 8.18

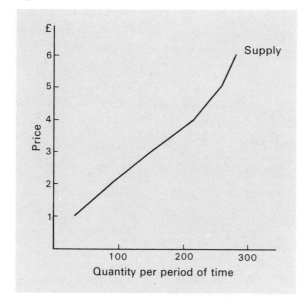

Quantity per period of time

2. A change in costs

The quantity that a firm is willing to supply will not only be influenced by the price it can obtain but also by changes in its costs of production. The firm analysed in Fig. 8.16 (page 137) was seen to respond

Fig. 8.19

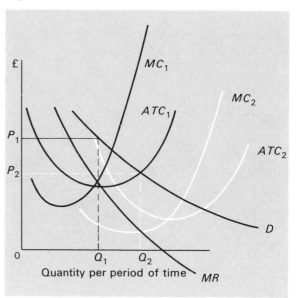

to a change in price brought about by a shift of the demand schedule, while operating within a certain cost structure. If, however, the cost structure changes, output will be associated with different average total costs and marginal costs.

The firm in Fig. 8.19 is initially maximising its profits at output OQ_1 where marginal cost is equal to marginal revenue. The existing cost curves are MC_1 and ATC_1 but these then change, perhaps because of advances in the technology employed in making the product. The level of output OQ_1 is no longer a level at which profits are maximised, as marginal revenue is now above the lower marginal cost curve MC_2 which reflects this improvement in technology. The firm is now in a position to increase profits by expanding output, as additional units of output will add more to total revenue than to total costs. Had the firm remained at OQ_1 it would have denied itself these profitable units of output. Profits will again be maximised at OQ_2, where again marginal revenue is equal to marginal costs, and where the difference between total revenue and total costs is now larger than that which existed at OQ_1. The firm was prepared to supply more, and to reduce the price of its product in order to encourage consumers to purchase the higher output, since extra units of output still raised profits because of the lowering of costs.

The effect of unfavourable changes in the firm's cost structure can be followed if one starts with the curves MC_2 and ATC_2 and replaces them with

MC_1 and ATC_2. If this happens, OQ_2 will not be a level of output where profits are maximised, as marginal cost as shown by MC_1 will be far in excess of the marginal revenue, and the firm will contract output to OQ_1 where it is maximising profits again but at a lower level of output.

Thus another conclusion about supply is that a fall in the costs of production will lead to an increase in the quantity supplied, while an increase in the costs of production will produce a fall in the quantity which producers are willing to supply at various price levels.

This reaction of producers to changes in costs can be seen in Figs. 8.20 and 8.21. The supply curve S_1 shows the relationship between price and the quantity supplied in a market for a product, on the assumption that all the other factors that influence supply remain unchanged. Developments that reduce the costs of production, such as an improvement in technology, a fall in the price of raw materials or a rise in the productivity of labour, will mean that the firms benefiting from these changes will be prepared to supply more at each price than previously. Although the price of the product has remained unchanged, the lower costs enable firms to produce what were previously unprofitable units of output.

This produces a rightward shift of the supply curve in Fig. 8.20 from S_1 to S_2, so that at a price of OP_1, for example, the quantity supplied will be OQ_3 rather than OQ_1. Similarly, at the price OP_2 the quantity supplied will now be OQ_4 rather than OQ_2. A rise in the costs of production, however, will indicate that firms are now prepared to supply less at each price than previously, as shown in Fig. 8.21 where supply at OP_1 falls from OQ_1 to OQ_3, while supply at OP_2 falls from OQ_2 to OQ_4.

However, a change in the price of the product itself will cause a movement along the relevant supply curve, as the supply curve provides this information on how supply changes with the price of the product itself.

Fig. 8.20

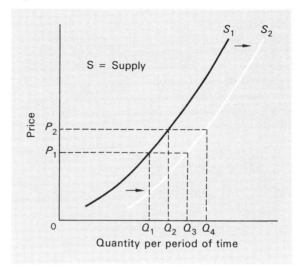

Fig. 8.21

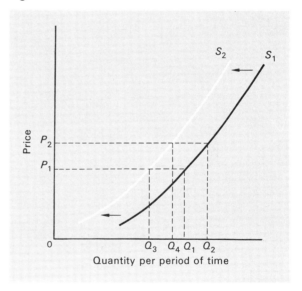

3. A change in relative profitability

A change in the prices of products will affect the relative profitability of firms operating in the respective markets for these products. A rise in the price of floor tiles, for example, perhaps caused by a change in tastes and preferences shifting the market demand curve to the right, will attract increased supplies from existing producers, and this will be shown by an upward movement along the existing market supply curve as these producers expand their output. After a period of time, however, firms engaged in other products and making lower – or even only normal – profits will see the manufacture of floor tiles as relatively more attractive. It may prove comparatively easy for firms engaged in similar products to move into tile production because their existing materials, items of plant and equipment and labour force may be flexible in this direction.

After a time lag, therefore, depending upon the nature of the product and the technical conditions governing production, the market supply schedule relating to floor tiles will shift to the right as in Fig. 8.20. This indicates that more is supplied at each price than previously, as more firms are now involved in the product. If the price and market demand of floor tiles remains at a sufficiently high level, so continuing to make this a relatively more profitable line of output, firms engaged in perhaps totally different products may eventually diversify into the production of floor tiles and the supply schedule will shift further to the right.

The result of this shift of resources into the manufacture of floor tiles will be at the expense of other products. This will be reflected in a leftward shift of the supply curves relating to these products, as shown in Fig. 8.21, whereby less is now supplied at each price than previously. This is an example of how resources are re-allocated according to changes in consumer demand, and this re-allocation will come to an end when relative profitability no longer makes such a transfer of resources worth while.

The elasticity of supply

This refers to the extent to which the quantity supplied responds to a change in price. Figs. 8.22 and 8.23 show that the same percentage rise in price from OP_1 to OP_2 and from OM_1 to OM_2 has produced a different response in the quantity supplied. Supply of product X in Fig. 8.22 is said to be elastic in that the percentage change in price has caused a larger percentage change in supply. Supply of product Y in Fig. 8.23 is said to be inelastic as the percentage change in price produces a smaller percentage change in the supply. The formula for the elasticity of supply (E^s) is as follows:

$$E^s = \frac{\text{percentage change in the quantity supplied}}{\text{percentage change in price}}$$

If, for example, when the price of wool is raised from £12 to £15 per unit, the supply is increased from 5 million to 6 million units per period of time, the change in price is 25 per cent and the percentage change in the supply of wool is 20 per cent. Using the above formula, this produces an E^s of 0·8. Thus for every 1 per cent rise in the price of wool, there is a 0·8 per cent increase in the supply of wool and, since the value of the E^s is less than one, supply in

Fig. 8.22

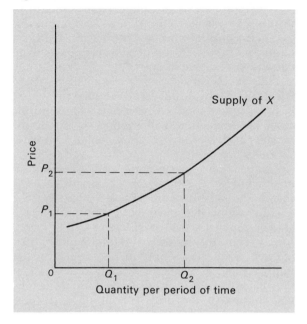

Fig. 8.23

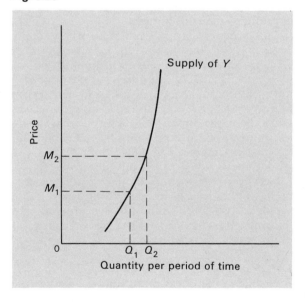

this price range is inelastic. If the value of the E^s is greater than one, supply is elastic.

As with all elasticities, the value of the E^s can also be established for a downward movement in the price level. The value of the E^s is important to firms, as they will wish to know how the supply of their inputs will be influenced by changes in the prices which they are willing to offer to attract additional quantities. They will also be concerned about how a price change is likely to affect the supply being put on to the market by their competitors.

Factors that influence the E^s

(a) *The response of firms to an increase in the price of a product will depend upon the rate at which costs increase as output is expanded to take advantage of increased profitability afforded by the price rise.* If firms are currently maximising profits, where marginal revenue is equal to marginal costs, a rise in price as shown in Fig. 8.16 (page 137) will allow firms to expand output. A cost structure that displays rapidly rising marginal costs will not provide the firms with much more scope to increase output. This is because the rapidly rising marginal costs associated with increased units of output will soon meet the marginal revenue resulting from the sale of these extra units. If, however, marginal costs rise very slowly, firms will be able to expand output by a much larger amount before marginal revenue again equals marginal costs.

Thus rapidly rising costs will tend to produce an inelastic supply, while costs that rise relatively slowly will produce an elastic supply. This is shown in Figs. 8.22 and 8.23. The cost structure involved in producing product X is such that a small percentage price rise will promote a large percentage increase in supply. But product Y requires a relatively large percentage rise in price even to call forth a small percentage increase in supply. At some point however, as shown in Chapter 6 all costs will start to rise at an increasing rate and thus all supply curves will become increasingly inelastic at higher levels of output.

(b) *Chapter 6 demonstrated that the ability of firms to adjust to a change in their market demand for their product depended very heavily upon the length of the time period considered.* The longer the time period the greater was the opportunity of firms to vary the employment of all factors of production in order to adjust more fully to the changed market conditions. The lower average total costs and marginal costs would then produce a greater response in supply, as firms were no longer operating within the constraints imposed by a capacity that was essentially designed for a lower level of output. Fig. 8.24 shows how supply will react according to the time period considered.

When the price is OP_1 the firms are prepared to

Fig. 8.24

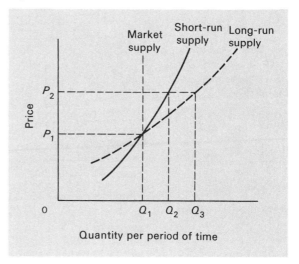

supply OQ_1. When the price rises to OP_2 there first exists what is known as a **market supply period**, and this is defined as a period of time during which the supply flowing on to the market cannot be increased and, as with all time periods, this depends upon the nature of the product and the technical conditions surrounding production. A sudden rise in the price of leather, for example, will not immediately lead to an increase in supply, and during this market supply period the quantity is said to be perfectly inelastic in that a percentage change in price has left supply unchanged, and thus $E^s = O$. In the short-run period, however, the firm is prepared to supply OQ_2 while in the long run it is prepared to supply OQ_3. Supply is thus more elastic the longer the time period considered, and this illustrates the economies of scale which firms can derive from a more complete adjustment to higher output.

In the very long run the application of advances in science and technology and the introduction of new materials, skills and management techniques will contribute to further improvements in productivity and other cost-saving developments. This will provide producers with additional scope for absorbing the impact of the long-run trend for the prices of their inputs to increase. A schedule that reflected the response of supply in the very long run to favourable developments in the market would therefore be even more elastic than the long-run supply curve illustrated in Fig. 8.24. The quantity supplied in the very long run would be correspondingly larger than OQ_3.

9. The Organisation, Prices and Markets

Market equilibrium

Having analysed the factors that influence both demand and supply, it is now possible to bring these forces together and discuss their interaction in a market, and the respective roles they play in determining market prices. Fig. 9.1 illustrates the market for product X and includes both the demand and supply curves and their relationship to the price of product X.

A price of OP_2 in this market will not produce a market equilibrium, as this is defined as a condition when neither of the economic forces of demand and supply show any tendency to change, and the market price is stable.

Fig. 9.1

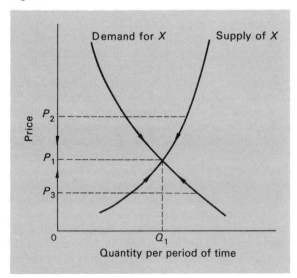

Quantity per period of time

At the price of OP_2 a situation of disequilibrium exists, in that the quantity which consumers are prepared to purchase is less than the quantity which firms are willing to supply at the price of OP_2. A surplus thus exists in this market, and the result will be a fall in price as consumers offer a lower price and firms reduce their price in order to sell this excess supply. This fall in price will rid the market of the excess supply, as not only will consumers be prepared to demand more as the price of X falls, but the fall in price will discourage some of the supply. Price will continue to fall until the excess supply has been removed from the market and this arises when the price is OP_1 as at this price the quantity which consumers are prepared to purchase will equal the quantity that producers are willing to supply. The price OP_1 has produced a market equilibrium in that neither demand nor supply will show any tendency to change and the quantity traded is OQ_1.

Similarly, OP_3 would not produce a market equilibrium because at this price the quantity which consumers are prepared to purchase is greater than the quantity producers are willing to supply at this price of OP_3. Excess demand exists at OP_3 and this will cause the price to rise as some consumers are prepared to pay a higher price to obtain product X, and firms are in a position to charge a higher price. This rise in price will remove the excess demand by pricing some consumers out of the market and encouraging a greater supply. The price rise continues until the excess demand has been completely removed, and this occurs when price is OP_1, as once again demand is equal to supply and a market equilibrium exists. The way a market price changes to produce a new equilibrium if any of the factors that influence demand and supply alter, can be seen in the following examples.

1. A rightward shift of the demand curve

Fig. 9.2 depicts the market for product X, which has produced an initial equilibrium at a price OP_1 and a quantity bought and sold of OQ_1. There is then a rightward shift of the demand curve, perhaps because of a rise in the price of a substitute, or a change in tastes and preferences in favour of the product. This market is now in a state of disequilibrium as the economic forces of demand and supply will show a tendency to change and this will be reflected in a movement of the price.

At the initial price OP_1, demand now exceeds supply by Q_1Q_3 and the price of X will start to rise, which will help to produce a new market equilibrium. The path towards the new

Fig. 9.2

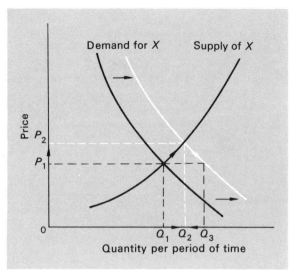

Fig. 9.3

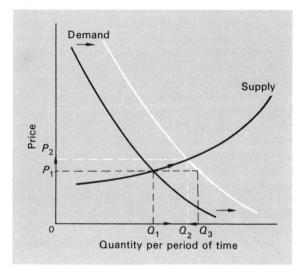

Fig. 9.4

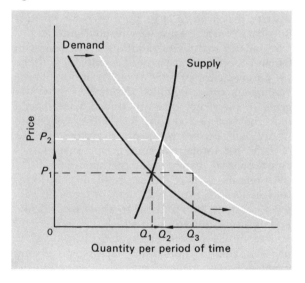

equilibrium can be traced by movements along the existing supply curve as they tell us how demand and supply can be expected to react to this increase in price. As the price increases, some of the excess demand is choked off while the higher price will at the same time encourage a greater supply. Eventually a new market equilibrium will be achieved at OP_2 where demand again equals supply at OQ_2. The end result is both an increase in price and an increase in the quantity bought and sold.

An interesting feature of this path towards a new equilibrium is that the excess demand of Q_1Q_3 was removed by an increase in supply of Q_1Q_2 and a fall of Q_3Q_2 in the initially higher demand as the price rose. The extent to which the shift of demand is met mainly by an increase in price that chokes off demand, or an increase in output that satisfies most of the demand, depends upon the E^s of the product. In Fig. 9.3 it is assumed that the supply of product X is elastic within the relevant price range, and thus only a small percentage price change is required to call forth a large percentage increase in supply from producers. The new equilibrium shows a small increase in price but a large increase in the quantity bought and sold. This suggests that the nature of product X and the methods of production are such that its output can readily be increased without a significant increase in marginal costs or encountering the problems associated with a lack of capacity.

This is in contrast to Fig. 9.4 where it is assumed that the supply of product X is inelastic. In this case,

a large percentage increase in price is necessary to produce even a small percentage increase in supply, and the new equilibrium is established with a large price rise and a small increase in the quantity bought and sold.

In this case product X represents the output from an industry where production and hence supply to the market cannot readily be expanded. This would be the case, for example, with an increase in the market demand for certain types of food and beverages, where the supply is limited to the size of the present crop, and various growing periods must elapse before more land can be given over to the increased production of such products. Moreover, in the case of coffee and cocoa it may be several years before the crop can be harvested from new plantings.

The supply of raw materials such as timber and rubber will also be restricted by the time that it takes for new trees to mature. The extractive industries are also likely to face difficulties in expanding the output of metal ores, for example. Sudden increases in demand from the manufacturing economies generally lead to large price increases once existing stockpiles have been exhausted and they are forced to rely upon the output from current production.

Thus the supply curve for many of industry's raw materials tends to be very inelastic. An increase in demand is met mainly by a rise in price rather than by any significant increase in the quantity traded. Similarly in the case of the various processing and refining industries, a lack of spare capacity may lead to large price increases as user industries compete for a very limited output.

So far the analysis of the impact of changes in demand upon markets has dealt essentially with the short-run reaction of firms to such changes, but the equilibrium towards which the market moves in terms of price and quantity traded will depend upon the time period considered. This is because supply will prove to be more elastic (or less inelastic) the longer the time period that elapses after the initial change in the market demand.

Although it is more difficult to predict the long-run reaction of a firm, as the state of technology is never constant, it is possible to show in principle the long-run equilibrium to which the market will tend to move. Moreover, further change in the market demand and other factors governing production may, in the meantime, move producers on to a different path of expansion or contraction.

A rightward shift of the demand curve in Fig. 9.5 is first met solely by a rise in price to OP_2 during the market supply period when supply is totally inelastic. In the short run, the type of supply curve dealt with in the previous analysis now operates, and shows how firms can expand output in response to this higher price, which then produces an equilibrium of OP_3 and OQ_3. In the long run, supply becomes more elastic and the price falls further to OP_4 and the quantity bought would be OQ_4.

Fig. 9.5

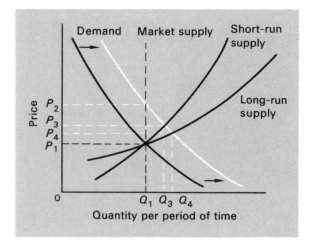

Fig. 9.6

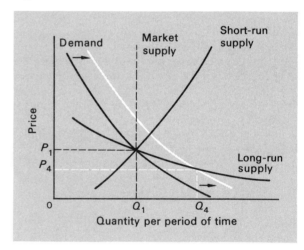

This gradual long-run adjustment to a higher level of output and more favourable market conditions eventually brings about a fall in the unit costs from the levels that they experienced in the short run. Thus the developments illustrated in Fig. 9.5 would eventually move the market towards a price of OP_4, which although not much higher than the original price of OP_1 still allows a significant increase in the output and hence supply to the market from the producers who make up the supply side of the market.

In the case of the products involved in the market shown in Fig. 9.6, then they must still be reaping very significant economies of scale, which are more than able to outweigh possible diseconomies and the rises in input prices that exert an upward pressure upon unit costs. This is demonstrated by the fact that the long-run supply curve is still falling, thus allowing producers to accept a price actually lower than the original level of OP_1, while still being able to expand their output and hence the supply to the market by a large amount, as is shown by OQ_4.

The question may then be asked as to why the firms that make up the market supply in Fig. 9.6 do not increase output beyond OQ_4. At first sight this would seem the logical development, as increased output that caused a further fall in average and marginal costs would be possible, even though the price would have to be lowered. However, the explanation as to why supply will not go beyond OQ_4 in Fig. 9.6 is that the fall in price necessary to sell the extra output, and the effect this has upon suppliers' total revenues, does not make it worth while despite the fall in average and marginal costs in the long run. After all, firms will produce only when it is profitable to do so.

At this point you should refer back to Chapter 6 and the section dealing with 'The very long run' (page 101). A more detailed description is given there of the reasons why developments on the supply side associated with advances in science and technology, materials, skills and management techniques, often supported by some form of integration, will help to further minimise cost increases. This helps to bring about a further fall in the level of real prices despite the long-run trend of increases in the actual prices paid for goods and services. The long-run fall in real prices is the result of household incomes rising faster than prices, so that the resulting rise in real disposable income and hence purchasing power allows consumers to buy more goods and services.

In terms of the demand and supply analysis used in this chapter, the rise in real disposable income would be reflected in a gradual rightward shift of the demand curve for a particular good or service. In the long run this higher demand is met increasingly by a greater supply and a price rise that is a smaller percentage than the typical pay increase that helped to produce the rightward shift of the demand curve.

If, however, producers in general are not able to offset any of the higher wages and salaries they pay to their employees by an improvement in productivity or other cost-saving programmes, then they will be obliged to raise their prices by the full amount of such a cost increase. In this case the rise in disposable income produced by the higher wages and salaries will be more or less matched by similar increases in the prices that producers are obliged to charge for their goods and services. In this case the rightward shift of the typical market demand curve is balanced by a leftward shift of the supply schedule, with the result that the quantity bought and sold remains unchanged while there is also a rise in price.

The rise in disposable incomes in this case has not led to an increase in sales in the typical market, because households in general have not experienced a rise in their real disposable incomes. This was because the general rise in incomes was met by a rise in the general level of prices.

Thus the more a producer can absorb the impact of the long-run increases in the prices paid for its inputs, especially labour, then the smaller are the increases in its unit costs and hence its prices. These are the producers that are best equipped to take advantage of increases in demand for those goods and services that are particularly sensitive to increases in real disposable income.

2. A leftward shift of the demand schedule

This fall in demand could be attributed perhaps to a fall in the price of a substitute or change in tastes and preferences away from the product in question. The analysis is similar to that in Fig. 9.2 (page 143) except that the direction of the developments is reversed.

In Fig. 9.7 the demand curve shifts to the left, which means that at the initial price of OP_1 a disequilibrium now exists in the market as at OP_1,

Fig. 9.7

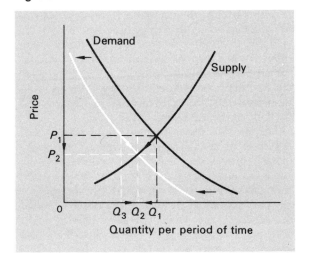

supply now exceeds demand by Q_3Q_1 and the price will start to fall. As the price falls, the reaction of demand and supply is shown by movements along the new demand curve and the existing supply curve. The fall in price encourages demand, while reducing some supply until a new equilibrium price is reached at OP_2, while the quantity bought and sold is now at OQ_2. The extent to which the increase in demand is met mainly by a fall in price or by a fall in quantity, will again depend upon the E^s relating to product X in this price range.

In Fig. 9.8 it is assumed that the supply of product X is elastic, and the new equilibrium is characterised by a relatively small fall in price but a relatively large reduction in quantity. If only a small percentage price rise was necessary to encourage a significant increase in supply, then this also implies that it takes only a similar price fall to make a large part of output unprofitable.

In the case of an inelastic supply in Fig. 9.9, however, the new equilibrium shows a relatively large fall in price compared with the reduction in quantity. If supply is inelastic, it means that very few extra units prove profitable despite a large price rise, and so the reverse of this is also true – that a large price fall makes relatively fewer units unprofitable.

There will be, for example, a very large fall in the prices of certain basic foods and beverages as the supplies coming on to the market will have been the result of production decisions taken in a much earlier period when the market demand may have been appreciably higher. Since many of the costs will already have been incurred the producers will still put their crops on to the market, and settle for whatever price they can obtain. Raw materials and the output of the processing and refining industries may also be subject to a large price fall as they are generally stockpiled as a means of meeting the needs of their customers and avoiding frequent changes in the utilisation of capacity. Producers may eventually be obliged to offload the growing stocks created by the fall in the market demand, and this will contribute to the fall in prices.

A feature of capital-intensive industries is that they tend to maintain production at relatively unchanged levels despite falling demand and prices. This is because reductions in output do not make significant savings, since the variable costs are not a large part of total costs. If they shut down a part of their capacity they would still be obliged to meet the fixed costs associated with the plant and machinery that is no longer being used, while

Fig. 9.8

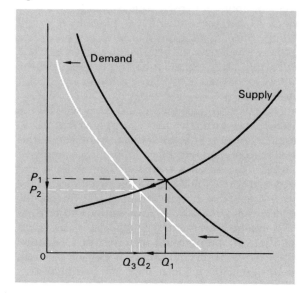

Fig. 9.9

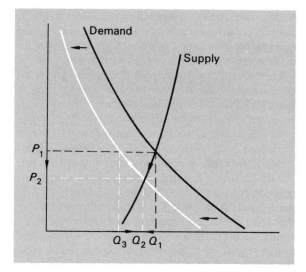

making only a relatively small saving on the variable costs of production. A producer may then consider maintaining a relatively high output and accept the lower price as long as the revenue derived from the sale of that output is sufficient to cover the variable costs incurred.

If, for example, the fixed costs of a particular plant operated by a producer amount to £2 m., the variable costs are £½ m. and the output from the plant earns £$\frac{3}{4}$ m., then the plant will make a loss of £1$\frac{3}{4}$ m. If, however, the producer closed this plant down, the loss would amount to £2 m., as the fixed costs still have to be met. Thus as long as output can earn enough to cover the variable costs of production then the producer will continue to operate the plant. But if the price falls to a level that produces revenue of only £$\frac{1}{4}$ m. then a loss of £2$\frac{1}{4}$ m. will be incurred if the plant is kept running.

The producer will also consider the extent to which the fall in demand and price is likely to be only temporary or of a more permanent nature. The decision to shut down the plant or maintain output must also take into account the effects of losing key personnel and breaking up experienced and closely knit groups of employees responsible for important aspects of the plant's operation and management. There may be difficulties in recruiting people of the same calibre and re-establishing equally efficient teams of employees if the market demand picks up again. A closure will also disrupt both the sources of supply and the existing distribution network, while the absence of the product from the market may leave the field open to competitors that have maintained their production and then benefit from any revival in the market demand.

The factors to be considered by a producer that is highly integrated both backwards towards the sources of supply and forwards towards the market will be even more complex. A decision to shut down a plant will have repercussions for a wide range of activities throughout the producer's operations.

It can be concluded that the market supply curve for certain types of product may prove to be relatively inelastic. A price fall does not lead to a significant reduction in the quantity traded. If the demand and price continue to fall, however, and these market developments show no real sign of reversing themselves, then after a time the supply will demonstrate a much greater reaction to a lower price. In the long run therefore, and even more so in the very long run, there will be a contraction in the overall scale of the industry's operations.

Eventually, however, the producers that have managed to survive will be able to adopt a method of production and introduce items of fixed capital that are more closely geared to a lower level of output. This will then be reflected in lower fixed costs per unit of output, and some units of output that were unprofitable when operating with plant that was geared to a much higher level of output

now become profitable once again. Thus the lower unit costs produced by a long-run adjustment to a lower demand will then allow something of a recovery in output despite the lower market price caused by the original fall in the market demand.

3. A rightward shift in the supply curve

A change in any of the factors influencing supply, such as a fall in the costs of production because of improved production techniques, will cause the market supply curve to *shift* to the right. This is because not only will existing producers be prepared to supply more at each price than previously, but the supply will be added to by new firms entering the market because of the change in relative profitability that may result from such a reduction in costs.

The result of a rightward shift of the supply curve relating to product X in Fig. 9.10 is that at OP_1 supply now exceeds demand and the price will start to fall. This in turn removes the excess supply by encouraging greater demand and discouraging some supply. This is shown by *movements along* the existing demand curve and the new supply curve. A new equilibrium is then established at a lower price of OP_2 and an increased quantity bought and sold at OQ_2. Elasticities are again important, but in this case the E^d will dictate the relative price and quantity changes. If the demand for product X is elastic, as in Fig. 9.11, only a relatively small fall in price is necessary to encourage a relatively large increase in demand to absorb the increased supply.

Fig. 9.10

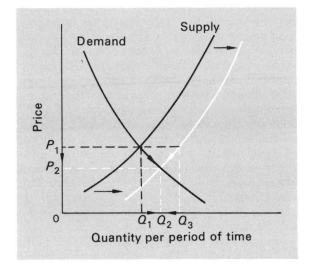

Fig. 9.11

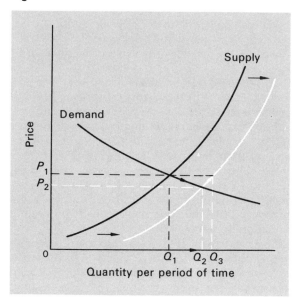

Fig. 9.12

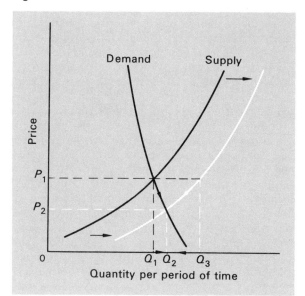

This will be the case, for example, if only a small price fall is required to attract buyers away from a close substitute, or if the product is now priced at a level that suddenly makes it much more attractive to an income group made up of a very large number of households. Fig. 9.11 also confirms our earlier prediction that a fall in the price of a product for which the demand is elastic will raise total spending on that product and hence the total sales revenue earned by the industry.

One can also identify here therefore the incentive that producers have to reduce their unit costs. If they can manage to reduce their prices by even a small percentage then they can expect a significant increase in their sales. If the market demand for the product in general is elastic then the demand for the output of any single producer will be even more elastic. Thus a fall in the general price of the product brought about by cost-saving developments in the industry as a whole will expand the total size of the market, while any single producer's share of the enlarged market will depend upon the price reduction that particular producer can afford and how it compares with the price cuts introduced by competitors.

In Fig. 9.12, where demand is shown to be inelastic, a relatively large fall in price is necessary to promote even a relatively small increase in sales. This illustrates the problems of producers involved in a market that has virtually reached saturation point; a very large price fall is required to encourage households to increase their consumption by even a very small percentage. This is the case with basic foods, beverages and household items, for example, where total demand is unlikely to respond to a fall in their prices.

Once again, however, if any single producer is willing to sell at a price below that charged by competitors then the demand for that producer's output will be much more sensitive when compared with the response of the total market demand to a general fall in the market price of that product.

Fig. 9.13 can be used to illustrate the problems faced by producers of basic food and beverage products. The market in Fig. 9.13 depicts a very inelastic demand and a vertical supply 'curve'. The supply being put on to the market will depend upon that particular year's crop or harvest, and no matter what then happens to the price that same quantity will be supplied, i.e. supply is totally inelastic.

The output of these products is very susceptible to climatic factors. If in any single year the weather proves to be particularly favourable for the growing of a certain food or beverage crop, then this will increase the total supply put onto the market. If, for example, there is a bumper sugar-

Fig. 9.13

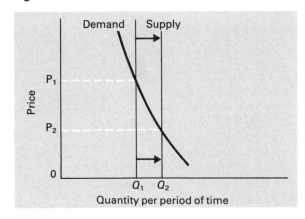

beet crop then the impact of this large increase in supply upon an inelastic demand is to produce a substantial fall in the market price. Households are very unlikely to increase their consumption; the food processing industry may substitute some of its artificial sweeteners with sugar, while its use as a source of industrial alcohol may become more viable. But any such increases in sales of sugar-beet is more than outweighed by the fall in the market price.

As shown in Fig. 9.13, the result of these developments in the market is a fall in the revenue of the producers. The position facing the producers of basic food and beverage products, and those that grow some of the raw materials required by various industries, is that in the long run improvements in productivity lead to further increases in supply. Advances in science and technology raise the productivity of items of capital and also lead to the use of new and improved pesticides and fertilisers, while research projects lead to higher-yield plants and seeds.

In some markets this has led to government intervention schemes that are designed to support the incomes of growers. When, for example, good weather conditions lead to a large increase in output, the government could intervene in the market once the price has reached a certain level, in order to prevent it from falling any further. It can do this by adding its own demand to that of the market and thus absorb the remaining excess supply that would otherwise have led to a further fall in the market price. In Fig. 9.13 this would be

reflected in a rightward shift of the demand curve. The extent of this intervention would depend upon what the government regards as the minimum price that producers should receive. If it is assumed, for the sake of simplicity, that OP_1 is the minimum price the government is seeking to guarantee to producers, then it must be prepared to buy up the quantity Q_1Q_2 from the market. If, however, the government had set a lower minimum price for producers then it would not have been obliged to buy up so much from the market.

Thus once the market has absorbed all that it is willing to buy at the price established by the government then producers will be able to sell their remaining output to the government at that same price. The income of producers is therefore protected from the large price fall that would otherwise have resulted from increases in output. In fact the higher their output, the larger their incomes will be. In the case of the minimum price OP_1 in Fig. 9.13, the producers will receive a total income of $OP_1 \times OQ_3$. They will have sold OQ_1 to the market at a price of OP_1, while the remaining output Q_1Q_3 would have been sold to the government at the same price. Without such a scheme the income of producers would have been $OP_2 \times OQ_2$.

A major problem confronting a government that wishes to support the income of such producers is at what level to set the minimum price. The more a government yields to the pressure from producers to set a relatively high market price then the lower the quantity the market will absorb at that price and the larger the quantity the government is obliged to buy up from the producers. There is therefore a conflict between what is in the interests of the buyers and what is in the interests of the producers.

Moreover, if the price is set too high then this may encourage overproduction, which is then further aggravated by the long-run improvements in productivity. The government may then be faced with the need to buy up increasing quantities of the product. Not only will the storage of the surpluses be costly; but in the case of some products there will be the problem of the surpluses deteriorating. How the government uses these surpluses is described in 4. below.

A scheme designed to support the prices and incomes received by producers would not work, of course, if buyers were able to purchase equivalent products from abroad at lower prices. In order to prevent this from happening the government would have either to prohibit their import

Fig. 9.14

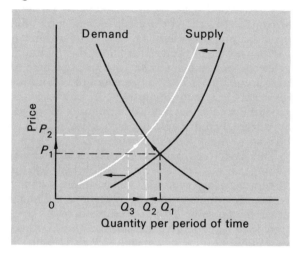

Fig. 9.15

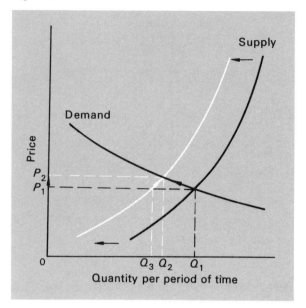

altogether or to put an import duty on them. Similar restrictions and duties would also have to be placed upon imports that were close substitutes.

4. A leftward shift of the supply curve

Given the current market price, a rise in the costs of production will make some units of output unprofitable. This will oblige producers to reduce their output and hence their supply to the market. The amount by which any single producer will have to cut output will depend upon how severely that producer's costs are affected by the rise in the prices of the industry's inputs.

If, for example, all the producers grant roughly the same percentage pay increase to their employees then those with the highest output per employee will be in a stronger position to absorb the extra labour costs. These more efficient producers will therefore experience a much smaller increase in their unit costs, and their output will be reduced by a smaller amount than those producers with lower output per employee. Similarly, higher raw material prices will have a less serious impact upon those producers that make more efficient use of such inputs.

The effect of an increase in the costs of production can be shown by a leftward shift of the market supply curve as depicted in Fig. 9.14. This shift indicates that less is now supplied at each price than previously. At the current general market price of OP_1 there is no longer a large enough supply coming on to the market to satisfy the demand at that price. This excess demand will exert

an upward pressure upon the general market price, and this price rise will choke off part of the demand, as some of the buyers will be priced out of the market and will turn to what they regard as substitutes. The price rise will also allow producers to restore some of those units of output that were made unprofitable by the initial increase in the costs of production. These developments in the market are shown in Fig. 9.14 by movements along the existing demand and the new market supply curve. The result of an increase in the costs of production is a higher market price and a reduction in the quantity bought and sold.

In the case of an elastic market demand, as in Fig. 9.15, only a relatively small percentage price rise is required to establish a market equilibrium. In this case the product must have very close substitutes, and this is confirmed by the large percentage fall in the quantity bought and sold.

In the case of the inelastic market demand shown in Fig. 9.16, the new equilibrium involves a large percentage increase in the price but a much smaller percentage reduction in the quantity bought and sold. The producers are able to obtain a much higher price for their output, and this enables them to restore a large part of the production that the rise in their costs had previously made unprofitable. If the demand for a product is inelastic, then the absence of a close substitute allows producers to charge a much higher price to help cover the

Fig. 9.16

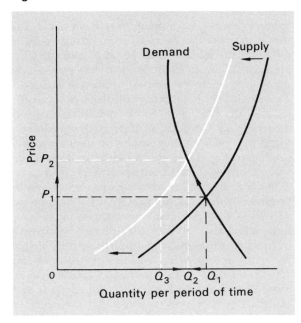

increased costs of production while experiencing a relatively small reduction in their sales.

The analysis will now return to the earlier description of the developments that can arise in the markets for agricultural products (see 3., page 149). The market demand for many of these products tends to be very inelastic indeed, and the effect of a large reduction in the supply caused by exceptionally bad weather is a sudden and large rise in the market price. Unlike the manufacturing industries, however, the rise in price does not then lead to something of a recovery in output, as a growing period must elapse before supply can respond.

If expressed diagrammatically this fall in the supply of an agricultural product would be depicted by a leftward shift of the supply 'curve'. The resulting excess demand would be removed from the market solely by a price rise rather than any response in the supply. The inelastic demand means, however, that a very large percentage increase in price is required to choke off this excess demand.

The government intervention scheme described in 3. above can now be used to protect buyers from such a large price rise. The government can prevent the price from rising above a certain level by drawing upon the surpluses which it has accumulated in the earlier years when it intervened

to maintain a minimum price for the producers. When stocks are released on to the market they will help to meet the demand and avoid the high price that would otherwise have been established. A side-effect of this intervention, however, is that the incomes of producers will be lower than those earned in years of larger output when the government bought up the surpluses.

This again demonstrates the problem facing the government in operating such a scheme, because if the price is allowed to reach a much higher level before it releases its stocks then this will benefit the producers, but buyers will have to pay the higher price. The dilemma facing the government is to set a price that satisfies both the producers and the buyers. In particular the government must avoid setting a price that produces a large 'mountain' of a product because over the years the additions to its stocks far exceed its drawings. The government may eventually be obliged to destroy these stocks or sell them in another part of the world for whatever price it can get.

The previous examples have served to illustrate not only how the economic forces of demand and supply interact in a market, but that both demand and supply are influenced by so many factors that many markets can be characterised by continual changes. A market may move towards an equilibrium and for a while perhaps reach such a position; but firms will have to be continually aware of the need to adjust to both developments in demand and the conditions governing their supply.

The 'marketing mix'

Having examined the more general developments likely to influence the total market demand for a good or service, it is now necessary to outline those variables that the firm itself can alter, which will affect the demand for its own particular good or service within the market as a whole.

Producers pay a great deal of attention to what is known as their 'marketing mix'. It is possible to view the marketing operation as being made up of a mixture of different 'ingredients' to which producers attach different degrees of importance. These areas embrace the features of the product itself, its price and its distribution, and promotion. The achievement of the organisation will depend upon ensuring that an appropriate balance is maintained between these various factors. If, however, the organisation's objectives were to change, then this may require that certain adjustments are made to the existing marketing mix. The organisation may decide that it should seek to increase its market share and that this objective is best achieved by concentrating more upon lowering price and increasing its sales outlets; this may involve less attention to certain features of the products and a saving on certain promotional activities.

The initial marketing mix will depend upon the **target market**. The producer cannot expect to provide a range of products with sufficient variations to satisfy all the customers that make up the market as a whole. The producer must first decide upon the segment of the market to aim for. The segment that offers the best prospects of achieving its objectives will then become its target market. The company marketing strategy will therefore be aimed at meeting the needs it has identified in relation to a clearly defined set of customers. The target area will be researched to identify what these particular customers are looking for, while also examining what is currently being offered by other producers to that same part of the market.

For example, a company may have decided to move into the production of microwave ovens rather than other types of appliance used in kitchens. It must then decide what part of the market for microwave ovens to concentrate upon. There will already be a range of such ovens on offer to the market in general and they will all incorporate a combination of factors that reflect the marketing mixes decided upon by their respective producers. Fig. 9.17 indicates some of the elements that may be associated with such a product.

In the case of the microwave oven being sold by producer A, it is relying heavily upon the product variables, with the next important element being its promotional activities. It could be a high-priced oven where the emphasis is upon the quality aspect, and this is supported by specific promotional activities aimed at this particular target market. Similarly, the distribution is limited to a few outlets, but they will be those that are generally frequented by its potential customers. Producer B, however, has opted essentially for a low-price oven

Fig. 9.17

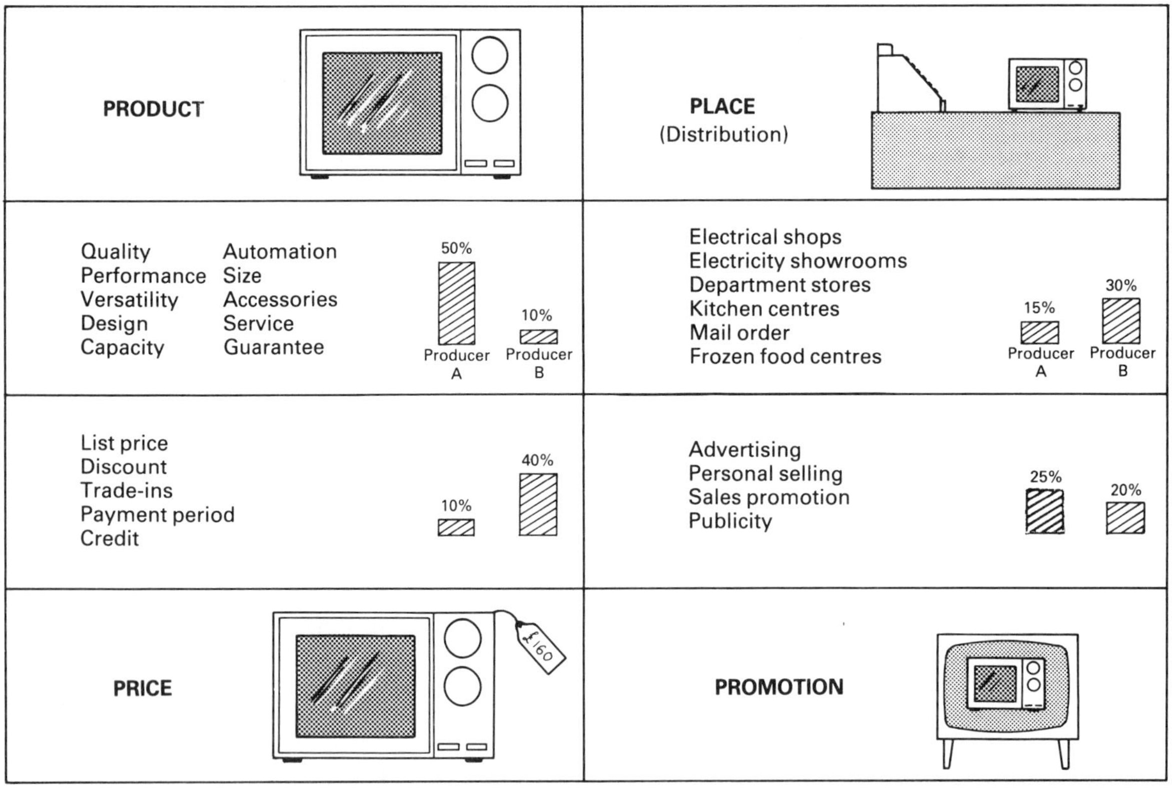

PRODUCT		PLACE (Distribution)	
Quality Automation	50% — Producer A; 10% — Producer B	Electrical shops / Electricity showrooms / Department stores / Kitchen centres / Mail order / Frozen food centres	15% — Producer A; 30% — Producer B
Performance Size			
Versatility Accessories			
Design Service			
Capacity Guarantee			
List price / Discount / Trade-ins / Payment period / Credit	10%; 40%	Advertising / Personal selling / Sales promotion / Publicity	25%; 20%
PRICE		PROMOTION	

with perhaps special discounts available during certain periods. Producer B supports this with a large number of retail outlets of the type where it will be able to reach its own particular group of potential customers. The emphasis here is upon price rather than quality or sophistication.

Having examined these and other products on the market, the new producer may decide to aim for the market where company A would be the closest competitor. The marketing mix adopted may have an even greater product ingredient as the new producer may have decided that this target market holds out the best prospects, particularly because its existing products in other markets have a well-established reputation for quality and style. It may, for example, emphasise the high-technology aspect of its oven, and this may be reflected in such features as programming controls and its overall design. It may be designed to appeal especially to those people in the market for the more expensive range of fitted kitchens, and its distribution will be limited mainly to large department stores and the specialist suppliers of fitted kitchens. Its overall image will be supported and perhaps even further enhanced by the appropriate complementary kitchen furnishings. Promotion could concentrate mainly upon certain magazines where glossy advertisements would be seen by the appropriate income groups. In-store demonstrations may be organised or run in conjunction with the producers of ranges of fitted kitchens. This marketing mix may be seen as a way of capturing potential customers from producer A.

Having decided upon an appropriate marketing mix, a producer must ensure that the various aspects of its marketing activities continue to support each other and do not pull in opposite directions. The new producer of microwave ovens, for example, would be unwise to engage in any significant degree of price discounting if the effect was to reduce its image of offering a high-quality product. Similarly, it would not be expected to use resources promoting its ovens in the average high-street multiple dealing with a whole range of middle-priced domestic appliances.

Market forms

Having discussed how prices and outputs are established in a market, it is now possible to describe the impact of changes in markets upon firms involved in them. The effect of market changes upon a firm will, however, depend heavily upon the nature of the market as a whole, where it

sells its product in terms of the degree of competition that it has to face. Changes in a highly competitive market will have repercussions upon the firms involved, which differ from those that arise out of a market where the forces of competition may be much weaker.

Imperfect competition

This description is used to predict events in a market where there are many producers selling products that, although basically the same in their main characteristics and eventual usage, do display a degree of product differentiation. There may, for example, be a large number of firms producing biscuits and each of them will attempt to make their respective products particularly attractive to consumers by attention to ingredients, shape and packaging.

The total market demand curve for biscuits will be downward, sloping from left to right, and the price E^d will depend upon how important biscuits are as a foodstuff. The overall price E^d for biscuits will be lower than the price E^d for the product of a single firm producing biscuits. The value of the price E^d facing a single producer will in fact depend upon the degree of product differentiation that the producer has managed to incorporate in its biscuits. The greater the product differentiation, the lower will be the E^d for its product and a rise in price will leave it with more consumers than would be the case if the product was less differentiated from some of its competitors. If, of course, the product was identical in every way, including packaging, and was equally convenient to purchase, then a rise in price would result in a total loss of demand.

A biscuit manufacturer is shown in Fig. 9.18, and is currently maximising profits at an output of OQ_1, where marginal cost is equal to marginal revenue. Since at this output OQ_1 the average total cost per unit is below the price received per unit sold, this firm is making not just profits but super-normal profits.

Imperfect competition is also characterised by the lack of any barriers that may exist to prevent firms moving into an industry. If the firm in Fig. 9.18 is typical of those in the biscuit industry, the existence of super-normal profits will be an incentive for existing firms to expand and new firms to enter the industry. The market supply curve will then shift to the right indicating that more biscuits will be supplied at each price than previously. Since there are now more firms in the industry the existing producers, as with the firm in

Fig. 9.18

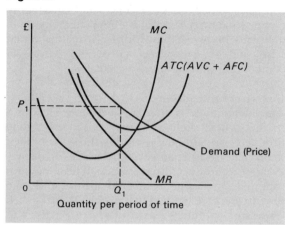

Fig. 9.19

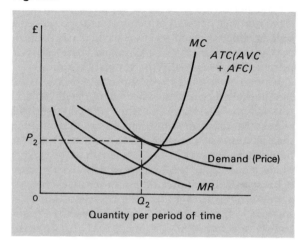

Fig. 9.18, can expect to sell fewer biscuits at each price than previously. The demand curve facing this particular firm now starts to shift to the left. Not only will the firm sell fewer biscuits at each price but it can expect the demand for its particular product to become more elastic. This is because the increasing number of firms in the industry will mean a wider range of biscuits from which consumers can select their purchases, and as a result the demand for any particular brand will be more elastic.

These developments will come to an end when there is no longer any incentive for new firms to enter the industry. This occurs when the typical firm is making only normal profits, which is the minimum return necessary to keep a firm interested in a particular line of output. Thus if the firm in Fig. 9.18 is typical of biscuit producers, the scale of the industry will cease expanding when the level of output produces a cost and revenue situation as exists in Fig. 9.19. At output OQ_2 total revenue is equal to total costs, as average costs is equal to price, and since normal profit is included in costs then this firm is making normal profits.

In the long run each firm is pushed into the position where it has excess capacity, as any attempt by a firm to produce at the level of output where average total cost is at a minimum would involve a range of output where marginal revenue was less than marginal costs. The firm can reduce average total costs in the long run by gearing itself more efficiently to produce OQ_2, but the super-normal profits that arise will again induce a further

increase in the market supply, until finally a long-run equilibrium is reached where normal profits are again being made with a margin of unused capacity.

From the point of view of consumers, this type of competition raises several points. The greater the degree of product differentiation that exists in a market, the greater the real choice available to a consumer. In this case the value of the E^d for any single product will be lower than if there was less product differentiation. Fig. 9.19, however, implies that the steeper the demand schedule, the further the long-run output will be removed from the level of output where average total costs are at a minimum. The smaller the degree of product differentiation, the less steep is the demand schedule and the closer will be the long-run output to that at which average total costs are at a minimum. The choice confronting consumers, if they were ever in a position to exert such a choice, would be between a more markedly differentiated product at a certain price, or products which are less differentiated at a lower price.

Imperfect competition in markets will also see a great deal of **non-price competition** by firms in the form of advertising, packaging and other marketing activities, in an effort to persuade consumers that their particular product is superior. Large sums of money may be spent to attract consumers from competing brands, and this will prove successful to the extent that consumers feel a need can be better satisfied by switching brands. In fact a producer that does not maintain its promotional campaigns may soon lose ground to competitors. If the total market is virtually saturated, in that the income E^d is approaching zero, then such advertising does not increase the total market for the product but seeks to maintain or increase the **market share** of the firm involved. A larger market share may then strengthen the position of a single firm from the point of view of take-overs.

If a firm gains an increasing share of the market, it loses many of the characteristics associated with imperfect competition. More significant economies of scale may be produced if the producer standardises the product to a greater extent, and this will then have to be judged according to the loss of choice available to the consumer. This loss of real choice, however, may already have occurred when the market was imperfectly competitive, as advertising campaigns and product development will seek to incorporate in the firm's product features almost identical to those attached to competing products. Thus consumers will believe that they perhaps lose nothing by switching brands in terms of these features, but rather gain from the additional qualities of the new purchase. Firms losing consumers will retaliate by adjustments in their product and marketing activities that include the new features of the more successful product and others of their own. This process is continuous and is reflected in the sudden emphasis by many producers on a common feature of the product once it has proved successful for another firm in the market.

Oligopoly

This is a market form about which it is far more difficult to make reliable predictions about the response of firms to changes in the market, or the extent to which they will initiate such changes. Oligopoly refers to a market in which there are very few producers of a product and is a strong characteristic of advanced manufacturing economies where growth has seen an increasing number of take-overs and mergers. This has resulted in the output of many products being heavily concentrated in relatively few but very large companies.

Where oligopoly exists, the policy of any one firm as far as pricing and output decisions are concerned will have a very significant effect upon the others. If the conditions influencing demand, for example, should change, the reaction of any single firm will be largely influenced by how the others are expected to react. But if all firms are

considering their policies in this way, the results are very unpredictable. If company A is considering the reactions of companies B, C and D, the reaction of these other companies may then depend upon what they believe company A thinks they will do. This of course is only one of many possibilities, but nevertheless generalisations can be made concerning the decisions of such companies and certain characteristics do exist to varying degrees in a market that is oligopolistic.

A very small number of firms with no real difference in strength in terms of profitability and market share may produce a situation where they recognise their degree of interdependence, and this will be all the more obvious the less the degree of product differentiation. They will be aware that direct competition that provokes retaliatory reactions in a cumulative fashion will make them all worse off. Since they start from positions of equal strength, no single firm will be confident in its ability to survive a competitive battle or indeed in whether the victor can readily recover from what may be the excessive costs of such a competitive struggle.

There may be some form of tacit agreement on what pricing policies should be adopted, and this is likely to be the case if firms not only recognise their interdependence but a leader emerges in the form of a producer that is the largest and becomes the **price leader**. Despite its strength this leader may still believe direct competition is undesirable. The other firms then follow this price leader and their adherence to the set price will be more readily achieved if the market conditions have produced a stable price or an upward pressure because of demand. If this is the case, they can all expect to gain from such price leadership. Tacit agreements will also be strong when they have similar opinions regarding anticipated market trends and changes in costs, so that any price change would be advantageous to all the companies in the light of these expectations.

However, in a rapidly changing market that produces a recession in demand, a tacit agreement on prices may prove increasingly difficult to hold, and a firm may be tempted to 'go it alone' in order to attract the demand that will be required to utilise spare capacity. A firm that makes this move first will achieve lower unit costs and will then be able to afford a further price reduction. The initial blow to the profits of other firms may place them at a disadvantage that then proves cumulative. This is because the firm instigating the move now succeeds in capturing an even larger share of the declining market as the greater utilisation of capacity allows further price reductions.

A tacit agreement on prices may also be motivated by a desire to keep out potential new competitors. If prices are kept too high the profits to be made make the costs of entering the market more acceptable to new firms who will be aware that a large capital investment will be required and a large share of the market necessary in order to be competitive. Obviously a risk will be involved, but if the prospects of a high return exist, it may more than compensate for this risk.

Therefore, there may be a common approach to a price reduction to forestall competition from firms displaying an interest in the market. The new firm, however, will then have to judge to what extent the existing producers can hold this price and whether it has sufficient financial resources to gain a foothold in the market. A potential competitor will also face the problem of the brand loyalty displayed by consumers to existing well-established products. A new entrant may find it difficult to overcome such non-price factors even if its own brand is competitively priced.

The larger the number of firms in an oligopolistic market, then perhaps the greater the degree of price competition, as this reduces the likelihood of many of them having equal strength, market shares, profitability, mutual interests and opinions regarding the future trends in their market. The possibility of a firm acting independently and engaging in direct competition thus increases. In particular, the most efficient firm may be less keen to assist other firms with a tacit agreement to raise prices, as this may hinder its plans for expanding its market share. Take-overs that reduce the number of independent firms in an industry would seem to suggest that tacit agreements are more difficult with a larger number of firms.

Markets that display oligopolistic features are monitored by government departments responsible for identifying **restrictive practices** and this provides limits to the extent to which firms can act in restraint of trade. The difficulty arises, however, in deciding the extent to which the government can promote competition on the basis of price. Many firms express a preference for non-price promotional activities that, although involving costs, do not initiate the substantial losses to revenue that would result from a more direct and fierce competitive struggle if one were ever to gather momentum. However, the end result of activities in an oligopolistic market may eventually be the creation of a monopoly.

Monopoly

This tends to be a very emotive word applied to the situation where there is only one producer of a product. There is, however, nothing inherently evil about this type of market form. A rational analysis of monopoly can show that, as with all market forms, there are both advantages and disadvantages from the point of view of the consumer, depending upon the way a monopolist conducts its business activities.

Since the monopolist is the only producer, the demand curve facing the firm is also the total market demand curve as this firm constitutes the whole of the industry. There may, for example, be just one producer of paint, ice-cream or car batteries, or one provider of a commercial service such as air freight. It should not be assumed, however, that a monopolist organisation can charge whatever price it wishes for its output and that the demand for its product is perfectly inelastic with a price E^d of zero. The demand curve facing the monopolist will be downward sloping, and the value of the price E^d will depend largely upon the availability of substitutes.

Whatever the market form, a firm cannot dictate both price and quantity, since if it wishes to raise price then it must accept a fall in sales, while an increase in sales will require a reduction in price.

The eventual price and output combination will be arrived at on the assumption that the monopolist wishes to maximise profits, and it will be where marginal cost is equal to marginal revenue, as shown in the case of imperfect competition, since the underlying analysis of profit maximisation is identical. There is no guarantee, however, that a monopolist will always make super-normal profits, as this will depend upon the cost structure and revenue situations at various levels of output. The revenue and cost situations may be such that only normal profits are made, and there is no reason why a monopolist should not make a loss.

The major difference, however, between monopoly and other market forms is that if super-normal profits are made, they will persist in the long run. A monopoly status exists because there are distinct barriers to entry whereby new firms cannot enter the industry. This means that super-normal profits will not allow the expansion of the industry to produce eventually a long-run increase in total supply and a fall in price. If this did occur through the entry of new firms, then by definition we would no longer have monopoly, but some other market form. The barriers that restrict entry may take the form of a patent or franchise granted to the producer that prevents direct competition in a particular line of output. Barriers may also exist in the form of the costs of entry, where the capital expenditure involved, and the market sales to make such a move worth while, involve a risk not outweighed by the prospective return. This will be the case especially if the monopolist is likely to foul such competition with a price-cutting war.

It is often suggested that a monopolist has no incentive to indulge in cost-reducing innovations as profits are protected from competition by the barriers to entry and if they are introduced the consumer will not benefit from lower prices. Such a suggestion, however, assumes that the monopolist is a breed apart and is not interested in maximising profits.

As has been demonstrated in Fig. 9.19 (page 154), a fall in costs will permit additional units of output since if output is not raised then the firm, regardless of the market form, would be operating in an area where marginal revenue is greater than marginal costs. Similarly, the increased output by a monopolist will require a reduction in price, so the end result is higher profits and larger output at a lower price to consumers. There are, however, additional incentives to innovate in that if the costs of production rise and the monopolist is forced to a situation of lower output and a higher price, this can influence the availability of substitutes. Products that could compete with that of the monopolist were perhaps not justified as a commercial venture because of the price of the monopolist's product. These potential substitutes, however, then become a viable proposition because of their stronger competitive position.

Even a rise in the price of car batteries, for example, may eventually provoke the development of a product that can fulfil many of the functions of the existing product. This will mean not only that the monopolist is faced with less demand at each price than previously, but the demand for the product becomes more elastic now that it has more substitutes. Similarly, a rise in the price of a particular type of energy under monopoly control will make the development of alternative sources a more viable proposition.

Innovations that reduce the necessity for a price rise can therefore weaken the threat from new substitutes. Indeed, one of the reasons for the granting of patent rights is that the profits derived from their application are made sufficiently secure to make research and development worth while. This bestows monopoly by creating a barrier to entry, and the absence of this barrier would erode profits as new firms entered a line of output utilising the same improved product or technology. Under these circumstances, the greater security of an adequate return on the capital expenditure involved may act as an incentive to innovate and from the point of view of the government can justify the provision of what amounts to monopoly power.

In highly competitive markets, the lack of any form of barrier to entry can result in lower prices and a higher output than would have existed under monopoly. If, however, output is spread between too many firms, there may be much duplication of effort and high unit costs as firms will be operating on a relatively small scale. This would then have to be compared with the possible economies of scale that may result from the concentration of output in fewer firms or even the creation of a monopoly. This is one of the economic motives behind nationalisation and the previous role of the Industrial Reorganisation Corporation and the National Enterprise Board in promoting rationalisation to achieve economies of scale, particularly in the face of strong international competition.

Governments have to steer a difficult course between their desire to see the benefits of competition, and the potential disadvantages of a very strong monopoly, or a group of firms acting in such a way that they virtually constitute a monopoly. This is reflected in the legislation that exists to control monopolies, mergers, take-overs and restrictive trade practices. The growth of competition that results from the dismantling of import barriers that sought to restrict entry into a market can be beneficial from the point of view of prices, but it may also provoke the growth of tacit agreements between firms on an international scale. The growth of monopolies on a global scale in the form of the multinational corporation is also a growing source of debate concerning their relative advantages and disadvantages.

Suggestions for Integrated Assignments

Assignment 1   An organisation

Situation: Students should carry out a study of an organisation with which they are familiar, e.g. full- or part-time place of employment, school or college, or club/society.

Indicative content

The individual and the organisation

Classification of organisations

Types of business objectives

Organisational structures

Raising of finance and purpose and uses of finance

Student activity

1. Select an organisation.
2. Identify sources of information – both written and from members of the organisation.
3. Collate, analyse and select relevant information.
4. Present written or oral report covering:
   (a) why the organisation was formed;
   (b) how the organisation was formed – including legal requirements;
   (c) scope and range of activities;
   (d) objectives;
   (e) finance;
   (f) structure – supported by a chart.

Skills

Learning and studying

Information gathering

Communicating

Working with others

People in Organisations

A Understand the principal features of organisational structures and operations and how these affect the communication system of an organisation.

B Give and exchange information.

E Present and disseminate information using appropriate means.

General Objectives

A Identify the nature, purpose of characteristics of different organisations.

B Examine the nature of and relationship between a business organisation's objectives, structure and policies.

J Examine the importance of the availability of finance in the acquisition of resources by organisations.

Finance

B Explain the various sources of finance which are available to fund different types of organisations.

Assignment 2   Technological change

Situation: Students should carry out an on-going investigation of a particular technological development and assess its implications for the products and/or processes of a named company.

Indicative content

Causes of change

Differing responses to change

Technical changes (in mode of production)

Development of processes

The relevance of technology

Nature of technology

Functions of the processes

Cost implications

Organisational impact

De-skilling and retraining

Student activity

1. Select a technology and a company.
2. Research media for relevant material.
3. Contact company for annual report and accounts and other sources of information.
4. Set up and maintain a system to monitor and record developments.
5. Analyse the implications of findings for products and/or processes and hence costs, revenues and profitability.
6. Adopt the role of an assistant in either the personnel, marketing or production department. Submit a written report to the department covering the opportunities provided by the technology and its potential contribution to the company's objectives.

Skills

Numeracy

Learning and studying

Information gathering

Communicating

Information processing

People in Organisations

B Give and exchange information.

General Objectives

D Consider the major forces creating change and the response of individuals and business organisations to change.

E Recognise the impact of change upon the operation of business organisations and their environment.

F Explore a range of technological processes used in local organisations.

G Assess the impact and implications of these processes on the organisation, its employees and its environment.

Finance

E Appreciate the construction of financial statements for private, public and social organisations in accordance with accounting concepts.

F Explain and illustrate the needs of management and others for financial information for planning, control and decision-taking.

Assignment 3   Staff recruitment

Situation: Students should organise and carry out a simulated recruitment of an employee for one of the following:

(a) fast–food restaurant;

(b) leisure and recreation centre;
(c) supermarket;
(d) garden centre.

Indicative content

Manpower planning

Personnel policies

Student activity

1. Identify position to be filled.
2. Produce a job description or obtain one from a local organisation.
3. Draw up a person specification.
4. Identify and select appropriate sources of recruitment and where appropriate an advertisement.
5. Design an application form.
6. Carry out interviews and make a decision.
7. Estimate the costs associated with the recruitment.

   Note: At least four students should fill in each application form and then be interviewed for the job.

Skills

Identifying and tackling problems

Learning and studying

Design and visual discrimination

Information gathering

Communicating

People in Organisations

A Understand the principal features of organisational structures and operations and how these affect the communications system of an organisation.

B Give and exchange information.

E Present and disseminate information, using appropriate means.

F Appreciate the importance of personal relationships and the social environment.

General Objectives

L Analyse the importance of people as employees, both as managers and workers and the factors determining their availability, suitability and efficiency.

Finance

F Explain and illustrate the needs of management and others for financial information for planning, control and decision-taking.

Assignment 4   A training programme

Situation: Students should design a suitable programme of training for the person recruited in Assignment 3.

Student activity

1. Identify the training requirements.
2. Assess the skill and knowledge aspects.
3. As an assistant in the personnel department draw up a programme covering:
   (a) on-the-job training;
   (b) off-the-job training;
   (c) the personnel, organisations and government agencies that may be involved.
4. Estimate the costs associated with the programme.
5. Design a follow-up procedure.

Indicative content

Identification of information needs

Sources of information

Purposes of information

Education and training

Manpower planning

Personnel policies

Industrial and human relations

Technical and economic efficiency

Evaluation of resource use through quantitative and qualitative measures of performance

Skills

Numeracy

Identifying and tackling problems

Learning and studying

Information gathering

General Objectives

K Recognise the role of information and knowledge as a resource within effective business organisations.

L Analyse the importance of people as employees, both as managers and workers and the factors determining their availability, suitability and efficiency.

M Analyse the concept of efficient resource use; examine its importance and the policies an organisation may pursue to improve its efficiency.

People in Organisations

B Give and exchange information.

F Appreciate the importance of personal relationships and the social environment.

Finance

F Explain and illustrate the needs of management and others for financial information for planning, control and decision-taking.

H Appreciate the influence of finance on organisational decision-making and its relation to other factors involved in management decisions.

Assignment 5   Savings survey

Situation: Students should carry out a survey of the outlets for household savings.

Indicative content

The individual and the organisation

Types of business objectives

Types and levels of policy

Choice between business units

Student activity

1. Visit a variety of financial institutions and collect information on savings schemes.
2. Adopt the role of a marketing assistant working on one of the financial institutions.
3. Present a report which assesses the competition from other financial institutions in connection with:

   (a) interest rates;
   (b) notice of withdrawal;
   (c) minimum deposits/contributions;
   (d) bonuses;
   (e) introductory offers;
   (f) opening hours;
   (g) customer services.

4. Make recommendations as to the measures that will strengthen the competitive position of the selected institution in order that it will attract more funds.

Skills

Numeracy

Identifying and tackling problems

Learning and studying

Information gathering

Communicating

People in Organisations

B Give and exchange information.

C Examine information systems and their impact upon an organisation's operations, in terms of the use of a range of formats for information handling.

General Objectives

A Identify the nature, purpose and characteristics of different organisations.

B Examine the nature of and relationship between a business organisation's objectives, structure and policies.

C Assess the varieties of contribution made by different forms of organisation to the working of a mixed economy.

Finance

A Recognise the importance of, and be able to apply accounting and financial analysis techniques in relation to personal finance.

Assignment 6   Integration

Situation: Students should investigate a major company to identify the extent to which its growth has been based upon various forms of integration.

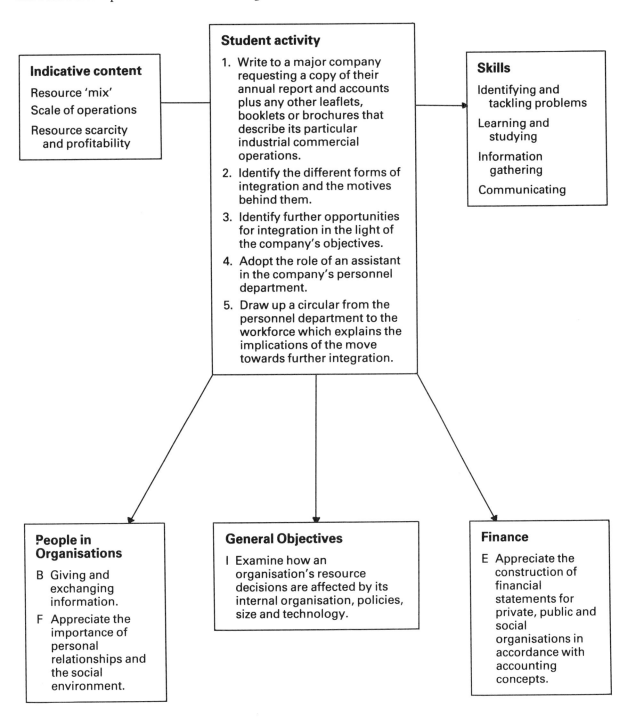

Indicative content

Resource 'mix'

Scale of operations

Resource scarcity and profitability

Student activity

1. Write to a major company requesting a copy of their annual report and accounts plus any other leaflets, booklets or brochures that describe its particular industrial commercial operations.
2. Identify the different forms of integration and the motives behind them.
3. Identify further opportunities for integration in the light of the company's objectives.
4. Adopt the role of an assistant in the company's personnel department.
5. Draw up a circular from the personnel department to the workforce which explains the implications of the move towards further integration.

Skills

Identifying and tackling problems

Learning and studying

Information gathering

Communicating

People in Organisations

B Giving and exchanging information.

F Appreciate the importance of personal relationships and the social environment.

General Objectives

I Examine how an organisation's resource decisions are affected by its internal organisation, policies, size and technology.

Finance

E Appreciate the construction of financial statements for private, public and social organisations in accordance with accounting concepts.

Assignment 7   Safety committee

Situation: Students should set up a safety committee in their college and carry out the duties of such a committee.

Indicative content

Personnel policies

Industrial and human relations

Employment law

Student activity

1. Divide into groups of four. Each group will be made up of two union representatives and two management representatives.
2. All members of the committee inspect the college either in their union or management role.
3. Union representatives prepare a list of the points which they wish to raise at the safety committee.
4. Management representatives discuss their findings and any measures they are prepared to take.
5. Hold meetings of the safety committees.
6. Each side produces a report on the issues discussed, the outcome and the financial implications.

Skills

Identifying and tackling problems

Learning and studying

Information gathering

Communicating

Working with others

People in Organisations

B Give and exchange information.

F Appreciate the importance of personal relationships and the social environment.

General Objectives

L Analyse the importance of people as employees, both as managers and workers, and the factors determining their availability, suitability and efficiency.

Finance

H Appreciate the influence of finance on organisational decision-making and its relation to other factors involved in management decisions.

Assignment 8 Marketing trainers

Situation: Students should carry out a survey to establish the factors that influence the sales of trainers.

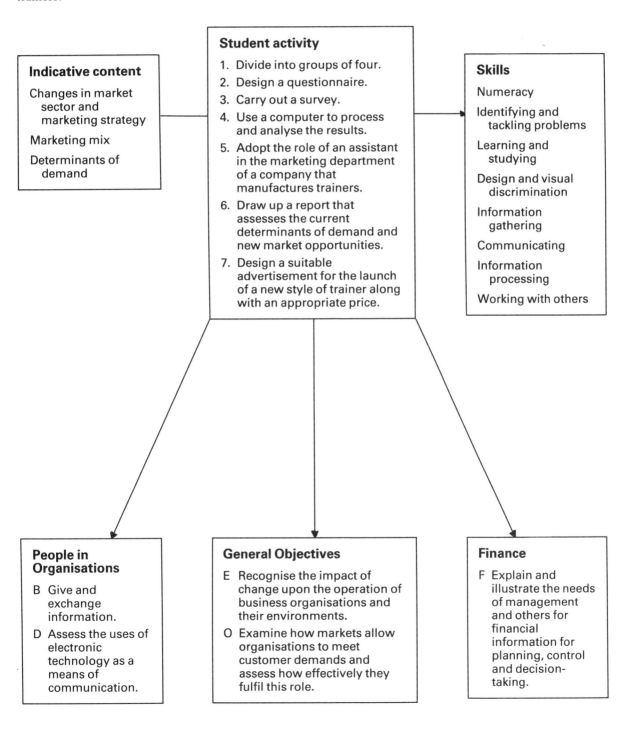

Indicative content

Changes in market sector and marketing strategy

Marketing mix

Determinants of demand

Student activity

1. Divide into groups of four.
2. Design a questionnaire.
3. Carry out a survey.
4. Use a computer to process and analyse the results.
5. Adopt the role of an assistant in the marketing department of a company that manufactures trainers.
6. Draw up a report that assesses the current determinants of demand and new market opportunities.
7. Design a suitable advertisement for the launch of a new style of trainer along with an appropriate price.

Skills

Numeracy

Identifying and tackling problems

Learning and studying

Design and visual discrimination

Information gathering

Communicating

Information processing

Working with others

People in Organisations

B Give and exchange information.

D Assess the uses of electronic technology as a means of communication.

General Objectives

E Recognise the impact of change upon the operation of business organisations and their environments.

O Examine how markets allow organisations to meet customer demands and assess how effectively they fulfil this role.

Finance

F Explain and illustrate the needs of management and others for financial information for planning, control and decision-taking.

Index

organisations – *continued*
  types (in mixed economy), 8–17
  in UK economy, 4–5
output
  economies of scale, 98–100
  law of diminishing returns, 91–8
  level, population and, 27–8
  unit costs, 88–91
overdrafts, 76, 77–8
overseas legislation, discriminatory, 112
overseas markets, 105
  see also foreign competition; multinational companies

partnerships, 5, 9, 76
patents, 104, 157
pension funds, 12, 85
pensions, 36
performance appraisal, 57–60
'person specification', 49, 51
personal flexibility schemes, 42
personal funds (financing source), 76
personal services, 118–19
personnel department (procedures), 48–52
policy making, 3–4
'political lobbying', 7
pollution, 40, 42
population
  explosion, 41
  size, 24–8
  structure, 28–32
power (objective), 6
preference shares, 10, 81–2, 87
Premium Bonds, 86
price(s)
  cross-elasticity of demand, 131–2
  elasticity of demand, 126–30
  influence on demand, 119–22, 125
  leader, 155
  market equilibrium, 142–51
  in oligopoly, 155–6
  real, consumer and, 101–2
  relative (of inputs), 101, 102
  revenue curves and, 133–5
  supply and, 132–41
  see also inflation
primary industries, 31
private joint stock company, 9–11
private sector, 4
  business organisations (types), 8–16
  objectives, 5–7
privatisation, 21–3
process innovation, 38–40
producer needs, 1, 2
product differentiation, 153, 154, 155
product innovation, 40, 41, 104
production, 4
  capital-intensive, 101, 146
  costs, *see* costs

products
  complementary, 121–2, 131, 132
  substitute, 120–21, 123, 129, 131, 150, 157
professional bodies, 50
profit, 81–2
  maximisation, 5–6, 88
  retained, 76 *bis*, 77
  -sharing schemes, 64, 67
profitability
  costs and, 88–91
  relative (changed), 139–40
  supply and, 132–40 *passim*
project approach (training), 56–7
promotional activity, 151–2, 153, 156
promotions/career development, 45, 48, 99
prospectus, 11
public corporations, 16, 82
public limited company, 5, 11–12
public sector, 4–5, 31
  acquisition of capital by, 82–7
  borrowing requirements, 22, 82–7
  business organisations (types), 16–17
  objectives, 7–8
purchasing (scale economies), 98–9

qualifications, 56
  genuine occupational, 111, 112, 113

racial discrimination, 109, 112–13
rationalisation, 103 *bis*, 157
raw materials, 100, 104, 146, 149, 150
recession, 89, 104
record-keeping, 4
recruitment, *see* labour (recruitment of)
redundancy, 47, 109, 117
regional policy, 32
Registrar of Companies, 10, 16
Registrar of Friendly Societies, 16
relationships, 17
  formal structure, 19–21
  informal structure, 21
relative price of inputs, 101, 102
research and development, 7, 13, 40, 73–4, 99, 157
resources, 1–2, 4
  see also raw materials
responsibility (in organisational structure), 17
restrictive practices, 156, 157
retail co-operative societies, 14–15
retail trade (groups), 9
retirement age, 29–30, 45, 47
revenue curves, 133–5
Ridley, Nicholas, 22
'rights' issues, 87
risk, 84
  integration to avoid, 103, 105
  profit and, 5, 6
  shareholders and, 10, 77, 78–80, 81